First World War
and Army of Occupation
War Diary
France, Belgium and Germany

19 DIVISION
57 Infantry Brigade
Worcestershire Regiment 3rd Battalion,
Worcestershire Regiment 10th Battalion,
Brigade Machine Gun Company
and Brigade Trench Mortar Battery
17 July 1915 - 20 October 1918

WO95/2086

The Naval & Military Press Ltd
www.nmarchive.com
Published in association with The National Archives

Published by

The Naval & Military Press Ltd

Unit 10 Ridgewood Industrial Park,

Uckfield, East Sussex,

TN22 5QE England

Tel: +44 (0) 1825 749494

www.naval-military-press.com

www.nmarchive.com

This diary has been reprinted in facsimile from the original. Any imperfections are inevitably reproduced and the quality may fall short of modern type and cartographic standards.

© Crown Copyright
Images reproduced by permission of The National Archives, London, England, 2015.

Contents

Document type	Place/Title	Date From	Date To
Heading	WO95/2086/1		
Heading	19th Division 57th Infy Bde 3rd Bn Worcestershire Regt. Jun 1918-Feb 1919 From 25 Div. 74 Bde		
Miscellaneous	57th Inf Bde	31/07/1918	31/07/1918
Miscellaneous	3rd Bde The Worcestershire Regt.	01/07/1918	01/07/1918
War Diary		01/06/1918	31/07/1918
Miscellaneous	57th. Inf. Bde.	22/09/1918	22/09/1918
War Diary		01/08/1918	30/09/1918
Miscellaneous	3rd. Bn. The Worcestershire Regt.	01/10/1918	01/10/1918
Miscellaneous	Routine Orders. By. Lt Con. P.R. Whalley D.S.O. Commdg Bn The Worcestershire Regiment.	28/09/1918	28/09/1918
War Diary		01/10/1918	26/10/1918
Miscellaneous	3rd Bn. The Worcestershire Regiment	01/11/1918	01/11/1918
Miscellaneous	57th. Inf. Bde.	04/12/1918	04/12/1918
War Diary		01/11/1918	27/11/1918
Miscellaneous	19th Division	14/11/1918	14/11/1918
Miscellaneous	3rd. Bn. The Worcestershire Regiment	01/12/1918	01/12/1918
Heading	10 Battn. Worcesters absorbed by 3rd Battn Worcesters in June		
War Diary		27/12/1918	08/02/1919
Heading	WO95/2086/2		
Heading	19th Division 57th Infy Bde 10th Bn Worcestershire Regt Jly 1915-Feb 1918		
Heading	10 Worcester Vol 9		
Heading	57th Ind. Bde. 19th Div. War Diary 10th Battn. The Worcestershire Regiment. July (17.7.15-31.7.15) 1915		
War Diary	Tidworth	17/07/1915	18/07/1915
War Diary	Boulogne	19/07/1915	20/07/1915
War Diary	Watten	20/07/1915	20/07/1915
War Diary	Bayenghem	21/07/1915	23/07/1915
War Diary	Renescure	23/07/1915	24/07/1915
War Diary	Aire	24/07/1915	30/07/1915
War Diary	Haverskerque	31/07/1915	31/07/1915
Heading	57th Inf. Bde. 19th Div. War Diary 10th Battn. The Worcestershire Regiment. August 1915		
War Diary	Merville	01/08/1915	03/08/1915
War Diary	Estaires	04/08/1915	04/08/1915
War Diary	Laventie	04/08/1915	10/08/1915
War Diary	Estaires	11/08/1915	14/08/1915
War Diary	Merville	15/08/1915	27/08/1915
War Diary	La Croix Marmuse	28/08/1915	28/08/1915
War Diary	Trenches (Ind II)	29/08/1915	30/08/1915
Heading	57th Inf. Bde. 19th Div. War Diary 10th Battn. The Worcestershire Regiment. September 1915		
War Diary	Trenches. (Ind II b.)	01/09/1915	07/09/1915
War Diary	Rue Des Chavattes	08/09/1915	12/09/1915
War Diary	Locon	13/09/1915	25/09/1915
War Diary	Le Hamel	25/09/1915	25/09/1915
War Diary	Locon	26/09/1915	27/09/1915
War Diary	Le Hamel	27/09/1915	27/09/1915

War Diary	Locon	28/09/1915	29/09/1915
War Diary	Ind II.	30/09/1915	30/09/1915
Heading	57th Inf. Bde. 19th Div. 10th Battn. The Worcestershire Regiment. October 1915		
War Diary	Trenches Ind II C.	01/10/1915	02/10/1915
War Diary	Le Hamel	03/10/1915	03/10/1915
War Diary	Ind IV A.	04/10/1915	08/10/1915
War Diary	Lacouture	11/10/1915	11/10/1915
War Diary	Vieille Chapelle	11/10/1915	13/10/1915
War Diary	Lacoutoure	13/10/1915	14/10/1915
War Diary	Trenches Ind IV A.	15/10/1915	18/10/1915
War Diary	Marais	20/10/1915	21/10/1915
War Diary	Reserve Trenches Ind I B.	22/10/1915	31/10/1915
Heading	57th Inf. Bde. 19th Div. 10th Battn. The Worcestershire Regiment. November 1915		
War Diary	Old British Line Ind I B	01/11/1915	05/11/1915
War Diary	Le Hamel	06/11/1915	08/11/1915
War Diary	Locon	09/11/1915	17/11/1915
War Diary	Trenches Ind II A.	18/11/1915	21/11/1915
War Diary	Le Touret	22/11/1915	23/11/1915
War Diary	La Tombe Willot	24/11/1915	24/11/1915
War Diary	Calonne	25/11/1915	30/11/1915
Heading	57th Inf. Bde. 19th Div. 10th Battn. The Worcestershire Regiment. December 1915		
War Diary	Calonne	01/12/1915	04/12/1915
War Diary	Bout Deville	05/12/1915	11/12/1915
War Diary	Trenches Ind IV A.	12/12/1915	15/12/1915
War Diary	Richebourg	15/12/1915	15/12/1915
War Diary	St Vaast	16/12/1915	19/12/1915
War Diary	Trenches Ind IV A.	20/12/1915	23/12/1915
War Diary	Richebourg		
War Diary	St Vaast	24/12/1915	27/12/1915
War Diary	La Croix Marmuse	28/12/1915	31/12/1915
Heading	19th Division 57th Infantry Brigade. March to June 1918 missing.		
Heading	10th Worcesters Vol. 7		
War Diary	La Croix Marmuse	01/01/1916	04/01/1916
War Diary	Trenches Neuve Chapelle	05/01/1916	08/01/1916
War Diary	Croix Barbee	08/01/1916	11/01/1916
War Diary	Trenches Neuve Chapelle	12/01/1916	17/01/1916
War Diary	Croix Barbee	18/01/1916	20/01/1916
War Diary	Robecq	21/01/1916	31/01/1916
Miscellaneous		02/06/1916	02/06/1916
War Diary	Robecq	01/02/1916	23/02/1916
War Diary	La Gorgue	24/02/1916	24/02/1916
War Diary	Trenches	25/02/1916	26/02/1916
War Diary	Pont Du Hem	27/02/1916	28/02/1916
War Diary	Trenches	28/02/1916	03/03/1916
War Diary	Pont Du Hem	04/03/1916	07/03/1916
War Diary	Robermetz	08/03/1916	13/03/1916
War Diary	Pont Du Hem	14/03/1916	14/03/1916
War Diary	Trenches	15/03/1916	21/03/1916
War Diary	Pont Du Hem	22/03/1916	25/03/1916
War Diary	Trenches	26/03/1916	29/03/1916
War Diary	Pont Du Hem	30/03/1916	31/03/1916
War Diary	Robermetz	31/03/1916	06/04/1916

War Diary	Pont Du Hem	06/04/1916	06/04/1916
War Diary	Trenches	07/04/1916	11/04/1916
War Diary	Pont Du Hem	12/04/1916	15/04/1916
War Diary	Trenches	15/04/1916	17/04/1916
War Diary	La Gorgue	17/04/1916	18/04/1916
War Diary	Robecq	19/04/1916	20/04/1916
War Diary	Marthes	20/04/1916	07/05/1916
War Diary	Amiens	08/05/1916	08/05/1916
War Diary	Vignacourt	08/05/1916	30/05/1916
War Diary	St Riquier	30/05/1916	10/06/1916
War Diary	Vignacourt	11/06/1916	11/06/1916
War Diary	Frechencourt	12/06/1916	12/06/1916
War Diary	Dernancourt	13/06/1916	30/06/1916
Heading	57th Inf. Bde. 19th Div. 10th Battn. The Worcestershire Regiment. July 1916		
War Diary	Albert	01/07/1916	02/07/1916
War Diary	Usna Tara Line		
War Diary	Village of La Boiselle	03/07/1916	03/07/1916
War Diary	Ryecroft Avenue	04/07/1916	04/07/1916
War Diary	Old British Line	04/07/1916	05/07/1916
War Diary	Albert	06/07/1916	08/07/1916
War Diary	Millencourt	09/07/1916	09/07/1916
War Diary	Hennecourt Wood		
War Diary	Lavieville	10/07/1916	19/07/1916
War Diary	Fricourt	20/07/1916	22/07/1916
War Diary	Bazentin-Le Petit	23/07/1916	23/07/1916
War Diary	Becourt Wood	24/07/1916	29/07/1916
War Diary	Bazentin Le Petit	30/07/1916	31/07/1916
Miscellaneous	10th. (S) Bn. Worcestershire Regt.	31/07/1916	31/07/1916
Miscellaneous Map	Casualty List. 1916.	26/07/1916	26/07/1916
Heading	57th Brigade. 19th. Division. 1/10th Battalion Worcestershire Regiment August 1916		
War Diary	Bresle	01/08/1916	02/08/1916
War Diary	Mouflers	03/08/1916	06/08/1916
War Diary	Dranoutre	07/08/1916	09/08/1916
War Diary	Trenches	10/08/1916	14/08/1916
War Diary	Brigade Reserve	15/08/1916	22/08/1916
War Diary	Dranoutre	23/08/1916	31/08/1916
War Diary	Brigade Reserve	01/09/1916	05/09/1916
War Diary	Trenches	06/09/1916	12/09/1916
War Diary	Divisional Reserve	13/09/1916	16/09/1916
War Diary	Trenches	17/09/1916	19/09/1916
War Diary	Divnl Rest	20/09/1916	06/10/1916
War Diary	Divl Reserve	07/10/1916	24/10/1916
War Diary	Trenches	24/10/1916	26/10/1916
War Diary	Rest	27/10/1916	29/10/1916
War Diary	Trenches	30/10/1916	02/11/1916
War Diary	Rest Billets	03/11/1916	05/11/1916
War Diary	Trenches	06/11/1916	06/11/1916
War Diary	Surrounding Gravel Point	08/11/1916	08/11/1916
War Diary	Trenches	09/11/1916	11/11/1916
War Diary	Rest Billets	12/11/1916	17/11/1916
War Diary	Trenches	18/11/1916	19/11/1916
War Diary	Aveluy	20/11/1916	20/11/1916
War Diary	Warloy	21/11/1916	22/11/1916

War Diary	Rubempre	23/11/1916	23/11/1916
War Diary	Montrelet	24/11/1916	24/11/1916
War Diary	Franqueville	25/11/1916	25/11/1916
War Diary	Bernaville	26/11/1916	26/11/1916
War Diary	Gezaincourt	27/11/1916	09/01/1917
War Diary	Amplier Trenches Hebuterne Area	10/01/1917	16/01/1917
War Diary	Bayencourt	17/01/1917	21/01/1917
War Diary	Bertrancourt	22/01/1917	01/02/1917
War Diary	Trenches	02/02/1917	21/02/1917
War Diary	Courchelles	22/02/1917	25/02/1917
War Diary	Euston Dump	26/02/1917	28/02/1917
War Diary	Trenches	01/03/1917	02/03/1917
War Diary	Arqueves	03/03/1917	04/03/1917
War Diary	Bus	05/03/1917	08/03/1917
War Diary	Louvencourt	09/03/1917	09/03/1917
War Diary	Gezaincourt	10/03/1917	10/03/1917
War Diary	Gezaincourt Bonnieres	11/03/1917	04/04/1917
War Diary	Acquin	05/04/1917	20/04/1917
War Diary	Locre	21/04/1917	23/04/1917
War Diary	Curragh Camp Locre	24/04/1917	30/04/1917
War Diary	St Lawrence Camp Poperinge	01/05/1917	01/05/1917
War Diary	Trenches Ypres Salient	02/05/1917	10/05/1917
War Diary	Scherpenberg	11/05/1917	24/05/1917
War Diary	Trenches	24/05/1917	26/05/1917
War Diary	Curragh Camp Locre	27/05/1917	31/05/1917
War Diary	Epsom Camp	01/06/1917	12/06/1917
War Diary	Murrumbidge	13/06/1917	13/06/1917
War Diary	Garden Camp	14/06/1917	16/06/1917
War Diary	Trenches	17/06/1917	19/06/1917
War Diary	Garden Camp	20/06/1917	20/06/1917
War Diary	Corunda Camp	21/06/1917	01/07/1917
War Diary	Garden Camp	02/07/1917	02/07/1917
War Diary	Trenches	10/07/1917	10/07/1917
War Diary	Irish House	11/07/1917	22/07/1917
War Diary	Corunda Camp	01/07/1917	01/07/1917
War Diary	Garden Camp	02/07/1917	02/07/1917
War Diary	Trenches	10/07/1917	10/07/1917
War Diary	Irish House	11/07/1917	23/07/1917
War Diary	Trenches	29/07/1917	29/07/1917
War Diary	Kemmel	30/07/1917	30/07/1917
War Diary	Shelters	31/07/1917	31/07/1917
War Diary	Trenches	23/07/1917	29/07/1917
War Diary	Kemmel	30/07/1917	30/07/1917
War Diary	Shelters	31/07/1917	31/07/1917
War Diary	Kemmel Shelters	01/08/1917	03/08/1917
War Diary	Trenches H.Q. in Denys Wood	04/08/1917	04/08/1917
War Diary	Support Line	05/08/1917	09/08/1917
War Diary	Corunna Camp	10/08/1917	11/08/1917
War Diary	Milles-Lez Blequin	12/08/1917	22/08/1917
War Diary	Escouelles	23/08/1917	28/08/1917
War Diary	Hondeghem	29/08/1919	29/08/1919
War Diary	Moolenacker	30/08/1917	06/09/1917
War Diary	Corunna Camp	07/09/1917	10/09/1917
War Diary	Camp at N.9.d.8.6 Sheet 26.	11/09/1917	11/09/1917
War Diary	Trenches	12/09/1917	14/09/1917
War Diary	Camp at N.9.d.8.5	15/09/1917	30/09/1917

War Diary	Hill 60	01/10/1917	05/10/1917
War Diary	Rossignol Camp	06/10/1917	11/10/1917
War Diary	Support Line	12/10/1917	13/10/1917
War Diary	Line	14/10/1917	17/10/1917
War Diary	Support	18/10/1917	19/10/1917
War Diary	Norton Camp	20/10/1917	27/10/1917
War Diary	Kemmel Shelters	28/10/1917	31/10/1917
Miscellaneous	Headquarters 57th Brigade	01/12/1917	01/12/1917
War Diary	Kemmel Shelters	01/11/1917	04/11/1917
War Diary	Trenches	05/11/1917	07/11/1917
War Diary	Spoil Bank	08/11/1917	09/11/1917
War Diary	Bois Confluent	10/11/1917	10/11/1917
War Diary	Moolenacker	11/11/1917	12/11/1917
War Diary	Blaringhem	13/11/1917	28/11/1917
War Diary	Tilques	29/11/1917	30/11/1917
War Diary	Le Sablioniere	01/12/1917	09/12/1917
War Diary	Etricourt	10/12/1917	18/12/1917
War Diary	Haurincourt Wood	19/12/1917	20/12/1917
War Diary	Reserve Front Suite	21/12/1917	27/12/1917
War Diary	Support	28/12/1917	31/12/1917
War Diary	Right Subsector 57th. Bde. Front.	01/01/1918	05/01/1918
War Diary	Reserve	06/01/1918	12/01/1918
War Diary	Trenches	13/01/1918	21/01/1918
War Diary	Vallulart Camp	22/01/1918	24/01/1918
War Diary	Support	25/01/1918	31/01/1918
War Diary	Eastwood Camp	01/02/1918	01/02/1918
War Diary	Havrincourt Wood	02/02/1918	28/02/1918
Heading	WO95/2086/3		
Heading	19th Division 57th Infy Bde 57th Machine Gun Coy. Feb 1916-Jan 1918		
Heading	57th M.G. Coy. Vol I		
War Diary	Grantham	08/02/1916	09/02/1916
War Diary	Havre	10/02/1916	13/02/1916
War Diary	Robecq	15/02/1916	19/02/1916
War Diary	Puresbecques	20/02/1916	24/02/1916
War Diary	Pont Du Hem	24/02/1916	31/03/1916
War Diary	Puresbecques Merville	01/04/1916	06/04/1916
War Diary	Pubesbecques	06/04/1916	06/04/1916
War Diary	Pont-Du-Hem	07/04/1916	17/04/1916
War Diary	Robecq	18/04/1916	19/04/1916
War Diary	Ham	20/04/1916	25/04/1916
War Diary	Pont-Du-Hem	26/04/1916	30/04/1916
War Diary	Ham	01/05/1916	30/05/1916
War Diary	St Riquier	01/06/1916	15/06/1916
War Diary	Rainneville	16/06/1916	27/06/1916
War Diary	Behencourt	28/06/1916	30/06/1916
War Diary	Vignacourt	01/07/1916	02/07/1916
War Diary	St Riquier	03/07/1916	10/07/1916
War Diary	Vignacourt	11/07/1916	26/07/1916
War Diary	Rainnerville	27/06/1916	27/06/1916
War Diary	Frawvillers Wood	28/06/1916	30/06/1916
Heading	57th. Inf. Bde. 19th Div. 57th Machine Gun Company. July 1916		
War Diary	Millencourt	01/07/1916	01/07/1916
War Diary	Albert	02/07/1916	07/07/1916
War Diary	Millencourt	08/07/1916	31/07/1916

Heading	57th Brigade. 19th Division. 57th Brigade Machine Gun Company August 1916		
War Diary	Nr Fricourt	01/08/1916	01/08/1916
War Diary	Bresle	02/08/1916	03/08/1916
War Diary	Bouchon	05/08/1916	06/08/1916
War Diary	Dranoutre	07/08/1916	01/09/1916
War Diary	Romarin	05/09/1916	06/09/1916
War Diary	Dranoutre		
War Diary	Romarin	07/09/1916	19/09/1916
War Diary	Outtersteen	20/09/1916	20/09/1916
War Diary	Borre	21/09/1916	06/10/1916
War Diary	Sarton	07/10/1916	07/10/1916
War Diary	St Leger	08/10/1916	17/10/1916
War Diary	Warloy	18/10/1916	21/10/1916
War Diary	Camp	22/10/1916	22/10/1916
War Diary	In The Trenches	22/10/1916	03/11/1916
War Diary	Aveluy	03/11/1916	07/11/1916
War Diary	In The Trenches	08/11/1916	12/11/1916
War Diary	Crucifix Corner	13/11/1916	17/11/1916
War Diary	In The Trenches	17/11/1916	19/11/1916
War Diary	Crucifix Corner	20/11/1916	21/11/1916
War Diary	Warloy	22/11/1916	22/11/1916
War Diary	Rubempre	28/11/1916	28/11/1916
War Diary	Canaples	24/11/1916	24/11/1916
War Diary	Franqueville	25/11/1916	25/11/1916
War Diary	Bernaville	26/11/1916	26/11/1916
War Diary	Lonquevillette	27/11/1916	30/11/1916
Heading	War Diary 57th. Coy. Machine Gun Corps. December 1916.		
War Diary	Longuevillette	01/12/1916	03/12/1916
War Diary	Hem	04/12/1916	05/12/1916
War Diary	Beauval	06/12/1916	12/12/1916
War Diary	Berneuil	13/12/1916	14/12/1916
War Diary	Beauval	15/12/1916	08/01/1917
War Diary	Autwieule	09/01/1917	10/01/1917
War Diary	Bayencourt		
War Diary	Hebuterne	10/01/1917	21/01/1917
War Diary	Bayencourt	22/01/1917	22/01/1917
War Diary	Courcelle	23/01/1917	27/01/1917
War Diary	Bus	28/01/1917	01/02/1917
War Diary	Courcelles	02/02/1917	01/03/1917
War Diary	Bus	02/03/1917	08/03/1917
War Diary	Move	09/03/1917	20/03/1917
War Diary	La Clytte	21/03/1917	31/03/1917
War Diary	Caestre Area	01/04/1917	01/04/1917
War Diary	Hazebrouck	02/04/1917	02/04/1917
War Diary	Wizernes	03/04/1917	03/04/1917
War Diary	Val D'Aquin	04/04/1917	20/04/1917
War Diary	Scherpenberg	21/04/1917	30/04/1917
War Diary	Hill Sixty-Hooge Sector	01/05/1917	11/05/1917
War Diary	Scherpenberg Area	11/05/1917	20/05/1917
War Diary	La Clytte	21/05/1917	31/05/1917
War Diary	Westoutre.	01/06/1917	06/06/1917
War Diary	In Action	07/06/1917	09/06/1917
War Diary	La Clytte	10/06/1917	12/06/1917
War Diary	Klondike Farm	13/06/1917	14/06/1917

War Diary	La Line	15/06/1917	21/06/1917
War Diary	M.15 C.6.5.	22/06/1917	30/06/1917
Miscellaneous	Appendix A 57th Brigade Preliminary Instructions For The Offensive Part 1	31/05/1917	31/05/1917
Miscellaneous	Extract From 19th Division Operation Order No. 136.	04/06/1917	04/06/1917
Miscellaneous	Correction to 19th Division Instructions For The Offensive which have already been issued.	18/05/1917	18/05/1917
Miscellaneous	10th R. War. R.	04/06/1917	04/06/1917
Miscellaneous	Machine Gun Barrage Chart.	19/05/1917	19/05/1917
Heading	57th. M.G. Coy. War Diary From 1st July to 31st. July. 1917.		
War Diary	In Westoutre (M15.c.6.6.)	01/07/1917	03/07/1917
War Diary	In Line Northern Section Fix Corps Front		
War Diary	In Line	03/07/1917	12/07/1917
War Diary	Kemmel	12/07/1917	22/07/1917
War Diary	In The Line	20/07/1917	25/07/1917
War Diary	In The Field	24/07/1917	27/07/1917
War Diary	In The Line	27/07/1917	31/07/1917
Operation(al) Order(s)	Operation Order No. 14	28/07/1917	28/07/1917
War Diary	In The Line Coy H.Q. O.9a.7.1.	01/08/1917	02/08/1917
War Diary	In The Line	03/08/1917	09/08/1917
War Diary	M 26 C.2.2.	10/08/1917	11/08/1917
War Diary	Watterdal	12/08/1917	22/08/1917
War Diary	Colombert	23/08/1917	28/08/1917
War Diary	St Aples	29/08/1917	29/08/1917
War Diary	Merris	30/08/1917	06/09/1917
War Diary	Westoutre	07/09/1917	11/09/1917
War Diary	M 9.a. 6.9. In The Line	12/09/1917	15/09/1917
War Diary	N 15 d 89	16/09/1917	19/09/1917
War Diary	In The Line	19/09/1917	22/09/1917
War Diary	M 15 D 89	23/09/1917	27/09/1917
War Diary	In The Line	28/09/1917	25/10/1917
War Diary	In The Field	26/10/1917	14/11/1917
War Diary	Racquinghem	15/11/1917	30/11/1917
Miscellaneous	57th Inf Bde		
War Diary	Racquinghem	01/12/1917	07/12/1917
War Diary	Pommier Area	08/12/1917	08/12/1917
War Diary	Etricourt	08/12/1917	09/12/1917
War Diary	In The Line	10/12/1917	31/01/1918
Heading	WO95/2086/4		
Heading	19th Division 57th Infy Bde 57th Lt Trench Mortar Bty Feb 1918-Mar 1919		
Map			
Miscellaneous			
Heading	57th L.T.M.B. Feby December 1918		
War Diary	Haussy	22/10/1918	31/10/1918
War Diary	Cauroir	02/11/1918	02/11/1918
War Diary	St Aubert	03/11/1918	03/11/1918
War Diary	Sepmeries	04/11/1918	04/11/1918
War Diary	Maresches	05/11/1918	05/11/1918
War Diary	Jenlain	06/11/1918	08/11/1918
War Diary	Malplaquet	08/11/1918	10/11/1918
War Diary	La Flamengrie	13/11/1918	14/11/1918
War Diary	Sepmeries	15/11/1918	15/11/1918
War Diary	St Aubert	17/11/1918	17/11/1918
War Diary	Cauroir	26/11/1918	27/11/1918

War Diary	Gezaincourt	28/11/1918	31/12/1918
Miscellaneous	Central Registry		
War Diary	Fienvillers	19/01/1919	19/01/1919
War Diary	Fienvillers	01/02/1919	07/02/1919
War Diary	Candas	07/02/1919	21/03/1919
War Diary	Belle Croix	01/12/1919	07/12/1919
War Diary	Pommier	08/12/1919	08/12/1919
War Diary	Etricourt	09/12/1919	09/12/1919
War Diary	Ribecourt	11/12/1917	14/02/1918
War Diary	Beaulencourt	18/02/1918	06/03/1918
War Diary	Barrastre	07/03/1918	21/03/1918
War Diary	Beaumetz Lez Cambrai	21/03/1918	23/03/1918
War Diary	Bancourt	24/03/1918	24/03/1918
War Diary	Miraumont	25/03/1918	25/03/1918
War Diary	Coigneux	26/03/1918	26/03/1918
War Diary	Warlincourt	27/03/1918	27/03/1918
War Diary	Bienvillers	28/03/1918	28/03/1918
War Diary	Famechon	29/03/1918	29/03/1918
War Diary	Doullens	29/03/1918	29/03/1918
War Diary	Kemmel	30/03/1918	31/03/1918
War Diary		01/01/1918	30/01/1918
Heading	57th Brigade. 19th Division. 57th Light Trench Mortar Battery April 1918.		
War Diary	Kemmel	01/04/1918	01/04/1918
War Diary	Messines	10/04/1918	15/04/1918
War Diary	Lindenhoek	17/04/1918	29/04/1918
War Diary	St Janter Biezen	01/05/1918	18/05/1918
War Diary	Moncetz	19/05/1918	30/05/1918
War Diary	Pourcy	31/05/1918	03/06/1918
War Diary	Hautvillers	10/06/1918	19/06/1918
War Diary	Oger	20/06/1918	20/06/1918
War Diary	Broussy-Le-Petit	21/06/1918	29/06/1918
War Diary	Semoine	30/06/1918	30/06/1918
War Diary	Mailly	01/07/1918	02/07/1918
War Diary	Wavrans	03/07/1918	11/07/1918
War Diary	Raimbert	12/07/1918	20/07/1918
War Diary	St Hilaire	21/07/1918	30/07/1918
War Diary	Raimbert	31/07/1918	04/08/1918
War Diary	Chocques	05/08/1918	05/08/1918
War Diary	Bethune	21/08/1918	24/08/1918
War Diary	L'Abbaye	29/08/1918	29/08/1918
War Diary	Bethune	31/08/1918	31/08/1918
War Diary	Lacouture	01/09/1918	03/09/1918
War Diary	Richbourg	07/09/1918	10/09/1918
War Diary	Hinges	11/09/1918	11/09/1918
War Diary	Bethune	12/09/1918	15/09/1918
War Diary	Rue Du Bois	16/09/1918	25/09/1918
War Diary	Shepherds Redoubt	26/09/1918	26/09/1918
War Diary	Rue Du Bois	28/09/1918	28/09/1918
War Diary	Bethune	29/09/1918	01/10/1918
War Diary	Raimbert	02/10/1918	02/10/1918
War Diary	Huclier	04/10/1918	05/10/1918
War Diary	Souastre	07/10/1918	07/10/1918
War Diary	Graincourt	09/10/1918	09/10/1918
War Diary	Anneux	10/10/1918	10/10/1918
War Diary	Cambria	11/10/1918	16/10/1918

War Diary   St Aubert   17/10/1918   20/10/1918

No 95/2086/1

19TH DIVISION
57TH INFY BDE

3RD BN WORCESTERSHIRE REGT.
JUN 1918 - FEB 1919

From 25 DIV. 74 BDE

7th Inf Bde.

Herewith War Diary
for month of July.

M Hargreaves Capt & adjt
for
COMMANDING 3rd WORCESTERSHIRE
31/7/18.

3rd Bn The Worcestershire Regt.

Casualties during June 1918

Date	Officers			Total Officers	Other Ranks			Total Other Ranks	Remarks
	K	W	M		K	W	M		
June 13th to 30th	-	2	-	2	-	13	-	13	Remainder 18th at duty.

H.D. 149
July 1st 1918

P.R. Whalley............ LIEUT. COL.
COMMANDING 3rd WORCESTERSHIRE REGT.

2nd West R.
7th S/7th 3rd Batta[lion] ?

WAR DIARY
or
INTELLIGENCE SUMMARY.
(Erase heading not required.)

Army Form C. 2118.

June, 1915

Place	Date	Hour	Summary of Events and Information	Remarks and references to Appendices
	June 5th to 19th		A detachment of the Bn. was in the forward area near BLIGNY forming a part of a composite Bn. which was composed of units of 25th Division	Refugees thro' SOISSONS 100,000
	June 5th		A composite company was formed from Wk[?] of Bn. at BEAUNAY.	Ret. found after CHALONS
	9th		Moved to REUVES where formed comp. of Bn [Lt.Col.?] R. Whalley DSO assumed command of Bn.	
	9th 10th		Training was continued at REUVES	Ret. found at ARCIS after
	11th 13th 14th 19th		Moved to MATIGNY	
	19th to 21st		Remainder of Bn. returned from the line	
	21st 22nd		Re-organizing + refitting of the Bn. Bn. transferred to 19th Division + joined 57th Inf Bde. at BROUSSY-LE-PETIT absorbing 10th Bn Worcesters Regt. Bn now over 800 strong. The Commdt was still sent to the base on this date. Comfort. of 10th Bn taken over.	Ref. found into CHALONS about
	24th		Bn moved to old Prisoners of War camp near CONNANTRE.	C.42 Ret French at ARCIS sheet

Army Form C. 2118.

WAR DIARY
or
INTELLIGENCE SUMMARY.
(Erase heading not required.)

Place	Date	Hour	Summary of Events and Information	Remarks and references to Appendices
	June 21st to 30th		Bn. exercises & training. Bn. marched to SEMOINE preparatory to entraining for the British Zone.	Ref. APCIS sheet

P.E. Whalley......LIEUT. COL.
COMMANDING 3rd WORCESTERSHIRE REGT.

WAR DIARY
or
INTELLIGENCE SUMMARY.
(Erase heading not required)

Army Form C. 2118.

3 Worcester

Vol 2

Place	Date	Hour	Summary of Events and Information	Remarks and references to Appendices
	July 1st		Day spent at SEMOINE	Ref. Map ARRAS
	2nd	1am	Bn. entrained for British zone.	
	3rd	6.30 am	Bn. detrained at HESDIN, & moved by bus to WAVRANS near ST. OMER.	M.P. HAZEBROUCK Sh 1/100,000
	4th to 10th		Bn. Training & refitting at WAVRANS. Some reinforcements joined Bn. during this period, making strength of Bn. about 900 other ranks.	
	11th		Bn. moved by bus to AUCHEL.	
	12th to 18th		Bn. training at AUCHEL.	
	19th		Bn. sports held on old aerodrome near AUCHEL. Very successful day.	Y.43
	20th	9.30am	Bn. marched to BOURECQ.	
	21st to 29th		Bn. in training at BOURECQ. No 16 Platoon won Bde. H.Q. anti-[aircraft?] competition on 29th.	"
	30th		Bn. marched to AUCHEL.	
	31st		Bn. at AUCHEL. Casualties during month - Nil	

31/7/18

.... LIEUT. COL.
COMMANDING 3rd WORCESTERSHIRE REGT.

57th Inf Bde.

2074

Herewith page 1 of War Diary for
August, which should have been
forwarded with the remainder of the
sheets. Error regretted.

Musgrave Capt & Adjt
for Major
Comdg 3rd Worcestershire Regt

22/9/18

19th Divn FA

Forwarded

22/9/18   Comdg 57 Inf Bde

WAR DIARY
or
INTELLIGENCE SUMMARY.
(Erase heading not required)

Army Form C. 2118.

Place	Date	Hour	Summary of Events and Information	Remarks and references to Appendices
	Aug 1st to 3rd		Bn training at AUCHEL	
	4th	4.30 pm	19th Division commenced relief of 2nd Division. Bn moved to CHOCQUES & became Bn in Reserve to 76th Inf Bde. 3rd Division.	
	5th		Bn relieved 1st Royal Fusiliers in the front line. AVELETTE sector.	
	6th	11 pm	Quiet day. Message received that enemy were withdrawing in front of Division on left. Patrols sent out. No signs of the enemy for at least 800 yds in front.	
	7th	9.30 am	Front line advanced & took up position K12a 38. to W12 central.	Map 36A/20,000
		7 am	to W12d 93. No signs of enemy. Ordered to advance to push Enemy back. Enemy were shelling line we are on. Flank willing active during afternoon & night.	
		2 pm	Line advanced to LIME STREET. Enemy now occupying houses in front of us & being a good deal of sniping.	

J.44

Army Form C. 2118.

WAR DIARY
or
INTELLIGENCE SUMMARY.
(Erase heading not required.)

Place	Date	Hour	Summary of Events and Information	Remarks and references to Appendices
	Aug 8th	5 am	Iine advanced. Enemy moving from W6 h.5.8. to X.1.C.8.5. to X.1.C.8.5. Enemy snipers very active; also artillery fire during night.	Ref Map 36A 1/40,000
	9th		No further advance. 2Lt P.G.S. Russell wounded in enemy shelling during night. 10 B'n & 10 R Warwickshire Regt relief line was as follows — W6 central – W6d.5.8. – X.1.c.8.5. & X.1.a.8.8.	
	10th		About 50 casualties during tour. B'n moved back to Supports, to Trenches east of HINGES.	
	11th	1.30am	B'n in Bde Support	
	12th			
	13th		B'n relieved by 10th R Warwickshire Regt & moved to Bde Reserve. B'n in Bde Reserve — 2 Coys & H.Q. at CHOCQUES, 2 Coys at VENDIN-LEZ-BÉTHUNE. Training carried out.	
	14th 15th 16th 17th 18th 19th 20th		Lt Col P.W. Ballroy DSO took over command of B'n. Capt. R.W. Ballroy DSO. T.F. Troutbeck DSO took over command of B. B'n moved into positions in the vicinity of AVELETTE. A Co. relieved two Coys of 2nd Platoons on front line, were under Orders of O.C. 8th North'd Staffs Regt.	
	21st			

Army Form C. 2118.

WAR DIARY
or
INTELLIGENCE SUMMARY.
(Erase heading not required.)

Place	Date	Hour	Summary of Events and Information	Remarks and references to Appendices
	Aug			
	27th to 28		H.Q. B, C, & D Coy moved back to GONNEHEM. 57th Inf Bde now Bde in Reserve.	
	29		Bn training at GONNEHEM.	
	23rd		A Coy withdrawn from front line & rejoined Bn at GONNEHEM.	
	29th		Bn 57th Inf Bde relieved 56th Inf Bde undergoing 8th N. Staff Regt & becoming Bn in Bde Reserve. Lt. Col Whalley DSO resumed command of Bn.	
	30th			
	31st		Bn still in same position	

Prundle........ LIEUT. COL.
COMMANDING 3rd WORCESTERSHIRE REGT.

WAR DIARY or INTELLIGENCE SUMMARY

Army Form C. 2118.

3 Worcesh. Regt

Vol 4

Place	Date	Hour	Summary of Events and Information	Remarks and references to Appendices
Bn in the Room on CANAL BANK.				Rd did to Zoaw
			Bn sdly in readiness from M.31.d.0.5 to S1.d.0.5 ham to that in which the advance through Meteren under which the Bn was taking part till the retirement of Warwicks left on its left met from of direct advance on to the Bn attack commenced. The enemy put up hostile M.G. fire and M.G. positions were very well dealt with by the Bn officers. Place was being entered by the Bn. The Germans from following from own night's front. PONT LOOG S.3 central. Battn's retreat had not been able to advance its [illegible] front was on forward with 4th Dav Cav.	
		6.30am	46th Drvn attacked hilled a barrage C&D Cos confirmed to their movements and as there were no evidence of its afternoon [illegible] revealed the two Old Bristol Fort were infact	L.45

WAR DIARY or INTELLIGENCE SUMMARY

Army Form C. 2118.

Place	Date	Hour	Summary of Events and Information	Remarks and references to Appendices
at NEUVE CHAPEL	Sept 4th		Reconnaissance Pn. escorted to front taken over from 2 Coy. 10th D.W. on other half Bn. in reserve from M3.8.8.2.0 to S.S.C.4.5.	Ref map Sh 36 1/20,000
	5th		During the day patrols were sent out to ascertain whether the old German front line was occupied. It was found that it was. Two patrols occurred on dive patrols LEARSTRA HALL. Many Fichers captured and 2 L.t. & N.C.O.s killed.	
	6th 7th 8th		Bn in same position. Active artillery fairly active especially at night. A few loose Germans infiltrated in the vicinity, one slug overstepping attacked as had succeeded only to down before relieved by 10th Royal Warwicks (left never took to support in their H.L. late)	
	9th 10th		Bn in same position. 5 L.t. Inf Bde relieved by 58 L.t. Inf Bde, the Bn being relieved by 2nd Wiltshire Regt. Moved back to reserve in HINGES and its vicinity.	
	11th to 15th 16th		Bn training and cleaning up at HINGES. Very wet weather	

WAR DIARY
or
INTELLIGENCE SUMMARY
(Erase heading not required.)

Army Form C. 2118.

Place	Date	Hour	Summary of Events and Information	Remarks and references to Appendices
	Sept 16th		Lt Col P.R.W. Inglefield assumed command of 8th Inf Bde and Major Retallack DSO of 1st Bn. 1/4 R.Berks Inf Bde in front line south of BOIS DE BIEZ.	
	17th		Quiet day	
	18th		Another quiet day. 2 Lt Dixon killed by sniper near morning (18th)	
	19th	6.30am	10th R War Regt attacked & captured the DISTILLERY & SHEPHERDS Ref Map RIENCOURT 1/10,000 A Co confirmed & pushed Adapt on to Le MASSEE & consolidated posts on the mound from SUCS 2 to SUCS 8	
		1.30pm	10th R War Regt driven out of DISTILLERY and SHEPHERDS by a counter attack. A Co held on to forward posts as long as possible, but in touch with the enemy & had been practically lost. A Co had to fall back to the original line carefully. B Co pushed out patrols which occupied during the day. B Co attacked they were still in SEVEN SISTERS.	
	21st		An uneventful day	
	22nd		Nothing of interest occurred. Lt Col B. Whalley DSO resumed command of Bn in 220	
	23rd		Bn relieved by 10 R Warwickshire Regt & moved to support line	

WAR DIARY or INTELLIGENCE SUMMARY

Army Form C. 2118.

(Erase heading not required.)

Place	Date	Hour	Summary of Events and Information	Remarks and references to Appendices
	5.1.15 24 25	3 am	Bn in line of Retention. Bn relieved 1 Gloucestershire Regt in right sub-sector from to showing CHEPHERD'S REDOUBT and the DISTILLERY.	R/ N of RICHEBOURG 1/10,000
		8 am	A Coy attacked behind SHEPHERDS REDOUBT and du DISTILLERY. All objectives captured about 80 known and 10 machine guns captured. Our casualties slight. Found however about 50 yds east of the LA BASSEE road. 10th Royal Warwickshire Regt were unable to return to our supports and left no Coy had to form a defensive flank, but were able to hold on to their line east of the road. The Bn on our right, 1/6 R.W.F. gained all objectives and took 55 Boches.	
		6 pm	was immediately opened with them. Enemy very heavy barrage put down behind our front line. Enemy immediately attempted to counter-attack, but was scattered by our rifle and lewis gun fire. Our men that advanced from their trenches to reset the enemy and to escape the barrage. Our had absolutely rested but Bn on our right fell back thus exposing our right left flank, as defensive flank had to be formed. One had up knees...	See Appendix 'A'

Army Form C. 2118.

WAR DIARY
or
INTELLIGENCE SUMMARY.
(Erase heading not required.)

Instructions regarding War Diaries and Intelligence Summaries are contained in F. S. Regs., Part II. and the Staff Manual respectively. Title pages will be prepared in manuscript.

Place	Date	Hour	Summary of Events and Information	Remarks and references to Appendices
	Sept 26	3 am	Bn on the right regained its position on the road, but had no ammn other than ½ hand grenades.	
		5.30am	Enemy again attempted to counter attack but was again repulsed by rifle & Lewis gun fire. For the remainder of the day no infantry action developed, but artillery was active on both sides. 2 Lt T.B. Mills M.C. and 2 Lt B. Newcomb were wounded during the day. Bn was relieved & Bn handed over the Brigade to 8 Gloucestershire Regt during night Sept 26/27.	
	27th 28th		Bn in support in line of Richebourg. Bn relieved by 2nd Middlesex Regt 58 Bde, and moved to Annexe at HINGES.	
	29th & 30th		Bn resting and refitting at HINGES.	

F. Rivolle .... LIEUT. COL.
COMMANDING 3rd WORCESTERSHIRE REGT.

3rd Bn The Worcestershire Regt
Casualties During September 1918

Dates	Officers K	W	M	Total Officer Casualties	Other Ranks K	W	M	Total Other Ranks	
Noon 1st to Noon 2nd						3		3	
3rd to 4th					5	23		28	1 Off. at duty / 20 OR Dof W
4th to 5th						3		3	
5th to 6th	1	1	1	2		6	1	7	
7th to 8th	1	-	-			1		1	
8th to 9th						1		1	Died of Wds
18th to 19th	1	-	-	1	1	1		2	
19th to 20th					1	2		3	
20th to 21st		1	-	1	3	15		18	
23rd to 24th						6		6	
24th to 25th					-	3		8	
25th to 26th		1	-	1	12	15	2*	29	*1 OR Dof Wds
26th to 27th		1	-	1		2*		2	*1 at duty 1 D of Wds
27th to 28th					1			1	
	2	3	1	6	23	131	3	157	

Total officer casualties 6
"   OR   " 157

1st October 1918   Frank Lee .... LIEUT. COL.
COMMANDING 3rd WORCESTERSHIRE REGT.

Appendix A

ROUTINE ORDERS.
BY
Lt. Col. P. R. WHALLEY D.S.O. Commdg. —ᵗʰ Bⁿ THE WORCESTERSHIRE REGIMENT.

EXTRACT   SEPTEMBER 28ᵗʰ 1918

Recent Operations.

The following messages are published for information and communication to all ranks.

—ᵗʰ Inf Bde.

"Please convey my hearty congratulations to Lt Col WHALLEY and all ranks of the —ᵗʰ Worcestershire Regiment on their fine performance in capturing SHEPHERD'S REDOUBT and the DISTILLERY and holding them against all counter attacks"

(Sgd) G. D. Jeffreys Major Genl
Commdg —ᵗʰ Division

26.9.18.

—ᵗʰ Worc Regt.

"I have the greatest pleasure in forwarding the attached congratulatory message from the G.O.C. the Division.

I desire also to place on record my own personal thanks for the courage, energy and determination displayed by all ranks during the past few days.

In addition I realise that the Regimental motto "FIRM" is as much inwardly implanted on the mind of every Officer and man of the —ᵗʰ Bⁿ The Worcestershire Regiment, as it is outwardly displayed."

Bde HQ
27.9.18
(Sgd) A. J. F. Eden Brig Genl
Commdg —ᵗʰ Inf Bde

[signature]
Captain
Adjutant —ᵗʰ Bⁿ The Worcestershire Regt.

Army Form C. 2118.

WAR DIARY
or
INTELLIGENCE SUMMARY.
(Erase heading not required.)

Instructions regarding War Diaries and Intelligence Summaries are contained in F.S. Regs., Part II. and the Staff Manual respectively. Title pages will be prepared in manuscript.

Place	Date	Hour	Summary of Events and Information	Remarks and references to Appendices
	Oct 1st		Bn relieved by 2/5 Royal Welsh Fusiliers 74th Division and moved by march route to AUCHEL, where the night was spent.	
	2nd		Bn marched from AUCHEL to TANGRY, where it was in Bn Bivouac & prepared to move at short notice.	Rft of 1 2nd LIEUT 11 /100 OR
	3rd		Training at TANGRY.	
	4th	20.00	Bn entrained at BRYAS for Third Army Area.	
	5th	09.00	Bn detrained at WANINCOURT and marched to SOUASTRE.	
	6th		Training at SOUASTRE. Transport left by road for GRAINCOURT.	
	7th	14.15	Bn entrained for GRAINCOURT.	
		22.15	Bn arrived in camp at GRAINCOURT.	
	8th		Bn at GRAINCOURT.	
	9th		Bn moved to camp near ANNEUX.	L &
	10th		Bn moved to northern suburbs of CAMBRAI	
	11th		Training etc. in CAMBRAI.	
	12th		Bn moved to south eastern suburbs of CAMBRAI.	
	13th		Church parade etc in CAMBRAI. R.C. service held in CAMBRAI Cathedral.	
	14th 15 16		Bn training at CAMBRAI.	
	17 18		Bn marched to ST AUBERT. Now Bn in support to 2nd Inf. Bde.	

Army Form C. 2118.

WAR DIARY
or
INTELLIGENCE SUMMARY.
(Erase heading not required.)

Place	Date	Hour	Summary of Events and Information	Remarks and references to Appendices
	Oct 17th	1600	Bn relieved 7th Northamptons in the HAUSSY sector. During the night D Coy advanced their line to railway cutting.	Ref Map SIA SE 1/20,000
	18th		During the day two platoons pushed across railway into the village.	
	19th	1400	Enemy found to have retired on C Coy front, but still in southern part of village.	
	20th	0200	10th R.War.Regt. & 9th Glosters attacked & captured HAUSSY & high ground beyond. Bn in support in HAUSSY	
	21st 22nd		Bn in HAUSSY	
	23rd	1200	Bn. moved to AYESNES in rest	
	26th	0900	Bn. moved to CAUROIR and resumed the training till Armistice.	

P R Whalley LIEUT. COL.
COMMANDING 3rd WORCESTERSHIRE REGT.

3rd Bn The Worcestershire Regiment
Casualties during October 1918

Dates	Officers			Total Officer Casualties	Other Ranks			Total Other Ranks	
	K.	W.	M.		K.	W.	M.		
Noon 18th to Noon 19th					3	14		17	20th Afoot
" 19th - 20					1	32*		33	
" 20th - 21					1	4		5	
" 21 - 22					2	3		5	
" 22 - 23					1*	2		3	Died in Hospital (sick)
" 23 - 24						2		2	
" 24 - 25					1*	3		4	1st Bn of Ado on Oct.10.18 Died in Hospital (sick)
" 25 - 26					1*	1		2	
	—	—	—	—	10	61	—	71	

Total Officer Casualties —
" O.R. --- 71

1st November 1918.   P R W .... LIEUT. COL.
COMMANDING 3rd WORCESTERSHIRE REGT.

57th Inf Bde.

Herewith original copy of War Diary for the month of November 1918.

J.W.E. Mullin
for Major
COMMANDING 3rd WORCESTERSHIRE REGT.

Army Form C. 2118.

WAR DIARY
or
INTELLIGENCE SUMMARY.
(Erase heading not required.)

Instructions regarding War Diaries and Intelligence Summaries are contained in F. S. Regs., Part II. and the Staff Manual respectively. Title pages will be prepared in manuscript.

J.47

Place	Date	Hour	Summary of Events and Information	Remarks and references to Appendices
	Nov 1918			
	1st		Bn training at CARDIR	
	2nd	0800	Bn moved to billets at ST AUBERT	
	3rd	1605	Bn moved to SEPMERIES starting for an attack at VENDEGIES	
	4th	0900	Bn moved to billets about ST HUBERT crossroads	
	5th	0944	Bn moved to billets at ETH.	
	6th	2300	Bn moved from ETH and relieved 6th K.S.L.I. in trenches S. WEST BANK of R. HORNEAU B. HQ at FLAMENGRIE	
	7th	0100	Brigade took R.Warnick on left and 24th Division on right attacked and captured with crossed EAST of the River HORNEAU and the village of BERMERIES. C & D Coys attacked, B in support. No other dispositions. A & C Coys reached final objective 1/2 hr Two Lieut G. GEORGE killed. We attacked fourteen German O.R.'s captured.	R.O. ref Sheet 51
	8th		Staff Sgt W. H. G. Halifax was hit on his arm but did not leave. Toronto 2nd Lieut JONES, PARKIN and J. W. WEBB assumed the duties of Q.M. as Capt BROWN, A.M. went sick. Evening billets over for (illegible) of M. (illegible) ... moving along town	

Army Form C. 2118.

WAR DIARY
or
INTELLIGENCE SUMMARY.
(Erase heading not required.)

3 Wmash

Instructions regarding War Diaries and Intelligence Summaries are contained in F. S. Regs., Part II. and the Staff Manual respectively. Title pages will be prepared in manuscript.

Place	Date	Hour	Summary of Events and Information	Remarks and references to Appendices
	9th		8th Glosters and and Bn and carried on the advance with 5 squadrons and by 11th Division on left and 5th Division on right into front line at the Brigade front. Bn. spent the night in billets at LES VENTS and LES BAIVENTS	
	10th		Bn moved back to billets at HEBUTERNE	
	11th		Armistice with Germany signed. Hostilities ceased 11/00 hours. Bn moved to LA FLAMENGRIE.	
	14th		Bn. moved to SEPMERIES	
	15th		Bn moved to ST AUBERT	
	16th		Bn moved to CAUROIR.	
	27th		Bn moved to FIENVILLERS.	

R.J. Tarte
Major
COMMANDING 3rd WORCESTERSHIRE REGT.

19th Division 57 Bde

WG197

Herewith War
Diaries of 3rd Worc.
R.

H. Horn
Weaver
for Brig Genl
Comdg 57th Bde

14/
11/
15

3rd Bn. The Worcestershire Regiment.
Casualties for Month of November 1918.

Period	Officers			Total Officer Casualties	Other Ranks			Total O.R. Casualties	
	K	W	M		K	W	M		
Noon Nov 3rd to noon Nov 4						8*		8	*D. of W.
" 7th " " 8		1		1	2	21*		23	*at duty
" 8 " " 9		1*		1*		14	5	19	at duty
Nov 9th	1 died			1					
Totals	1	2	-	3	2	43	5	50	

Total Officer Casualties — 3
Total O.R. Casualties — 50
53

1st December 1918.

Major
Commanding 3rd Worcestershire Regt.

MEMO

From

To

June 18
pm 3
pm. 6/9
——————191——————

10 Batt. Worcesters
attached to Batt. Worcesters
3rd Batt. Co.—

6/9.

Army Form C. 2118.

3 Worcs

WAR DIARY
or
INTELLIGENCE SUMMARY.

(Erase heading not required.)

Place	Date	Hour	Summary of Events and Information	Remarks and references to Appendices
	2nd		Bn at FIENVILLERS whole month. Training carried out, and a great deal of football played. Demobilisation began. Pivotal men and coalminers despatched to England throughout the month. Bn. Colour were fetched from Worcester Cathedral, on Colour party commanded of Capt E. LATTEY M.C. Capt L.J. VICARAGE No 9297 R.S.M. S.F. BYRON No. 200843 C.S.M. A.H. JONES D.C.M. and No 10058 Sgt REDEY One draft of 119 joined Bn. on 11st.	

Prinkle .... LIEUT. COL.
COMMANDING 3rd WORCESTERSHIRE REGT.

Army Form C. 2118.

3 Worcesters

WAR DIARY
or
INTELLIGENCE SUMMARY.
(Erase heading not required.)

Instructions regarding War Diaries and Intelligence Summaries are contained in F. S. Regs., Part II. and the Staff Manual respectively. Title pages will be prepared in manuscript.

T.49

Place	Date	Hour	Summary of Events and Information	Remarks and references to Appendices
January			Bun at BIENVILLERS whole month.	
	1st		Training, divisional & inspection's carried out.	
	11th		Dangerous areas made more safe.	
	25th		Bn. received through the ensuing fortnight CAPT E. LATTEY MC., CAPT VICKERS and also various unnamed ranks.	
			Bn. also sent to 8th GLOUCESTERSHIRE REGT. & 10th R. WARWICKSHIRE REGT. various parties of whom to instructs 9th CHESHIRE REGT.	
			4 M-G-N OFFICERS & 80 ORS (CONS 19th DIV)	
	27th		Bn. football team won the Div. Commander's cup football cup, beating 9th CHESHIRE REGT in final.	
			Bn. also won the Div. Cross Country Run held during the month.	

P. Whalley
LIEUT. COL.
COMMANDING 3rd WORCESTERSHIRE REGT.

Army Form C. 2118.

WAR DIARY
or
INTELLIGENCE SUMMARY

3 Worcester

Place	Date	Hour	Summary of Events and Information	Remarks and references to Appendices
	Feb		Bnt at FIENVILLERS for whole month. Demobilization of all miners men except dost so completed during the month.	
	28		Draft of 6 officers and 193 Other Ranks sent to 2nd Bn Worcestershire Regt. Education carried out during the whole month	

28/2/19

Prevulee .... LIEUT. COL.
COMMANDING 3rd WORCESTERSHIRE REGT.

NO 95/2086/2

19TH DIVISION
57TH INFY BDE

10TH BN WORCESTERSHIRE REGT
JLY 1915 - FEB 1918

~~DIARIES MISSING:-~~
~~DEC. 1916 AND~~
~~MAR - JUNE 1918.~~

Amalgamated with 3 BN

10 Worcesters
Vol 9

57th Inf.Bde.
19th Div.

Battn. disembarked
Boulogne from
England 19.7.15.

WAR DIARY

10th BATTN. THE WORCESTERSHIRE REGIMENT.

J U L Y

(17.7.15 - 31.7.15)

1 9 1 5

6
Feb '18

WAR DIARY or INTELLIGENCE SUMMARY

10th Worcestershire Regt.

(Erase heading not required.)

Instructions regarding War Diaries and Intelligence Summaries are contained in F.S. Regs., Part II and the Staff Manual respectively. Title Pages will be prepared in manuscript.

Place	Date	Hour	Summary of Events and Information	Remarks and references to Appendices
TIDWORTH	17/7/15	10:30 a.m.	1st line Transport, Machine Gun Detachment, Officers Chargers, 5 Officers and 107 other ranks proceeded to SOUTHAMPTON and entrained for HAVRE.	
"	18/7/15	6:30 p.m.	Head Quarters and A & B Companies left by train at 6:30 p.m. for FOLKESTONE	
BOULOGNE	19/7/15		C and D Companies left at 7 p.m. for FOLKESTONE. The first train was formed by the 2nd train on arriving to the relieving for changing trains through collision of trains at Tidworth. The Battalion crossed to BOULOGNE on two ships and marched to rest camp at OSTROHOVE	
"	"	—	Remained at OSTROHOVE all day.	
"	20/7/15	6:30 a.m.	Marched to PONT DE BRIQUES railway station and entrained for WATTEN, where met advance party.	Ref 100,000 HAZEBROUCK 5A
WATTEN	"	4:30 p.m.	Marched from WATTEN to billets at BAYENGHEM-LES-EPERLECQUES.	
BAYENGHEM	21/7/15	—	Remained in billets.	
"	22/7/15	9 a.m.	was on battalion route march through NORTLEUHNGHEM and MENTQUE.	
"	23/7/15	7 a.m.	Marched off to occupy fresh billets between RENESCURE at LYNDE. 2½ kils. from ST. OMER.	
RENESCURE	"	5 p.m.	Arrived at the new billets.	
"	24/7/15	7:30 a.m.	Marched off to occupy fresh billets at NEUFPRÉ and PECQUEUR near at the East of AIRE.	
AIRE	"	12 noon	Had dinner at AIRE.	
"	25/7/15	—	Remained at NEUFPRÉ and PECQUEUR.	
"	26/7/15	—	" "	
"	27/7/15	—	" "	
"	28/7/15	—	" "	
"	29/7/15	10 a.m.	Battalion Route March through BOESEGHEM.	
"	30/7/15	9 a.m.	Marched off to occupy billets at HAVERSKERQUE. Arrived 1 p.m.	
HAVERSKERQUE	31/7/15	11:45 a.m.	Billets at FEULES PURESBECQUES having left HAVERSKERQUE at 12:25 p.m.	Officer comm'g 10/Worc 3rd A. Sheet 3½.A.

57th Inf.Bde.
19th Div.

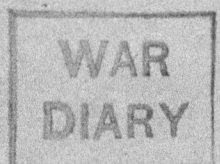

10th BATTN. THE WORCESTERSHIRE REGIMENT.

A U G U S T

1 9 1 5

INTELLIGENCE SUMMARY

(Erase heading not required.)

10th Worcestershire Regt.

Place	Date	Hour	Summary of Events and Information	Remarks and references to Appendices
MERVILLE.	Aug 1st	—	In billets.	
"	2nd	10:30am	The Battalion was inspected by Lt. Gen. Sir James Willcocks, Comdg. Indian Army Corps.	
"	3rd	8:30am	The Battalion marched to billets at ESTAIRES.	
ESTAIRES.	4th	5:0 pm	The Battalion marched to billets at LAVENTIE. A Coy went into the trenches for instruction with 2nd Bn. Black Watch (Bareilly Brigade)	
LAVENTIE.	5th	8:0 pm	In billets at LAVENTIE. A Coy in the trenches. C Coy working party of 150 diggers worked at support-trench	
"	"	—	of F Sup section (58th Rifles + 44th Deogras) from 10 p.m. to 2 a.m. (6"). D Coy working party of 200 diggers	
"	"	—	worked at support trench of E Sup section (2nd Black Water, to relief of A Coy. D Coy working party to Fortification	
"	6th	8:0 pm	B Coy to trenches into 2nd Black Water, to relief of A Coy. D Coy working party to Fortification (Bareilly Brigade)	
"	7th	8:0 pm	C Coy to trenches into H.Q. Black Water. A Coy working party to Fortification.	
"	8th	8:0 pm	D Coy to trenches into 2nd Black Water, to relief of B Coy. (3 casualties - wounded - 2 C Coy + 1 B Coy)	
"	9th	6:0 pm	C Coy relieved by a company of 1st 8th Gloucestershire Regt. B Coy working party which * suspected (2 casualties - wounded - 1 C + D)	* died 10th inst.
"	10th	5:0 pm	The Battalion less A + D Coy returned to billets at ESTAIRES. D Coy returned after being relieved by a Coy of	
"	"	—	1st 8th Gloucestershire Regt. A Coy remained at LE DRUMEZ, being attached to the Bareilly Brigade for	
ESTAIRES.	11th to 14th	—	work in the front line.	
"			Battalion less A Coy remained in billets.	
MERVILLE.	14th	4 p.m.	Battalion marched to join same billets at LES PURESBECQUES. Route to north of MERVILLE.	
"	15th to 27th	—	Battalion remained in billets at LES PURESBECQUES.	
"	17th	7 p.m.	A Coy returned from LE DRUMEZ	
"	26th	9 a.m.	4 Officers proceeded to trenches of JULLUNDUR BRIGADE for 48 hours instruction.	
"	22nd	"	" " " " " " " " " "	
"	24th	"	" " " " " - SIRHIND " " " "	
"	6th	"	" " " " " " " " " "	

INTELLIGENCE SUMMARY

18th Worcestershire Regt.

(Erase heading not required.)

Place	Date	Hour	Summary of Events and Information	Remarks and references to Appendices
MERVILLE	August 27.	3 p.m.	The Battalion marched to LA CROIX MARMUSE to new billets.	
LA CROIX MARMUSE	28.	5 p.m.	The Battalion moved to his trenches (IND II) and relieved the 1st Bn. Royal Welsh Fusiliers. Relief completed 10.30 p.m. Headquarters in la firing line each side of Peloton is supporttrench. front line: QUINQUE RUE to FARM CORNER.	
Trenches (IND II)	29. to 31.		Front received from QUINQUE RUE to PIPE Communication trench and no cog withdrawn to Reserve trench at TUBE STN. Work done each night:- Strengthening & raising of front parapets.	
"	30.		1 casualty (slightly wounded)	

A.V. [signature] Colonel
Comdg. 18th Worcestershire Regt.

57th Inf.Bde.
19th Div.

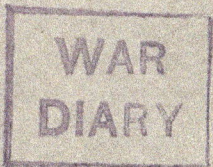

10th BATTN. THE WORCESTERSHIRE REGIMENT.

S E P T E M B E R

1 9 1 5

INTELLIGENCE SUMMARY 10th Worcestershire Regt.

(Erase heading not required.)

Place	Date Sept.	Hour	Summary of Events and Information	Remarks and references to Appendices
Trenches. (INDI b.)	1st	4 p.m.	The Battalion occupied the trenches (IND II b) for this period. QUINQUE RUE to PIPE Communication trench.	
	2nd		5 casualties on (Br. inf.) (all wounded) German cap (apparently had Hijaz*) rifle numbered 13.R.8.2.17, + hand grenade were captured. *This might read 13th Reserve Regt. 8th Company 12.17 being the Company number, this Regiment belongs to the VII Reserve Corps. Extract from "Khaki Corps" Intelligence Summary 4. 3/9/15.	
"	3rd		Casualties nil.	
"	4th		Casualties: 1 killed and 1 wounded.	
"	5th		" 2 killed and 3 wounded (including Lieut. R. Huxley wounded)	
"	6th		" 5 wounded.	
"	7th		Relieved in Trenches by 10th Bn. Royal Warwickshire Regt. Relief completed by 1.30 a.m. Three Companies proceeded to billets at RUE DES CHAVATTES and one company garrisoned its following posts:- CHAVATTES, EPINETTE.N, HAYSTACK, PATH, CHOCOLATE, DEAD COW, DITCH, BRIGADE ADVANCED POST, LE TOURET; lce whole Battalion forming Brigade Reserve. Total casualties during 10 days in trenches 3 killed and 17 wounded including Lt. R. Huxley.	
RUE DES CHAVATTES.	8th	1.30 a.m.	Found following working parties :- 70 men to construct new Brigade Advanced Post near RUE CAILLOUX	
		7 p.m.	200 men to carry stores for Machine Gun Company, 100 men to INDIAN VILLAGE and	
		8.30 p.m.	100 men to HAYSTACK POST. A working party of 30 men joined 10th Battalion.	
"	9th	8.30 a.m.	Working party of 70 men to RUE CAILLOUX.	
		7.15 p.m.	" 200 " to INDIAN VILLAGE.	
		7.30 p.m.	" 200 " to HAYSTACK.	
"	10th	8.30 a.m.	" 70 " to RUE CAILLOUX to complete Brigade Advanced Post.	
"	11th	7.15 p.m.	" 300 " to INDIAN VILLAGE.	
"		7.30 p.m.	" 100 " to HAYSTACK POST.	

INTELLIGENCE SUMMARY of 10th Worcestershire Regt.

(Erase heading not required.)

Instructions regarding War Diaries and Intelligence Summaries are contained in F.S. Regs., Part II. and the Staff Manual respectively. Title Pages will be prepared in manuscript.

Place	Date	Hour	Summary of Events and Information	Remarks and references to Appendices
RUE DES CRAVATTES	Sept. 12th	3 p.m.	The billets of the battalion were taken over by the 7th Battn Royal North Lancashire Regt. also. Its posts occupied on 7th inst.	
LOCON.	13th		The Battalion marched to new billets in the neighbourhood of LOCON and occupied the five following posts :— MESPLAUX N-E- and W, LE HAMMEL, LAWE.	
"	14th	3.30 p.m.	A working party of 400 were driven in 19 Divl Artillery wagons to ESTAMINET CORNER for work on communication trenches.	
"	15th	5.0 a.m.	Working Party returned.	
"	—	3.30 p.m.	Same working party proceeded to ESTAMINET CORNER.	
"	16th	5.0 a.m.	Working Party returned.	
"	"	10.45 a.m.	The 2nd Battalion of the Regt. marched over from its billets to BETHUNE and paraded with the battalion; a square being formed and speeches made by Lieut. G. F. Lenton D.S.O. and Major W.A. Lenox Conyngham. The Officers and men fell in for about ½ hour; the 2nd Battalion then left and was marched away by the bugle band of the 10th Battalion. Battalion remained in billets.	
"	17th	"	"	
"	18th	"	"	
"	19th	4 p.m.	Working party of 200 men proceeded to ESTAMINET CORNER.	
"	—	5 p.m.	" 200 men " " HAYSTACK POST.	
"	20th	—	"	
"	21st	—	"	
"	22nd	9.30 a.m.	The Battalion went for a route march in the "new light- marching order."	
"	23rd			
"	24th		Received orders to proceed to bivouac at LE HAMEL.	
"	25th	3.0 p.m.	Battalion proceeded into bivouac at LE H AMEL	

Instructions regarding War Diaries and Intelligence
Summaries are contained in F.S. Regs., Part II.
and the Staff Manual respectively. Title Pages
will be prepared in manuscript.

INTELLIGENCE SUMMARY 10th Worcestershire Regt.

(Erase heading not required.)

Place	Date Sept.	Hour	Summary of Events and Information	Remarks and references to Appendices
LE HAMEL	25th	8.30 a.m.	Battalion was ordered to proceed to a point 1 mile E of GORRE.	
		9.51 a.m.	Battalion was ordered to proceed further E to MARAIS to get in touch with the 10th Royal Warwickshire Regt. then proceeding in support of the 5-8th Brigade which had been launched to attack enemy's position to the N.E. of GIVENCHY LEZ LA BASSÉE.	
		10.20.	The 57th Brigade to which the Battalion belonged was placed at the disposal of the G.O.C. 2nd Division, to support the 5th Brigade which had been attacking the enemy's trenches situated on the N. side of the AIRE — LA BASSÉE canal and to the E. of GIVENCHY LEZ LA BASSÉE.	
		10.30.	At Staff Officer of the 19th Division H.Q. Staff conveyed an order to the Brigadier of the 57th Brigade, cancelling this latter order.	
		11.2.	The Battalion was ordered to proceed to LE PLANTIN to support the 10th Royal Warwickshire Regt. and endeavour to keep touch on its left with the 58th Brigade, the objective being the further trenches in the enemy's line to the E. of GIVENCHY LEZ LA BASSÉE, which was strongly held.	
		11.20.	When the head of the Battalion had reached LE PLANTIN, the order was cancelled and the Battalion withdrawn to its position W. of MARAIS, the order for the attack on the trenches N. of the line having been rescinded and the troops directed to retire on and hold the line BRITISH line of trenches.	
	4 p.m.		The Battalion remained in support till this hour when it reoccupied a reserve line of trenches in support of the 5-8th Brigade.	
LOCON.	26th	9.30.	The Battalion was ordered to return to its billets in the vicinity of LOCON.	
"	27th	5.45 p.m.	The Battalion remained in billets awaiting orders to move at short notice. The Battalion was ordered to reoccupy at Brigade H.Q. at LE HAMEL, which it reached about 7 p.m.	

INTELLIGENCE SUMMARY

(Erase heading not required.)

Place	Date Sept.	Hour	Summary of Events and Information	Remarks and references to Appendices
LE HAMEL.	27th	7.40pm	Orders were received to return to billets at LOCON and be prepared to rendezvous at LE HAMEL within about 40 mins notice.	
LOCON.	28th		The Battalion remained in billets in the vicinity of LOCON.	
"	29th	4.45pm	The Battalion left billets and proceeded to the trenches IND II to relieve the 7th Bn. East Lancashire Regt, holding the line from S.27.b.4.3. on left to BARNTON ROAD on right.	
IND II.	30th	12.30 a.m.	The relief complete. 2 men wounded by a bomb. A shorter line of the trenches was allotted to the battalion, namely from the centre of ROTHESAY BAY to S.27.b.4.3.	
"	30/9/15.			

A. Mooney.
Colonel.
Comdg 10th (S) Bn. Worcestershire Regt.

57th Inf.Bde.
19th Div.

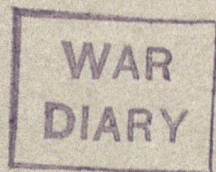

10th BATTN. THE WORCESTERSHIRE REGIMENT.

OCTOBER

1915

Instructions regarding War Diaries and Intelligence Summaries are contained in F.S. Regs., Part II. and the Staff Manual respectively. Title Pages will be prepared in manuscript.

WAR DIARY or INTELLIGENCE SUMMARY 10th Worcestershire Regt:-

(Erase heading not required.)

Place	Date Oct.	Hour	Summary of Events and Information	Remarks and references to Appendices
Trenches IND II C.	1.	9.30 a.m.	Working party of 2 Officers and 100 men proceeded to ROTHESAY BAY to construct dugouts under the supervision of 94th Coy. R.E.	
	2.	8.30 p.m.	3 Companies of the Battalion were relieved by the 9th Gorkhas. These Coys and Headquarters marched to bivouac at LE HAMEL.	
LE HAMEL.	3.	8.45 p.m.	The Battalion relieved the 7th Bn. Sealorn Regt in IND IV A; 1st Company took remainder in See IND II C. Hijemd. Section held by Battalion. PIPE Trench to FARM CORNER.	
IND IV A.	4.			
"	5.	3 a.m.	Very heavy gun and rifle fire on our extreme left. One man wounded. Lieut. L. F. Tree wounded.	
"	6.			
"	7.	6 p.m.	The relief of the Battalion by the 10th Royal Warwickshire Regt commenced. The Battalion relieved the 8th Gloucestershire Regt in Brigade Reserve and was distributed as follows:- A Coy — Reserve line of trenches by EDWARD ROAD. B Coy — 1 Platoon in Reserve trenches by ALBERT ROAD and the remainder of the Coy occupied the following posts:- CHOCOLATE, DEAD COW, HAYSTACK, PATH, Z. ORCHARD, ALBERT, CATS, DOGS, FACTORY. C Coy — Reserve line of trenches by ALBERT ROAD. D Coy — 3 Platoons in following posts:- RICHEBOURG WORKS, SCOTT, HUNTER, RAGS, BONES, ANGLE and GROTTO. The remainder of D Coy and Bn. H.Q. at X.5.c.8.6. (LACOUTURE) Relief complete.	
LACOUTURE.	8.	12.2 a.m.	Remained in Brigade Reserve until this date when relieved by 8th North Staffordshire Regt. Relief complete about 11 p.m.	
VIEILLE CHAPELLE	11. "		The Battalion went into billets at VIEILLE CHAPELLE relieving the 8th Gloucestershire Regt and took over the following posts:- VIEILLE CHAPELLE, FOSSE and ZELOBES.	

INTELLIGENCE SUMMARY 10th Worcestershire Regt.

(Erase heading not required.)

Place	Date Oct. 1915	Hour	Summary of Events and Information	Remarks and references to Appendices
VIEILLE CHAPELLE	12		Day spent by the men getting hut built at the Brewery.	
	13.	3:30 p.m.	The Battalion returned to billets in the neighbourhood of LACOUTURE in the afternoon.	
LACOUTURE	"	6:15 p.m.	The vicinity of Battalion H.Q. was heavily shelled by gas shells - one barn being hit, killing 2 men and wounding 6; one of the 2 killed was killed by gas. The remainder of the men were moved to another billet.	
"	14.		The Battalion remained in billets.	
Trenches IND IV A.	15.	6:30 p.m. 6:20 p.m.	The Battalion relieved the 10th Royal Warwickshire Regt. in the Trenches. Section IND IV A. Relief complete. B and D Coys in front line. A + C Coys in Reserve line. 2 men wounded by shell.	
MARAIS.	20.		The Battalion was relieved by the 2/3rd Gurkhas and 39th Garhwal Rifles. Relief complete by 8 p.m. A Coy occupied FESTUBERT EAST & LE PLANTIN POST EAST and remainder of Company and B, C, and D Coys occupied the Reserve trenches at MARAIS taking over from the 5th A- Serv of Lt Debra Dun Brigade.	
"	21.		The 2 posts taken over by A Coy were handed over to the 34th Walls Borderers. (Pioneers)	
Reserve Trenches IND I B.	22.		The Battalion moved to the OLD BRITISH TRENCH & Section IND I.B. took and garrisoned the following posts :- FESTUBERT, FESTUBERT. E, LE PLANTIN. N. S. and E.	
"	26.	11:30 a.m.	LE PLANTIN heavily shelled in morning. Casualties :- Lieut. R. Hartley killed and 3 men wounded.	
"	27.			
"	28.			
"	29.			
"	30.	10 a.m.	LE PLANTIN again shelled. Lieut. A.G. Bishop wounded.	
"	31.			

B. E. F. France
31/10/15

M H Leman/Longman Major
Comdg 10th Worcestershire Regt.

57th Inf.Bde.
19th Div.

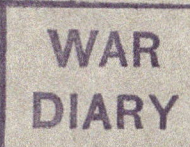

10th BATTN. THE WORCESTERSHIRE REGIMENT.

N O V E M B E R

1 9 1 5

WAR DIARY or INTELLIGENCE SUMMARY — 10th Worcestershire Regt.

Place	Date Nov.	Hour	Summary of Events and Information	Remarks and references to Appendices
OLD BRITISH LINE. INDI B.	1	Evening	Relieved line and in FESTUBERT and LE PLANTIN posts by 10th Royal Warwickshire Regt.	
IND I B.	2	12.30 a.m.	The Battalion relieved the 8th North Staffordshire Regt. in Section IND I.B. Relief not complete until 12.30 a.m. 2nd inst. owing to the impassable state of the trenches, heavy rain having caused considerable damage to the line. Shelter-dugouts have collapsed, communication and fire trenches are all flooded in many places, parapets and parados falling in. Men have no shelter and have to stand up to neck out waist in water all night.	
"	3.		No shelling, 2 wounded, and 1 broken leg.	
"	4.		2 men killed, 2 wounded, and 1 broken leg.	
"	5.		1 man wounded.	
"			The Battalion was relieved by the 8th North Staffordshire Regt. and went into billets at LE HAMEL and B Coy occupying dummy posts with garrison of 1 in each :- LOISNE. N), and E. TUNING FORK. W) and E, ROUTE A. Relief complete.	
LE HAMEL.	6 7 8		The Battalion remained in billets.	
LOCON	9 10 11 12 13 14 15.		The Battalion went into billets in the neighbourhood of LOCON taking over from 7th East Lancs Regt.	

The Battalion was inspected by Major General C.B. Fasken. C.B., Commanding 19th Division

INTELLIGENCE SUMMARY — 10th Worcestershire Regt.

(Erase heading not required.)

Place	Date 1915	Hour	Summary of Events and Information	Remarks and references to Appendices
LOCON.	Nov 16.		Battalion in billets.	
"	17.		The Battalion relieved the 9th Cheshire Regt in the Trenches. Section IND II A. relief complete by 8.15 p.m.	
Trenches. IND II A.	18.			
"	19.		In the Trenches Section IND II A. Casualties 5-killed and 6 wounded.	
"	20.	8.30 a.m	2 hour bombardment of German line opposite of CANADIAN ORCHARD.	
"	21.	8.20 p.m	The Battalion was relieved in the trenches by the 10th Royal Warwickshire Regt, and went into billets as follows:- A & B Coys billets at LE TOURET, C Coy billets in RUE DES CHAVATTES. "D" Coy into ruined houses in RUE DE L'EPINETTE.	6th Wilts page
LE TOURET	22		Remained in billets.	
"	23.		The Battalion moved into billets to LA TOMBE WILLOT taking over from the 6th Lincoln Regt. The 4th Lincoln Regt of 46th Division moved into our billets at LE TOURET.	
LA TOMBE WILLOT.	24.		Remained in billets.	
CALONNE.	25.		The Battalion moved into billets on the CALONNE — ROBECQ Road. left LA TOMBE WILLOT at 10 a.m. and arrived in new billeting area at 12.30 p.m. The day was occupied by Platoon training.	
"	26.		Improving billets, renovating the transport lines anyhow, and motor transport, erecting attention lintels, latrines etc.	
"	27.		do	
"	28.		do	
"	29		Company Training.	
"	30		do	

30/XI/15.

R L Cheney Colonel.
Comdg 10th Worcestershire Regt.

57th Inf.Bde.
19th Div.

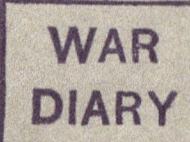

10th BATTN. THE WORCESTERSHIRE REGIMENT.

D E C E M B E R

1 9 1 5

INTELLIGENCE SUMMARY

(Erase heading not required.)

10-(5) Bn. Worcestershire Regt.

Place	Date Dec 1915	Hour	Summary of Events and Information	Remarks and references to Appendices
CALONNE.	1.		Battalion established in billets on the ROBECQ – CALONNE Road.	
"	2.			
"	3.		The Battalion was inspected in marching order by Lt. G.O.C. 57th Infantry Brigade.	
"	4.	9 a.m.	The Battalion moved into fresh billets as under :– H.Q. A and C Coy to BOUT DEVILLE and B and D Coys to LES 8 MAISONS. The 19th Div being taken away from XI Corps.	
BOUT DEVILLE	5.		H.Q. A and C Coy has moved back to the trenches owing to the 46th Div being taken away from XI Corps.	
"	6.			
"	7.			
"	8.			
"	9.			
"	10.			
"	11.		The Battalion remained in billets.	
Trenches IND. IV.A.	12.	7.40 p.m.	The Battalion relieved the 9th Cheshire Regt. in trenches Section IND IV A, relief complete by 7.40 p.m. A Coy in reserve and occupying HENS and EDWARD Posts, B Coy in support occupying FACTORY, ALBERT, DOGS and CATS Posts, C and D Coys in front line.	
"	13.	6.30 p.m.	"C" Coy 15th Welch Regt. arrived for instruction – one platoon attached to each company. Our artillery was fairly very active. Retaliation by enemy was practically nil.	
"	14.		On 14th inst.	
"	15.		The Battalion was relieved in trenches by the 16th Royal Warwickshire Regt. Relief complete by 7.15 p.m. Russian horses were occupied in RICHEBOURG ST VAAST and following posts :– RICHEBOURG, ANGLE, GROTTO, SCOTT, HUNTER, RAGS and BONES.	
RICHEBOURG ST VAAST.	16.		A Coy in support. B Coy in Reserve. C and D Coys in Front Line. Casualties were provided with a sentries installed in front line. 9. H.E. shells were dropped in the village, namely near Batn. H.Q. (similar for forty yards) (3 men wounded + 2 mules)	
"	17.			
"	18.			
"	19.			
Trenches IND. IV A	20.	4.30 p.m. 6.30 p.m.	The Battalion relieved the 16th Royal Warwickshire Regt. in the trenches Section IND IV A, relief complete by 6.30 p.m. A Coy in support. B Coy in Reserve. C and D Coys in Front Line. C Coy 15th Welch left the Battalion. "C" Coy 14th Welch Regt. arrived for instruction – one platoon attached to each company.	

INTELLIGENCE SUMMARY

10-(S)Th. Worcestershire Regt.

(Erase heading not required.)

and the Staff Manual respectively. Title Pages will be prepared in manuscript.

Place	Date Dec 1915	Hour	Summary of Events and Information	Remarks and references to Appendices
Trenches INDIA	21.	Dusk	Companies in front line were relieved by Coys in Support and Reserve.	
"	24.	2 a.m.	Companies in Support and Reserve were moved up to OLD BRITISH LINE; the whole battalion stood to arms to intended gas and bombing attack on our left by 9th Welch Regt. Which was intermittent, or attack was postponed. Companies returned to their original positions.	
"	22.	2.45 a.m. 9 p.m.	An attempted bombing raid by 1st 12th Division took place. A heavy artillery duel, which lasted for about an hour. A draft of 20 arrived from the Base. The Battalion was relieved in the trenches by 7th Royal Warwickshire Regt. Relief complete	
"	23.	about 7.30 p.m.	Ruined Louvres was reoccupied in the trenches of RICHEBOURG ST VAAST and the following posts by D. Coy:-	
RICHEBOURG ST VAAST.	24.	10 a.m.	RICHEBOURG, ANGLE, GROTTO, SCOTT, HUNTER, RAGS and BONES. The Regimental Transport was inspected by O.C. 19th Divisional Train. Working parties 260 strong worked under the R.E.	
"	25.		The village was shelled a little in the morning.	
"	26.		A draft of 36 arrived from the Base.	
"	27.		Working parties 260 strong worked under the R.E. The village was heavily shelled from 10 a.m. till 3.30 p.m. Considerable damage was done to the Remains of the church; the shells were from 5.9" and 8" howitzers.	
"	"	4.15 p.m.	The Battalion was relieved by 1st 7th. R. Lancs Regt. by the 37th Brigade. The Battalion marched to billets by companies to LA CROIX MARMUSE, which passed	
LA CROIX MARMUSE.	28.	about 7 p.m. morning	Following posts were reinforced:- LESTREM. S, PARADIS. N, EPINETTE. The 6th Wilts Regt. of 58th Brigade relieved the two Letter Posts. The following officers joined for duty:- 2nd Lieuts B.J. Ellis, R.G. Rolfe Rogers, A.M. Dickinson and C.F. Kinder.	
	29.		The Battalion remained in billets.	
	30.			
	31.			

A.L.[Maloney], Colonel
Comdg 10th Worcestershire Regt.

19th Division
57th Infantry Brigade.

March to June 1918 missing

The Battalion was absorbed by 3rd Worcesters on 22nd June 1918.

10th BATTALION

WORCESTERSHIRE REGIMENT

WAR DIARIES MARCH TO JUNE 1918 MISSING

also
Dec '16 missing

July '15
to
Feb. '18

7.D.

SECRET

Army Form C. 2118

Instructions regarding War Diaries and Intelligence Summaries are contained in F.S. Regs., Part II. and the Staff Manual respectively. Title Pages will be prepared in manuscript.

WAR DIARY
or
INTELLIGENCE SUMMARY   10th (S) Bn. Worcestershire Regt.

(Erase heading not required.)

Place	Date 1916	Hour	Summary of Events and Information	Remarks and references to Appendices
LA CROIX MARMUSE	1.		In Billets.	
"	2.			
"	3.	11 a.m.	The Battalion was inspected by Major General G.T.M. Bridges, C.M.G., D.S.O. Comdg. 19th Division, who made very.	
"	4.	8.30 p.m.	The Battalion relieved 10th Gloucester Regt. (57th Brigade) in Trenches (NEUVE CHAPELLE) occupying from OXFORD ST. at night to SIGNPOST LANE in day. Cal Drop & front line and A & B Coys. in Support. Trenches in most letter condition, much mud and deep water. B Coy of 16th Welch Regt was pulled up at CROIX BARBEE but taken in to line for instruction. The whole company being for in la front line.	
NEUVE CHAPELLE	5.	5 p.m.	A and B Coys were moved up to the front line owing to the departure of A,B Coy 16th Welch. Companies in front line now occupy line as follows:— C Coy OXFORD ST to FIFTEENTH ST. A " FIFTEENTH ST to BREWERY ROAD. B " BREWERY RD to CHATEAU ROAD. D " CHATEAU RD to SIGNPOST LANE.	
"	6.	dusk	C Coy moved from front line to night support to make room for 120 cyclists of 19th Divisional Cyclist Coy, who now held the line from OXFORD ST to BREWERY ROAD.	
"	"		"D" Coy 10th R Warwickshire Regt. were sent up as a Local Reserve to the Battalion, at MOGG'S HOLE. The Headquarters of Battn H.Q. was shelled.	
"	7.	10 a.m.		
"	"	6 p.m.	An Officers Patrol of 10th R. War Regt. went out-attacked on left company (D) composed of Lieuts Ward and Stong and a N.C.O.— Lt. Ward was killed and Lt. Stong was badly wounded.	
"	8.	10 a.m.	NEUVE CHAPELLE West was heavily shelled.	
"	"	2 p.m.	Battn H.Q. neighbourhood was shelled with H.E. Retaliation for our trench mortar batteries fine.	
"	"	11 a.m.	Sharp Br Barrage visible on trenches.	
"	"	7.30 pm.	The Battalion was relieved by the 10th R. Warwickshire Regt. and moved back into billets at CROIX BARBEE. B Coy occupied the following posts:— EUSTON, CURZON, LORETO. Casualties during the 4 days:— Killed and Wounded.	
CROIX BARBEE				

SECRET

Army Form C. 2118

Instructions regarding War Diaries and Intelligence Summaries are contained in F.S. Regs., Part II. and the Staff Manual respectively. Title Pages will be prepared in manuscript.

WAR DIARY
or
INTELLIGENCE SUMMARY 15 (S) Bn. Worcestershire Regt.

(Erase heading not required.)

Place	Date	Hour	Summary of Events and Information	Remarks and references to Appendices
CROIX BARBÉE	9. 10/16			
"	10.		Battalion remained in billets.	
"	11.			
Trenches. NEUVE CHAPELLE.	12.	10.15 p.m	The Battalion relieved the 10th Royal Warwickshire in the trenches (NEUVE CHAPELLE). Coys were distributed as follows:— C Coy on right of front line, then A Coy (2 platoons), then B Coy (3 platoons), then D Coy on left of front line. CHATEAU REDOUBT. B Coy (1 platoon) CHURCH KEEP A Coy (1 platoon) HILL'S REDOUBT. A Coy (1 platoon). A Coy 10th R. Warwickshire Regt at MOGG'S HOLE in Local Reserve.	
"	13.			
"	14.	dusk	The 2 platoons of A Coy retired into support to make room for the 19th Div. Cyclists in front line.	
"	15.			
"	16.			
"	17.	7.30 p.m.	The Battalion less D Coy was relieved in the trenches by the 10th R. Warwickshire Regt. D Coy joined Local Reserve to 10th R. War. Regt at MOGG'S HOLE; A Coy reinforced the following Posts:— EUSTON, CURZON at LORETTO, the remainder of the Coy and B and C Coy to billets at CROIX BARBÉE. Total casualties for the 5 days in trenches:— 1 killed at Killed & wounded	
CROIX BARBÉE.	18.		Remained in above Posts and Billets.	
"	19.			
"	20.			
ROBECQ.	21.	10 a.m	The platoon of A Coy and B & C Coys marched to rest billets at ROBECQ arriving about 3 p.m. March was very muddy. The Battalion was relieved by the 15th Welsh Regt. 1114th Brde.	
"	22.	9 p.m.	The remainder of "A" Coy arrived at ROBECQ, having been relieved in the Posts by the 15th Welsh Regt.	

SECRET   Army Form C. 2118

Instructions regarding War Diaries and Intelligence
Summaries are contained in F. S. Regs., Part II.
and the Staff Manual respectively. Title Pages
will be prepared in manuscript.

WAR DIARY
or
INTELLIGENCE SUMMARY 10th (S) Bn. Worcestershire Regt.
(Erase heading not required.)

Place	Date Jan 1916	Hour	Summary of Events and Information	Remarks and references to Appendices
ROBECQ	23.	3p.m.	D Coy arrived from trenches having been relieved by 1st Wilts Regt.	
"	24.	10a.m.	The G.O.C. Brigade inspected the billets of the battalion.	
"	25.		Refitting and cleaning up.	
"	26.			
"	27.		Training Programme commenced.	
"	28.		" Continued	
"	29.		" "	
"	30.		" "	
"	31.		Demonstration of method of putting up a wire entanglement by 1st S.W.B'n.	

A.T. Chesney
COLONEL,
COMDG., 10TH (S) BN THE WORCESTERSHIRE REGt

O. i/c A.G's Office
  Base.

    Herewith duplicate copy of "War Diary" for February 1916., the original copy sent you in March last not having reached you.

2. 6. 16.

        Pigott
        Lieut. COLONEL,
COMDG., 10TH (S) BN THE WORCESTERSHIRE REGT

SECRET.   XIX   Army Form C. 2118

Vol 8

WAR DIARY or INTELLIGENCE SUMMARY
16 (S) Bn. Worcestershire Regt.

(Erase heading not required.)

Place	Date Feb 1916	Hour	Summary of Events and Information	Remarks and references to Appendices
ROBECQ	1.			
"	2.	9.30 a.m. 10 a.m.	Regt Transport was inspected by the G.O.C. 37th Inf. Brigade. Battalion Spiritual service.	
"	4.			
"	7.	8.45 a.m.	Battalion (A Coy) left for a route march. – ST VENANT – GUARBECQUE – BUSNES.	
"	8.		1st day of inoculation against typhoid.	
"	9.	}		
"	10.		Re-inoculation of Battalion again at typhoid.	
"	12.		Col Cleaver relinquishes command of Battalion owing to ill health.	
"	13.	11 a.m.	Battalion (less A Coy) paraded for Divine Service with 10th R Warwickshire Regt. and held Divisional Band.	
"		2 p.m.	A Coy fired 10 rounds per man on Range near FORÊT DE NIEPPE. B.C. & D.Coy fire 10 rounds per man on Range near FORÊT DE NIEPPE.	
"	14.	9 a.m.	Battalion route march. ST. VENANT – GUARBECQUE – BUSNES.	
"	15.	9 a.m.	Battalion route march. ROBECQ – ST. VENANT – QUARBECQUE and return.	
"	16.		Brigade route march	
"	17.		Major Q.D. Heapte. D.S.O. took over command of Battalion	
"	19.	1 a.m.	Battalion moved into billets at LAGORGUE. A B & C up billeted in the square at L.34.l.9.8. Leave given to 1st Battalion.	
"	20.	}		
"	22.		Battalion remained in billets at LAGORGUE.	

Lieut. Col. A.G. Thynne took the charge of 2 Command. Brig Chief W.A. Lenox Conyngham who proceeded to the United Kingdom on sick leave.

Army Form C. 2118

WAR DIARY
or
INTELLIGENCE SUMMARY

16 (S) Bn. Worcestershire Regt.

(Erase heading not required.)

Place	Date 1916	Hour	Summary of Events and Information	Remarks and references to Appendices
LA GORGUE	24	3.15pm	The Battalion paraded to march to the trenches to relieve the 6th Bn Wilts Regt & 15th & 16th in the left sector of the 19th Division Front (MOATED GRANGE entrance to ERITH POST.)	6th Bn Wilts Regt 15th & 16th Worcestershire Regt
Trenches	25	8.25pm	Relief complete. A, C, & D Coys in front line and B Coy in Support. Coys (TILLELOY N. DREADNOUGHT, ERITH, GRANTS.) Y Coy & 17th West Yorks Regt 35th Division was attached to the battalion for instruction. Weather very cold while had frosts, snow on ground.	
	26		Heavy fall of snow in evening which continued till midnight 25/26. Commanding Officer was hour from his last night. 4 Generals visited Battn H.Q.	
			2nd in command out early morning 26th to adjust – during morning	
	"	8.15pm	The Battalion was relieved by the 10th R. Warwickshire Regt and moved back with B Coy at MIN & LONELY POSTS.	
PONT DU HEM	27	2pm	at PONT DU HEM and LA FLINQUE. B Coy overstayed MIN and LONELY POSTS. A heavy barrage in at most of mars in happened concentration and overhead posts. The Battalion carried out a practice alarm as stand to defence positions. Y Coy 17th West Yorks Regt. left.	
	28	1pm	Y Coy 19th Durham Light Infantry arrived, and is being attached to the battalion for instruction.	
Trenches	"	6pm	Coys marched to trenches to relieve 10th R. Warwickshire Regt. A, B, & D Coys in front line and C Coy in Artillery Posts.	
		11.10pm	Relief complete.	
	29	6pm	Rockets were sent up for practice purposes, as men were most found to be uncertain on	
			Casualties from 24th inst. to date, 2 killed and 1 wounded.	

Mogden Pigott Lt Col
Commdg 16th Worcestershire Regt.

SECRET.

Army Form C. 2118

Instructions regarding War Diaries and Intelligence Summaries are contained in F.S. Regs., Part II. and the Staff Manual respectively. Title Pages will be prepared in manuscript.

WAR DIARY or INTELLIGENCE SUMMARY 16th (S) Bn. Worcestershire Regt.

(Erase heading not required.)

Place	Date 1916	Hour	Summary of Events and Information	Remarks and references to Appendices
Trenches.	1.			
"	2.			
"	3.	9.15pm	The Battalion was relieved in the trenches by the 16th R. Warwickshire Regt. and moved into billets at PONT DU HEM and LA FLINQUE. Casualties during the 4 days in the trenches 2 killed and 4 wounded.	
PONT DU HEM.	4.		Considerable snow during last night and during the morning. A draft of 148 N.C.O.s & men mostly old soldiers from an Irregular battalion arrived at 11.30 p.m.	
"	5.	1.30pm	A Coy billets at LA FLINQUE were half shelled :- casualties 1 Killed and 2 wounded, also 2 A/lts 19th D.L.I. Killed and 1 wounded. The Coy was taken out for 2 or 3 hours and returned in the evening.	
"	6.			
"	7.	8.45am	The Battalion marched to billets (Divisional Reserve) in the neighbourhood of ROBERMETZ, via LA GORGUE and MERVILLE. Arrived at 11.30am. The 19th D.L.I. (Bantams) took over our billets in PONT DU HEM. Heavy fall of snow at night.	
ROBERMETZ	8.			
"	9.			
"	10.	7.30am	C and D Coys were conveyed in G.S. wagons to FME L'EPINETTE for working parties with 1st R.E. Very little work was done owing to an artillery bombardment, which the R.A. failed to cele Mr R.E. was coming in.	
"	11.	3pm	Officers' patrol from D Coy was conveyed to PONT DU HEM by motor lorry. They did a reconnaissance No Man's land "jump N" of the BIRDCAGE in view of a future raid by the Battalion.	
"	12.	5am	Patrol returned.	
"	13.		A patrol from C Coy went out on the same errand.	
PONT DU HEM.	14.	9am	Battalion left by Coys to march to billets at PONT DU HEM, arriving about 12 noon. The four front line Coys relieved the 106th B.M. 35th Division the following night. The Battalion relieved the 19th D.L.I. & the 106th B.de in the trenches (Left Sector MOATED GRANGE)	
Trenches.	15.	10pm	Relief complete by 10 p.m. B, A and D Coys in front line, C Coy in (Pts):- DREADNOUGHT, ERITH, TILLELOY, N. and GRANTS. The dugouts in front line were strongly impregnated with gas from Lachrymatory shells fired the previous day when about 150 to 18 officers N.C.O.s & men of the 19th D.L.I. including the C.O. Vomited violently.	

1875 Wt. W593/826 1,000,000 4/15 J.B.C. & A. A.D.S.S./Forms/C.2118.

WAR DIARY or INTELLIGENCE SUMMARY

Army Form C. 2118

10ᵗʰ (S) Bn. Worcestershire Regt.

Place	Date	Hour	Summary of Events and Information	Remarks and references to Appendices
Trenches	16.			
"	17.	10 p.m.	C Coy. who relieved by B Coy 8ᵗʰ N. Staffs Regt. on the left and D Coy was relieved by B Coy 10ᵗʰ R. Warwickshire Regt. in the centre and proceeded to billets at RIEZ BAILLEUL and PONT DU HEM respectively. The relief took place owing to threatened attack on enemy's trenches in our sector.	
"	18.		A Coy moved to the boats and B Coy moved to the left sub-sector.	
"	19.		Orders were received in the morning that the battalion would be partially relieved to-night. In the afternoon fresh orders were received to the effect that a normal relief would take place tomorrow night. These orders were again cancelled at about 8 p.m. The intended raid on the German trenches has also been cancelled. If having been estimated that in cost would have been £80,000.	
"	20.	10 p.m.	Snipers was extended by no under the German artillery opposite to BIRDCAGE and a raiding party of 3 officers and 70 men of the North Staffs Regt. bombed the front-line German trenches. Their casualties were 15 wounded. It is thought they accounted for 15-20 germans. Their co-operated with rifle and machine gun fire for 48 mins. Enemy retaliation was very mild and their fire appeared to be very weakly held. Our B Coy on the left co-operated with rapid rifle and machine gun fire for this hour. A few his coming from their support trench. Very few of their shells came the action. 35000 rounds SAA was expended by us.	
"	21.	10-15 a.m.	The enemy bombarded our front-line and Keeps very violently for an hour up till 11:15 a.m. and again between 12.15 p.m. and 1 p.m. Our casualties were 4 & 2 slight wounded.	
"	"	8.25 p.m.	The Battalion was relieved by the 10ᵗʰ R. Warwickshire Regt and returned to billets at PONT DU HEM. "D" Coy occupying MIN and LONELY Posts.	
PONT DU HEM	22.		Leave vacancies have been allotted at the rate of 10 and 11 every day; the largest-scale we have ever had since being out – too good to last we all think.	
"	23.		Companies were employed in cleaning up and bathing. Much colder – heavy fall of snow at night.	

SECRET.

Army Form C. 2118.

WAR DIARY
or
INTELLIGENCE SUMMARY.

10th (S) Bn. Worcestershire Regt.

(Erase heading not required.)

Instructions regarding War Diaries and Intelligence Summaries are contained in F.S. Regs., Part II and the Staff Manual respectively. Title pages will be prepared in manuscript.

Place	Date 1916.	Hour	Summary of Events and Information	Remarks and references to Appendices
PONT DU HEM.	24.		Snowed hard most of the morning — 3 to 4 inches deep, however it soon thawed.	
	25.		More snow during the night. Battalion was engaged on various working parties throughout the day and half the night. No cases of Trench feet.	
Trenches.	26.	9 p.m.	The Battalion relieved the 10th R. Warwickshire Regt in the left sector (MOATED GRANGE). C., D., & A. Coys in front line. B Coy in Posts:- GRANTS, TILLELOY N, ERITH, & DREADNOUGHT. Bombers in WINCHESTER Post. Trenches was found to be in a very bad condition owing to enemy shelling and rain. TILLELOY. N. is now evacuated by day as it is always heavily shelled — Also GRANTS —	
"	27.	2-4 p.m.	Our centre (D) Coy and left (A) Coy were bombarded with trench mortar bombs — about 50 — 1 man Killed and 1 wounded.	
"	28.		Relief much quieter now as LONELY ERITH STREET is boarded & can be used —	
"	29.	8.30 p.m.	The Battalion was relieved by the 10th R. Warwickshire Regt. 2 platoons of A coy proceeded to MINN & HONEY Posts, Remainder of battalion to billets at PONT DU HEM.	
PONT DU HEM	30.		30 new shelters were erected and sandbagged & fire-line & parts same	
	31.		The Battalion marched to billets at ROBERMETZ and rested on 8th inst. The 1st Herts Regt	
ROBERMETZ	"		moving into our billets at PONT DU HEM. MINN & HONEY were relieved by 1st Herts Regt on 8th inst.	

[signature] Lt Col
Comdg 10th Worcestershire Regt.

Army Form C. 2118.

WAR DIARY or INTELLIGENCE SUMMARY.

16-(S) Bn. Worcestershire Regt.

(Erase heading not required.)

Place	Date 1916	Hour	Summary of Events and Information	Remarks and references to Appendices
ROBERMETZ	1.		Battalion in billets – Brigade Reserve.	
"	4.	10 a.m.	C & D Coys inspected by the Commanding Officer – Kits and in Coy drill etc.	
"	5.	10 a.m.	A & B " " " " " "	
"	6.	1.30 p.	The Battalion returned to PONT DU HEM, marching by Coys, and came under orders of the 106th Bde until 57th Bde returns to LAVENTIE tomorrow.	
PONT DU HEM	-			
Trenches	7.	9.13 p.m.	The Battalion relieved the 1st Cambridgeshire Regt of 106th Bde in the left ano section of the MOATED GRANGE Section. Trench H.Q. now at GLOSTER HOUSE instead of WINCHESTER HOUSE, which has been evacuated owing to shelling. A,D & B Coys in front line and C Coy in Support Pots. Relief completed by 9.13 p.m. Weather very fine and very exceptionally quiet.	
"	8.		R.F.C. reported shelling trench bombs at intervals along top of German parapets to S of my section.	
"	9.		R.F.C. to-day report that three trees have been removed.	
"	10.		The artillery fired on the roads behind the German lines as a relief was in progress – this information was gained from a prisoner captured on my right.	
"	11.		Considerable activity transported by the R.F.C. in the BOIS DU BIEZ and the enemy trenches in front of NEUVE CHAPELLE. The prisoner reported that in common with LILLE that NEUVE CHAPELLE would not be attacked.	

SECRET.

Instructions regarding War Diaries and Intelligence Summaries are contained in F.S. Regs., Part II. and the Staff Manual respectively. Title pages will be prepared in manuscript.

Army Form C. 2118.

WAR DIARY
or
INTELLIGENCE SUMMARY. 10th (S) Bn. Worcestershire Regt.

(Erase heading not required.)

Place	Date 1916	Hour	Summary of Events and Information	Remarks and references to Appendices
Trenches	11	6 p.m.	Battalion H.Q. transferred from GLOSTER HOUSE to WINCHESTER HOUSE.	
Trenches	11	9.10 p.m.	The Battalion was relieved by the 10th Royal Warwickshire Regt. and moved back to Billets at PONT DU HEM, B Coy occupying MIN and LONELY Posts.	
PONT DU HEM	12			
"	13		All leave stopped for the battalion.	
"	14			
"	15	9.35 p.m.	The Battalion relieved the 10th R. Warwickshire Regt. in the same pro-portion of the trenches as before. A Coy on left, C centre and B on right. D Coy in Posts. Relief complete by 9.35 p.m. Bright moonlight night and enemy remarkably quiet.	
Trenches	"	"		
"	16	Noon	The C.O. and several officers of the 13th R.W.F. 113th Bde visited the trenches before taking over tomorrow. Rats are becoming a great pest and are increasing in numbers.	
"	17	9.54 p.m.	The Battalion was relieved in the trenches by the 13th R.W.F. 113th Bde and marched back to billets at LAGORGUE. by midnight. Casualties during 2 days :- 2 wounded.	
LA GORGUE	"			
"	18	9.30 a.m.	The Battalion marched to ROBECQ, parading at 9.30 a.m. Roads were very muddy and bad and the march was made during trying for the men by the high head wind and showers of rain. Reached ROBECQ by 12.45 p.m.	
ROBECQ	"			
"	19		Refitting and resting at ROBECQ.	
"	20		The Battalion started at 9.30 a.m. for march to MARTHES where it will be billeted	

SECRET.

Army Form C. 2118.

WAR DIARY
or
INTELLIGENCE SUMMARY: 10th (S) Bn. Worcestershire Regt.

(Erase heading not required.)

Place	Date 1916	Hour	Summary of Events and Information	Remarks and references to Appendices
MARTHES.	20.		On 12day's training in 1st Army Training Area. Route taken - LA PERRIÈRE - GUARBECQUE - MOLINGHEM - LAMBRES - WITTERNESSE - BLESSY. The march was to Brigade fronk. Entrained place to WITTERNESSE. Fine day but very cold & strong head wind. Only 2 men fell out. Reached MARTHES at 4/5.p.m. Platoon training was commenced.	
"	21.			
"	22.		2nd day of Platoon training was commenced in area MARTHES vicinity. Much rain prevented much being done.	
"	24.		Company Training on Area 1.A.	
"	25.		Company Training on Area 2.A.	
"	26.		Battalion Training on Area 3.A.	
"	27.		Battalion Training on Area H.A.	
"	28.		Companies fired on Lt. LINGHEM Range from 6.a.m. to 12.noon. Each company being allotted 1 hour.	
"	29.	9.15.p.l	Brigade Night Operations. An advance across the open and an attack at dawn.	
"	30.	6.a.m	Return to billets.	

Martin Pigott
Lt-Col.
Comdg 10th Worcestershire Regt.

SECRET.

Army Form C. 2118.

WAR DIARY
or
INTELLIGENCE SUMMARY. 10th (S)/Bn. Worcestershire Regt. Vol II

Instructions regarding War Diaries and Intelligence Summaries are contained in F.S. Regs., Part II. and the Staff Manual respectively. Title pages will be prepared in manuscript.

(Erase heading not required.)

F. Bevan   11.D

Place	Date 1916	Hour	Summary of Events and Information	Remarks and references to Appendices
MARTHES.	1.	9.30am	The Battalion took part in Brigade Operations. (Attack on Village of ENGUINEGATTE and holding it in a state of defence afterwards.) G.O.C. 19th Division witnessed these operations.	
"	2.	10 a.m.	Brigade Operations. (Village of ENGUINEGATTE again attacked by us in direction of ERNY ST JULIEN, very violent thunderstorm broke about 3 p.m. and through wetted all ranks.)	
"	4.	7.30am	Battalion took part in Divisional Operations. (Village of ENGUINEGATTE was attacked again by BERQUIGNY WOOD — 57th Bde was in Reserve.) These operations were witnessed by the Commander in Chief, Sir Douglas Haig. Battalion returned to billets at 6 p.m.	
"	5.		The C.O. and Signalling Officer with Signallers and Runners took part in a Staff Ride over the same ground as yesterdays Operations. Very hot day. 19th Divisional Band and Aircraft gave on the Village Square during the evening.	
"	6.		Aircraft & band.	
"	7.	8.15pm	The Battalion paraded for march to AIRE station where it entrained for LONGUEAU at about 10.30 p.m. The train left at 11.45 p.m. — travelling all night.	
AMIENS.	8.	8a.m.	Train reached LONGUEAU at 8 a.m. the Battalion the detrained and marched through AMIENS to VIGNACOURT (16 Kilometres). Breakfasts were eaten outside AMIENS	
VIGNACOURT	"	3pm	and the new billeting area was reached at about 3p.m. Marching was slightly impeded by a high wind and frequent showers. The 19th Division now belongs to the III Corps of the IV Army.	

SECRET.

Army Form C. 2118.

WAR DIARY
or
~~INTELLIGENCE SUMMARY.~~ 16th (S) Bn. Worcestershire Regt.

(Erase heading not required.)

Instructions regarding War Diaries and Intelligence Summaries are contained in F. S. Regs., Part II. and the Staff Manual respectively. Title pages will be prepared in manuscript.

Place	Date 1916	Hour	Summary of Events and Information	Remarks and references to Appendices
VIGNACOURT	8.		Leave re-opened for the battalion at the rate of 2 vacancies for seven but closed again on receipt of a telegram at about 9 p.m.	
"	9.		The day was spent in cleaning up clothing, equipment, billets etc.	
"	11.		The Battalion went for a route march.	
"	12.		Leave re-opened for the battalion at the rate of 2 vacancies a day.	
"	13.		The Battalion went for a route march. A draft of 24 joined.	
"	15.		The Rifle Range at BOIS DUCROQUET was allotted to the battalion, 2½ hours for each Company. 25 rounds fired by each man.	
"	16.		The Battalion went for a route march.	
"	17.		Battalion took part in a Brigade Scheme.	
"	18.		" " " " "	
"	19.		Rifle Range at DOMART. 2½ hrs per Coy.	
"	20.		Battalion took part in a Brigade training scheme.	
"	22.		The Battalion in the attack — hasty deployment from a wood, hasty entrenchments	
"	23.		Battalion route march to R. SOMME where the men bathed.	
"	24.		Rifle Range at BOIS DUCROQUET. 1½ hours per coy. A draft of 15 joined.	=

Army Form C. 2118.

WAR DIARY
or
INTELLIGENCE SUMMARY. 10th Worcestershire Regt.
(Erase heading not required.)

Place	Date	Hour	Summary of Events and Information	Remarks and references to Appendices
VIGNACOURT.	May 1916. 25.		Battalion Route March.	
"	26.		Rifle range at BOIS DUCROQUET. the few Coy. Running fourties with another Platoons in.	
"	27.		Divisional Sports near FLESSELLES. Battalion won the Obstacle Race and Lewis gun competition.	
"	29.		Battalion was inspected by the G.O.C. 57th Brigade.	
"	30.	8 a.m.	The Battalion marched with the Brigade to ST RIQUIER via ST OUEN and GORENFLOS - dinners at 12 noon near the latter place. arrived at 4 p.m.	
ST. RIQUIER.			Half the battalion is billeted in the historical town in which the third form of Arm was left a prisoner before his trial.	

M. C. E. Pyote Lt.Col.
Comdg 10th Worcestershire Regt.

SECRET

Army Form C. 2118

WAR DIARY or INTELLIGENCE SUMMARY

1/8*(S) Bn. Worcestershire Regt.
Vol 12 June

(Erase heading not required.)

Instructions regarding War Diaries and Intelligence Summaries are contained in F.S. Regs., Part II. and the Staff Manual respectively. Title Pages will be prepared in manuscript.

Place	Date June 1916	Hour	Summary of Events and Information	Remarks and references to Appendices
ST. RIQUIER	1.		The Battalion took part in a Brigade Attack on the ST. RIQUIER training area. Companies practised the attack on their own.	
"	2.		Same exercise as on 1st inst.	
"	3.		Battalion attack practice.	
"	5.		Brigade field day. Weather was very bad and the men got very wet. Operations were watched by the III Corps Commander.	
"	6.		The Battalion defended the enemy in an attack by the 58 Brigade.	
"	7.		Capt Sergt Major T. M. Ryan has been awarded the D.C.M. for courage in a wounded man under heavy rifle fire near FESTUBERT on the 3rd November 1915.	
"	8.		The Battalion took part in a Brigade field day.	
"	9.		Battalion took part in a Divisional field day which was watched by the 4th Army Commander.	
"	10.	8 a.m.	The Battalion returned with the Brigade to its former billets at ST. VIGNACOURT, midday halt and dinner near ST. OUEN. VIGNACOURT was reached at about 4 p.m.	
VIGNACOURT	11.	9.30 a.m.	The Battalion marched to FRÉCHENCOURT via FLESSELLES, VILLERS BOCAGE, MOLLIENS AU BOIS, at ST. GRATIEN had midday halt and dinner near MOLLIENS AU BOIS, arrived FRÉCHENCOURT at about 4 p.m.	
FRÉCHENCOURT	12.	10.30 a.m.	The Battalion marched to DERNANCOURT via BÉHENCOURT, FRANVILLERS and near ALBERT road, midday halt and dinner about 3 miles from destination, which reached at about 3.30 p.m.	
DERNANCOURT	13.	3.30 p.m.	The Battalion is encamped in 3 fields, and will be at the disposal of the CE III Corps at Heavy artillery III Corps for working parties for the next week or 10 days. This small village resembles a bee hive. The numbers of troops in this place is a perfect lesson in systematic & hygienic overcrowding.	
"	14.		4 officers & N.C.O.s at 2 servants went up to visit the trenches.	
"	15.		The Sig Sb is aiming in drabbels. 1.3 mi at last H battalions have arrived up to date. Another party of 4 officers, 4 N.C.O.s & 2 servants proceeded to visit the trenches.	

SECRET

Army Form C. 2118

Instructions regarding War Diaries and Intelligence Summaries are contained in F.S. Regs., Part II. and the Staff Manual respectively. Title Pages will be prepared in manuscript.

INTELLIGENCE SUMMARY — 10th (S)Bn. Worcestershire Regt.

(Erase heading not required.)

Place	Date	Hour	Summary of Events and Information	Remarks and references to Appendices
DERNANCOURT	June 1916 16.		Brigadier C.C. Onslow assumes command of the 57th Inf. Brigade.	
"	17.		A draft of 21 joined the battalion, 20 of whom were machine gunners.	
"	19.		Captain D.M.M. Sale is appointed 2nd in Command of the battalion and granted the local rank of Major during the absence of Major Lord A.G. Thynne.	
"	20–23		Walking parties continued under the C.R.E. III Corps and Heavy Artillery, III Corps.	
"	24th	U Day	Artillery bombardment continued throughout the day by our guns. A 12" Naval Gun took up its position on the railway line about 20 yds from our camp and fired some shots at intervals throughout the day.	
"	25th	V Day	2nd day of bombardment; there was retaliation on ALBERT mostly. 3 coys moved to another camp about ½ mile N. of to ALBERT railway as retaliation is expected on the village.	
"	26th	W Day	3rd Day of Bombardment. Bn. Hd. Qrs. moved to the new camp. Village was shelled slightly afternoon.	
"	27th	X Day	4th Day of Bombardment. Weather very bad — frequent heavy rain.	
"	28th	Y Day	5th Day of Bombardment. Heavy rain. The Battalion has just commenced to move to Preliminary assembly trenches to the E. of MILLENCOURT at 4 p.m. when a message was received to stand fast for 48 hours. (now postponed 48 hours) Imperative specialists in fighting now. Batting in R. ANCRE.	
"	29th	Z Day		
"	30th	4 p.m.	The Battalion moved to preliminary assault trenches to the E. of MILLENCOURT approximately 700 strong all ranks — 17 officers and a proportion of NCO's are to remain with first line transport to replace casualties — These numbers include Maj. Sale (acting 2nd in C.) and staff numbers for Adjutant, machine gun Qr. m., and Bombing officer.	

Maydrin Bagot Lt. Col.
Comdg 10th Worcestershire Regt.

57th Inf.Bde.
19th Div.

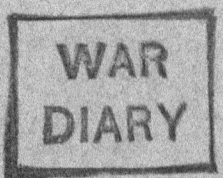

10th BATTN. THE WORCESTERSHIRE REGIMENT.

J U L Y

1 9 1 6

Attached:

Casualty Lists.

SECRET.   Army Form C/2118

WAR DIARY
or
INTELLIGENCE SUMMARY — 16th S. Bn. Worcestershire Regt.

Instructions regarding War Diaries and Intelligence Summaries are contained in F. S. Regs., Part II. and the Staff Manual respectively. Title Pages will be prepared in manuscript.

(Erase heading not required.)

Place	Date	Hour	Summary of Events and Information	Remarks and references to Appendices
ALBERT	July 1st 1916.	9am	At 9am the Battalion moved up to the Assembly Trenches to its N.W. of ALBERT where it lay in support. As the attack had started at 7.30am rumours & alarms were frequent.	
		9.15pm	At 9.15pm the Battalion was ordered to proceed to our original front line to support an attack. In the communication trench confusion reigned — wounded were being brought out — we were trying to get in — carrying parties were trying to get the same way — it was raining & the trench was knee deep in mud. By about 1am A, B & C Coys from the Battalion were in the front line of USNA REDOUBT — D Coy were placed to remain in reserve of USNA REDOUBT. The attack which was due to begin at midnight had to be put off — leaving the WARWICKSHIRE REGT to 2nd line A B & C Coy made their way back to the USNA – TARA Line — the remainder being thoroughly exhausted. Everyone slept which was greatly interrupted by the Germans bombardment of LA BOISELLE.	
USNA TARA Line.		1pm	At 1pm the O.C. 2/Lt (2nd i.c.) Capt Evans 2/Lt Dwyer (name Aff) 2/Lt Kimber 2nd Lt Lloyd (name Burbot)? attended a conference concerning attacking the were summoned from to transport & returned to the Bgt. It was also affecting attack. They returned to the Bgt. It was also at MILLENCOURT. During the afternoon the 58th Brigade attacked LA BOISELLE — Late at night the 57 Brigade were ordered to move up in support. The C.O. leaving	
		9pm	called a conference at 12 midnight, the Battalion moved in lines	

Army Form C. 2118

INTELLIGENCE SUMMARY

10th (S) Bn. Worcestershire Regt.

(Erase heading not required.)

Place	Date	Hour	Summary of Events and Information	Remarks and references to Appendices
Village of LA BOISELLE	July 1916 3rd		3 Platoons in fours across country & lay down behind our old Front line facing LA BOISELLE. The Battalion was seen & came under a heavy & hurtful fire causing considerable casualties. The advance was made in three lines, one platoon of each company being in front. The Battalion went forward with great dash & after a long fight captured three lines of trenches. Small parties penetrated right through the village of LA BOISELLE but running short of bombs were forced to retire. Intense fighting with varying success continued till about 12 midday when a line was consolidated behind the Church. Coming to our sufficient two companies of the WARWICKSHIRE REGT. held the front line while we consolidated about 30 yards behind.	
		2 am		
		2nd		
		4 pm	Casualties were heavy - An offensive is attacked. Reserve Officers from Transport arrived & took over the Battalion. There quickened down considerably & the line was firmly consolidated. During the night 3 weak bombing attacks by the enemy were easily stopped by Machine Gun fire.	
	4th	9 am	The South Lanc. Regt. came up in support of the Brigade. The Battalion withdrew to RYECROFT AVENUE after wandering some distance over the 12 country side endeavouring to find the trench. In the afternoon we were partly shelled	
RYECROFT Avenue.		2 pm	chiefly by 59 cm guns which. One shell obtained a direct hit on a party of men killing 5 & wounding two more. As always seems the case top were of the best men in the Battalion. The mud in the trench was very bad & to make matters worse it rained hard for a couple of hours.	

INTELLIGENCE SUMMARY

10th (S.) Bn. WORCESTERSHIRE Regt.

(Erase heading not required.)

Place	Date 1916	Hour	Summary of Events and Information	Remarks and references to Appendices
OLD BRITISH LINE	July 4th	9pm	The Battalion was ordered to move down to the Old British Line. On arriving there, by way of ANDREWS AVENUE which place was up to its knees in water, we found the STAFFORDSHIRE Regt. in possession. After frantic telephoning to Brigade we eventually fitted in a bit of KEATS REDAN in the Old British Lines where we spent a most miserable night.	
	5th	10am	We withdrew to the TARA-USNA line, being on the left of USNA REDOUBT. Fine sunny day. Dulwich we made the most to dry our clothes &c.	
ALBERT		9pm	Proceeded to billets in ALBERT in RUE DES TRAM RAILS	
do.	6th		Cleaning & refitting. Divisional Band played in afternoon	
do.	7th		Spent an afternoon. Wet most of the day	
do.	8th	11.30am	Inspection by Maj. Gen Bridges D.S.O. C.M.G. – Mr Monument. He allowed all officers & Sergts. & frankly my letter what we had done assumed in that position & would go down in history – He made us number First as trained officers M.G.s we must not throw away our lives & should rather sacrifice our fight materials. Nevertheless he was extremely pleased with the Division.	
		8.30pm	Divisional Band played on the afternoon. We went to Welch Regt. Transport to the North of MILLENCOURT. Received a draft of 68 men two Subalterns were within to wounds being myrighty kutul.	
MILLENCOURT	9th		Rested cleaned up.	
HENNECOURT WOOD	9th	7pm	Move to HENNECOURT WOOD & bivouaced in a field.	

INTELLIGENCE SUMMARY.

(Erase heading not required.)

16th (S) Bn. Worcestershire Regt.

Place	Date July 1916	Hour	Summary of Events and Information	Remarks and references to Appendices
LAVIÉVILLE	10"	3pm	Returned to original lines of MILLENCOURT. Before arriving here the Battalion was diverted into billets at LAVIÉVILLE.	
do.	11"		Received a draft of 206 men chiefly from Bedfordshire Regt. (also Essex Regt.) Parade under O.C. Coy.	
do.	12"		do.	
do.	13"		Lunfanken by Lt. Gen. Pulteney Q.O.C. III Corps. Having intent losing side to infect Lt. W.S. Seaward Camp Commandant 19 Div. reports for duty more posted to "C" Coy.	
do.	14"	4pm	advanced Brigade.	
do.	15"	3pm	Parade under O.C. Coy. Moved to MEAULTE. Objecting to harstage to relieve a Brigade of the 34" Division at POZIERES. Order cancelled at 8pm. Returned to Billets.	
do.		8pm	2/Lt O.A. Hicks reported for duty & posted to B Coy.	
do.	16"	2.15pm	Church Parade in afternoon. Capt. A.W. Burton (Li Worc) reported for duty with reinforcements from men. Capt. Burton assumes command of S/Lt Capt. while announced commanding the Battalion. Major Sills assumes rank of S/Lt. Col. Wet most of day. Move forward another 24 hours. Weekend Hunter spent his parking kit.	
do.	17"		Move again bothered at the the 11 hour.	
do.	18"		Parade under O.C. Coy.	
"	19"	3.30pm	Orders received to move at 6pm. Moved to MILLENCOURT where we remained till 10.45pm. it still being how we proceed to a point West of FRECOURT about 3 am. arriving about 3 am. F.2. c.9.3	

INTELLIGENCE SUMMARY. 10th/14th Bn. Worcestershire Regt.

(Erase heading not required.)

Place	Date 1916	Hour	Summary of Events and Information	Remarks and references to Appendices
FRICOURT	July 20"		Rested in bivouac all day.	
		8pm	Proceeded to relieve first North of BAZENTIN-LE-PETIT to relieve 98th Brigade. On arriving at Bde. HQ. found everything and everyone moving to our transport lines owing to our troops being driven out of HIGH WOOD. Great confusion during the Relief owing to guides not knowing tracks or the village being shelled with Tear shells.	
	21st		The Battalion eventually took up a line just before dawn as follows S.2.a.8.7 East to S.2.d.8.2. - The from S.2.b.5.8 to WINDMILL at S.9.a.3.0 where we tried with the 2nd Worc. Regt. The 2 Staff: Regt were in support in a line running WINDMILL - CEMETERY - S.8.b.3.8. During the morning WINDMILL which was used as an O.P. was shelled. About 12 a.m. the Bn moved to Quarry in D Coy.	
		3 pm	Attempted to capture German Machine gun about S.3.d.1.7 with Bomber Lewis gun in support. Attack failed & gun was lost. Another attack was made after dark with strong patrols, who were heavily fired upon & forced to retire. Patrols succeeded in locating his about by 3 separate German line to our front. They were partly successful in locating his about 400 yds away behind reverse slope of DOWNHILL.	
	22?	10 am	C Coy closed into to right towards HIGH WOOD took place being taken by Nothac. Regt. S.E Side - B Coy fell back at right angle to C Coy facing East. And were in support. Another attack was made on the machine Gun from by 2 Platoons of C Coy on North side of Bt BAZENTIN - HIGH WOOD road by 2 platoons of B Coy on South side. The attack was a failure also Gunners fact that the 2 platoon of C Coy were missing believed prisoners. It was afterwards reported by troops who were on charge of attacking Platoon of C Coy that the Machine Gun was firing from Barricade at S.3.c.6.5. This N.C.O. about 2 days in ago. went back to Barricade lost himself in lot of dead S.3.c.4.4. was trailed by M. Gun from (S.E Bn) behind his lot back, his companion being killed.	

INTELLIGENCE SUMMARY. 10th (S) Bn. Worcestershire Regt.

Place	Date 1916	Hour	Summary of Events and Information	Remarks and references to Appendices
BAZENTIN-LE-PETIT	July 23	11.30 am	About 11.30 a.m. Germans were observed in the High Wood road running into Bazentin Cemetery & chance was extended to Captain McIntosh's Machine Gun. The Germans would have been fair quarry at 200 have the attack would be launched. Attempted to Barricade Dug-outs. Machine Guns notified by situation. The signal was a failure. No Zero hour was notified since the "Hurrah" finish. Captain Laurey went over to own advanced line. Troops were driven back by M.G. fire & shrapnel. They had considerable casualties including 2Lt K.S.H. Whittuck.	
		8pm	Orders were received to attack Germans. His located in sunken running from S.3.c.6.5. to S.2.d.4.9. The 8. Glouc. Regt. would attack on the left. At 9.30pm. the order was cancelled. Lt. Col. WAR. Regt. would retire in a stack. Erstwhile cover from Infantry & Artillery fire from. The attack was to commence by 12.30am	
	23	1am	The village was heavily shelled by Germans & by Warwicks told to arrive in trenches at about 1am. An attack was made with attention to Springfontein which resulted in a bad fall & heavy casualties to the Regiment encountered. (Glouc - R.WAR.Reg.). The Battalion held South of BAZENTIN-LE-PETIT woods about S.14.c.2.7 & remained there for remainder of the day.	
BECOURT WOOD	24, 25	5pm	At the present attack to BECOURT WOOD in Bivouac. Rested. Cleaned up. ditto	Casualty list = 4 officers - also Most

INTELLIGENCE SUMMARY.

10 (S)B. WORCESTERSHIRE Regt.

(Erase heading not required.)

Place	Date 1916	Hour	Summary of Events and Information	Remarks and references to Appendices
BECOURT WOOD	26		Parades under O.C. Coys.	
"	27		ditto	
"	28		ditto	
"			Bn. As usual were warned to move up to line to relieve 58'. Received orders to move up to line to relieve 24 hrs later.	
"	29	4 p	Moved up to line East of BAZENTIN-LE-PETIT. Fusiliers by 9.10pm. Two platoon attack Coy. were in the front line from S.2.d.4.2. to S.2.d.9.2. (Cruicifix Corner) to S.2.d.9.2. - and went on from B Coy to try to make INTERMEDIATE LINE. Came across party of Germans in shell hole about 200 yds from our Front Line. Intermittent shelling all night mostly on our own Line. Relief completed with R. WELCH Fusiliers on our original line from S.8.6.5.8. to remainder in new original line from S.8.6.5.8.	
BAZENTIN LE PETIT.	30		Beautiful fine day. Headquarters extremely connection with Contact Aeroplane at 10.30 am. Orders were received for a general attack on its INTERMEDIATE LINE - 57: Bde to attack troops from track S.2.c.8.5 to S0b at S.2.d.2.B in following order from left to right. Public Wore- R. W.G.R. King's own suffolks by 8th F.a Coy R.E. 2.5: S.W.B. There would be a slow bombardment of the line of "Reserve" during today ending with an intense bombardment for 1 min. before Zero which was at 6.10 p.m. The Assault would take place in two lines - The first line would creep up to top of ridge & work to former line immediately	

762a
SB

INTELLIGENCE SUMMARY. 10th (S.) Bn. Worcestershire Regt.

Summaries are contained in F.S. Regs., Part II and the Staff Manual respectively. Title pages will be prepared in manuscript.

(Erase heading not required.)

Place	Date 1916	Hour	Summary of Events and Information	Remarks and references to Appendices
BAZENTIN LE PETIT.	July 30th		The Barrage lifted supposedly by to 22 Lies 75 yds behind. Thus 10 W'k Battalion until the clear of the trenches before 6.10 p.m. This was possible as to pursue his was on the Reserve side of the Ridge. The Attack as far as the Battalion was concerned was a complete failure. The KING'S OWN & R. WAR. Regt. captured the German Trench on our right but the latter Regt. went too much to the right thus leaving our right flank exposed. East Coy. of the Battalion attempted to fill in the gap to the Barrage. Sufficient [crossed out illegible lines] [crossed out] & Several Germans were seen leaving the trench during the "mad minute". The Battalion tried to consolidate a line just below the ridge but were continually under direct enfilade M.G. fire - they were badly shelled at dusk & it became obvious that line to our original line. Our trenches were very heavily shelled during the night. The STAFFORDSHIRE Regt. who had taken our places in the front line was attacked & withdrew at dawn - Before this there were some confusion as to what was our front line & all communication was exceedingly difficult. Meanwhile the R. WAR. R. had firmly established themselves in	CASUALTIES OFFICERS Killed 2/Lt E.M. France Wounded Capt. E.F.N. Evans OTHER RANKS Killed - 13 Wdd - 59 Missing - 10. TOTAL = 82.
	31st			

763c

INTELLIGENCE SUMMARY 10(S) Bn. WORCESTERSHIRE Regt.

Place	Date	Hour	Summary of Events and Information	Remarks and references to Appendices
BAZENTIN LE PETIT	31st July 1916	5a	The Bn. manned Trench shafts down to 1st S.W.B. and dug a trench from the road leading to HIGH WOOD to the WARWICK'S (left about S.2.d.9.7. — Bn. Hqs. started moved up to front line with orders to organise dug-out at S.6.c.0.3. The day passed fairly quietly except for Spasmodic Shelling. Relieved by 11th SUFFOLK Regt in the evening — Relief complete 2.9.pm. The Battalion withdrew by Companies to bivouac about E.6. central. The following officers were tried between 27th — 29th July — 2 Lt. Gude & N. Stoffer (attached for the attack) Cookesey (concussed) Michie } Franco (killed in action) Stone (concussed) Lutton Porley (Gunshot Wds) Stenan	7643 MB

D. M. F.B. Lt. Col.
Commdg. 10.(S.)Bn. WORCESTERSHIRE REGT.

10th (S.) Bn. Worcestershire Regt.

CASUALTIES.

OFFICERS
July 3rd 1916.

Killed.
Capt. G.A. Ricardo. Pipter. D.S.O.
Maj. F. Stg. Tucker.
Capt. R.G. Tasker.
Capt. A.R. Thomas.
2 Lt. G.M. Foster.

Missing believed Killed.
Lt. C. Huntingdon.
2 Lt. B.W. Pigg.
2 Lt. C.V. Holley.
2 Lt. Askem.

Died of Wounds
Lt. R.W. Jennings.

Wounded
Capt. H.A. Gillum Webb
2 Lt. C.G. Perkins

Wounded (contd)
2 Lt. A.M. Dickinson.
2 Lt. F.G. Miller.
2 Lt. F.T. Pearson.

OTHER RANKS

Killed. 44.
Wounded. 197.
Missing. 106.

TOTAL = 347

La Boiselle.
July 3rd 1916.

CASUALTY LIST

1916.   20–23 July

OFFICERS.

Lt. W. F. TREE } Killed
2 Lt. H. S. H. WALLACE } 22ⁿᵈ July
2 Lt. J. FISH. } 1916.

2 Lt W. M. HARTLAND   21ˢᵗ }
2 Lt O. A. HICKS   21ˢᵗ }
Lt I. N. MARTIN   22ⁿᵈ } WOUNDED
Lt W. S. SCAMMELL   22ⁿᵈ }
2 Lt C. G. WELD   22ⁿᵈ }

OTHER RANKS.

Killed   18
Wounded   71
Missing   64

TOTAL = 153.

2/7/16

57th Brigade.
19th Division.

1/10th BATTALION

WORCESTERSHIRE REGIMENT

AUGUST 1 9 1 6

WAR DIARY

INTELLIGENCE SUMMARY

10th (S) Bn. WORCESTERSHIRE Regt.

(Erase heading not required.)

Army Form C. 2118

Place	Date Aug 1916	Hour	Summary of Events and Information	Remarks and references to Appendices
BRESLE	1st	11.30 h	At 11.30 hr Battalion paraded on ALBERT to Billets in BRESLE – Draft of 51 men received – 50 soldiers Derby Men.	
"	2nd		Brigade Inspection by Gen. Pulteney G.O.C. III Corps. He thanked us for what we had done, saying he regret that we were leaving his Corps. Transport and all officers taken the defaulters en route to LONGPRÉ. Entrained at MERICOURT – arrived at LONGPRÉ 1 pm. Marched to MOUFLERS.	
MOUFLERS	3rd	8.30 am	Ordinary Parades.	
"	4th		Inspection by G.O.C. 57 Bde. at 10.30 am	
"	5th		Church Parade. Football Match against 7 Battalion. We won 1–0	
"	6th		Mrd to LONGPRÉ – entrained at 4.50 am arrived BAILLEUL at 2 pm	
DRANOUTRE	7th	2 am	Marched to DRANOUTRE – billetted in tents.	
"	8th		Ordinary Parades.	
"	9th		Ordinary Parades.	
TRENCHES	10th		Relieved 10 R. War. R. in front line from about N29.d.9.4. to N36.a.4.6. D Coy in support. C Coy in PICADILLY SPORT GUARDS Quiet night. Little Machine Gun fire.	
"	11th	3 pm	Front of Suffolks was subject to Trench Mortar & Shrapnel fire.	
"	12th	3.15 am	Left working party was dispersed off ride BULL RING by our own fire. Leaving five	

Army Form C. 2118.

WAR DIARY
INTELLIGENCE SUMMARY   10/(S) Bn. Worcestershire Regt.
(Erase heading not required.)

Place	Date 1916	Hour	Summary of Events and Information	Remarks and references to Appendices
TRENCHES	13th	2 am	Patrol under 2nd Lt Williams went out to B Coy right. Reported enemy wire strong but cut in places by our artillery. Opposite E.14 there is no M.G. post in enemy wire - During the night a relief was in effect	CASUALTIES 13th - 14th
		6.30 pm	owing to relieve 7 M.G. fire. Belgian aeroplane flew over lines.	OTHER RANKS Killed 2 Wounded 6.
	14th	1 am	Trench Mortars fired from right of B Coy. Artillery response to left of King George who waited for KEMMEL HILL running North South. Gunners retaliated with 4 or 5 salvos of shrapnel -	
		4 am	Trench N.33.a. The trenches held by the Battalion were in a bad state - The gravel to enfiladed from almost all sides were not built up. Between trenches of HAPPY MOMENTS waterfield Glocesters there was 150 yds of trench unknown. HAPPY MOMENTS cleaned out. Shelters were - Parapets Parados shelters - HAPPY MOMENTS Battalion situated in Brigade Reserve relieved by 10 R War. R by 9 pm. Also at DAYLIGHT CORNER, B.C.D at AIRCRAFT FARM.	76.
BRIGADE RESERVE	15th 16th 17th 18th 19th 20th 21st 22nd	}	Brigade Reserve.	
			Battalion relieved 10 R WAR. R in same sector of trenches as previously work carried out as before - Very quiet - only fire very slightly wounded	

Army Form C. 2118

WAR DIARY or INTELLIGENCE SUMMARY 10' (S) Bn. Worcestershire Regt.

(Erase heading not required.)

Place	Date 1916	Hour	Summary of Events and Information	Remarks and references to Appendices
BRANDHOEK	Aug 23		Divisional Reserve.	
"	24			
"	25		Close Order Drill.	
"	26		Handling of Ammn. etc.	
"	27			
	27		Relieves R.WAR.R in trenches.	
	28	12.30pm	Bombardment of enemy's trenches by Stokes Mortars & Artillery.	
		4pm	Enemy working parties dispersed.	
	29	11am	BULL RING bombarded by Minenwerfers	Casualties
		12mn	Officers' patrol returned. Germans working in front of parapet. Fired on by Lewis Guns.	OTHER RANKS- Wounded 3.
	30		Quiet day. Violent thunderstorm during afternoon & evening.	
	31		Considerable artillery activity on left side. Relieved by R. WAR. R. & withdrew into Brigade Reserve.	

761a
Eff

AW Stte Lt Colonel
Comdg. 10th (S) Bn THE WORCESTERSHIRE REGT

Army Form C. 2118

WAR DIARY
or
INTELLIGENCE SUMMARY 10" (S) Bn. Worcestershire Regt.

(Erase heading not required.)

Place	Date 1916	Hour	Summary of Events and Information	Remarks and references to Appendices
Brigade Reserve	1		Draft of 14 men all 10th Battn. men.	
"	2		1 Off & 40 men found daily at 8 am & 7 am.	
"	3		Baths at RANCOURT all & 10th Battn.	
"	4	pos	Battn. Working party of 6 Officers & 160 O.R. moving T1 & C0 & T2 were relieved. The Battalion moved from AIRCRAFT FARM at 1.30pm to RED LODGE and relieved the 10th Royal Inniskilling Fusiliers. Route RANOUTRE - NEUVE EGLISE. Road in T21 & d at T.M. D9.8 a shell burst on road and killed 8 and wounded 13 men.	
"	5		Cleaning up the camp owing to the dirty state in which it was left by the 10th Royal Inniskilling Fusiliers.	
Trenches	6		Relieved the 10th Royal Inniskilling Fusiliers by 9.30 PM	
"	7		Our own artillery active all day.	
"	8		A Gully heard at LE PETIT DOUVE FARM Artillery activity.	
"	9		Line of trench Ref N8 c.9.5 (Sheet 28 S.W. 1:10,000) also showed a considerable amount of enemy wiring. Enemy patrols enemy wire in front. Countered at N6 & 9.4 (28 S.W.) Enemy artillery did considerable damage to our trenches in front of our line. Officers patrols Lance Corpl. Skippy & another went out. They found that their wire was very much cut and shell holes in front. No men in front arrived.	9.15 = N8 c.8
"	10	9.30 AM / 1.15 AM	Both enemy & our own artillery very quiet during day, very active during night. 10 Rifle grenades, 2 working parties of N.C.O. & 10 men formed daily one 8/9/16 working under R.E.'s. Patrols under 2/Lt Bignon thoroughly examined & reported the new trench at 8/6.08, also they found a German listening post in the front wire of this new trench. They believe that the enemy had listening post a	

1875 Wt. W593/82.6 1/000,000 4/15 T.B.C. & A. A.D.S.S./Forms/C. 2118.

Army Form C. 2118

WAR DIARY
or
INTELLIGENCE SUMMARY 10th (S) Bn Worcestershire Regt
(Erase heading not required.)

Place	Date 1916 Sept	Hour	Summary of Events and Information	Remarks and references to Appendices
Trenches	10 11	6.30 pm	Company in Subsidiary Line relieved company in right front line. The company in left support of our front line. Very little artillery activity on either side. Enemy working party observed at W8.a.9.1¼. A Wanchope was observed at E left of LA PETITE DOUVE FARM. Sent into enemy's frogs into with shrapnel round.	
"	12		The Battalion was relieved by the 1st Royal Warwickshire Regt. Relief complete by 6.30 pm. The Battalion took over billets at LE ROMARIN. Very little artillery activity on either side.	
DIVISIONAL RESERVE	13 14 15 16		Cleaning up of Camp. Baths. Musketry. Parties of NCO's were formed for Bomb Squad Drill. Also during Bayonet Fighting. Box Respirators demonstration. Working party of 11 NCO's & men.	
"			" " "	
"			" " "	
"			" " "	
TRENCHES	17	9.30 pm	A bombing raid was made on enemy trenches at the party succeeded in getting into the German front line trench. It was very slightly held. The German casualties were estimated at 12 to 15 killed. Our party did not succeed in bringing back a prisoner or any form of identification. Our casualties were slight. 2 other ranks Bayoned. Shrapnel Bullet being wounded. 1 OR. 4 wounded. 1 missing	
"	18		The Battalion relieved the 1st R Warwickshire Regt in the same trenches. Relief complete by 6.40 pm. Very little artillery activity. Rifle & Machine gun fire normal. Enemy searching Kemmel in New Front line & shelter Bay on outskirts for life winds with rise from 10 pm to 5 am 7 to 8 pm 50 rounds per Stokes Gun. Exchanged artillery bombardment by our guns of NCO & 10 rds. shrapnel at 4 pm to finish. A battery which kept from W.8.a. 4.½.½ bombarded about W.8.c.4.½.½ and one hundred rds howitzer shrapnel at W.8.C.4.5.1¼.	
	19		The Battalion was relieved in the trenches by the 2nd Queens. Relief complete by 4.30 pm. Battalion then moved to Aldershot Huts.	

WAR DIARY or INTELLIGENCE SUMMARY

Army Form C. 2118

10th (S) Bn Worcestershire Regt

(Erase heading not required.)

Secret

Instructions regarding War Diaries and Intelligence Summaries are contained in F.S. Regs., Part II. and the Staff Manual respectively. Title Pages will be prepared in manuscript.

Place	Date 1916 Sept	Hour	Summary of Events and Information	Remarks and references to Appendices
Crosslie Rest	20th		Bn Battalion moved from ALDERSHOT HUTS to OULTERSTEENE AREA marched in billets by 2:30 PM. a draft of 1 off & 10 men refrented	
"	21st		The Battalion moved from OULTERSTEENE AREA to PETIT SEC BOIS AREA & settled in billets by 12.45 PM. A draft of 200 men arrived from Base.	
"	22nd		30 admits (for return) medical inspection by M.O. to all companies. arm drill & bayonet fighting. Lynn trainy.	
"	23rd		Parades left to O.C. Coys, but at least 6 hours work to be put in.	
"	24th		Church Parade & Baths for 1 company	
"	25th		5 hours work put in recenting to programme of work	
"	26th		Baths & sighted arms drill & programme as for previous	
"	27th		Arm drill & inning inspection of brigade in afternoon by army commander	
"	28th		5 hours work according to programme of work	
"	29th		" " " " " " "	
"	30th		" " " " " " "	

MMBrown Major
Comdg 10th (S) Bn Worcestershire Regt

Secret 57/A Vol 16

WAR DIARY or **INTELLIGENCE SUMMARY**
(Erase heading not required.)

10th (S)Bn Worcestershire Regt

Army Form C. 2118

Place	Date 1916	Hour	Summary of Events and Information	Remarks and references to Appendices
Point Rest	Oct 1		Church parade.	
	2		5 hours work according to programme of work	
	3			
	4		Brigade instruction by S.O. of Belgians	
	5		5½ hours work according to programme of work	
	6		Battalion moved from Point St Paris to AMPLIER	
	7		AMPLIER to BOIS du WARNIMONT	
Bois du Reserve	8		Cleaning up & forming huts. Charged operations orders. Party of 1st Officers stood as sufficient Battalion	
	9		5 hours work with O.C. Companies. A South East Coy (Captain) Battalion Companies practising artillery formation in Bois du Warnimont in 2 Coy & 1 in support. Both companies practising artillery formation.	
	10		Brigade field day practising the attack from artillery formation. Battalion	
	11		" "	
	12		Church parade. Steady company and Coy advancing behind a barrage.	
	13		Battalion field day practising to attack from artillery formation	
	14		Battalion moved from WARNIMONT WOOD to WARLOY	
	15		Cleaning up billets which were taken over by us in a filthy condition. Steady arm drill	
	16		The Battalion started to move to BRICKFIELDS ALBERT, but was recalled halfway	
	17		Early morning gymnastics. Practising extending from artillery formation, steady arm drill	
	18		Bayonet fighting.	
	19		Battalion marched from WARLOY to Bivouacs at Brickfields, ALBERT	
	20		Battalion relieved 8th Border, 8th K.S. Lancs & 11th Cheshires in trenches.	
	21		The enemy shelled our front line support very heavily during the night of 22nd/23rd & the 23rd	16 D
	22		Casualties Killed 13 O.R. Wounded 38 O.R. Missing 1 O.R. Shell Shock 1 O.R.	
	23		Enemy artillery very active but casualties not so heavy. Killed 1 O.R. Wounded 1 Officer, 2nd Lieut Binns T. + 5 O.R. O. Patrol went out & report a trench (unoccupied) about half way between	
	24			

Army Form C. 2118

SECRET

WAR DIARY
INTELLIGENCE SUMMARY

10th (S) Battn. Worcestershire Regt.

Place	Date Oct	Hour	Summary of Events and Information	Remarks and references to Appendices
Trenches	24/10/15		REGINA TRENCH & the enemy's lines. Battalion was relieved in the line by the 10th R. War. Regt. Battalion rested as far as was possible & then dug shelters & small dug outs. Two working parties found, one of 4 Officers & 200 men to pitch tents, the other 150 O.R. repairing & boarding communication trench.	
	25			
	26			
Rest	27		Battalion rested	
	28		"	
	29		Battalion relieved Royal Welsh Fusiliers	
Trenches	30		Heavy British Artillery activity during most of the day. Enemy artillery very active between 4 p.m. & 6 p.m. Patrols sent out & reported no wire in front of new trench.	
	31		The new trench is deep & in fairly good condition.	

E.W.Sturt. Capt. for Major.
Comdg. 10th (S) Batn. Worcestershire Regt.

SECRET
5/19 Vol 7

WAR DIARY or INTELLIGENCE SUMMARY
(Erase heading not required.)

Army Form C. 2118

10th Bn Worcestershire Regt

Place	Date Nov 1916	Hour	Summary of Events and Information	Remarks and references to Appendices
Trenches	1		Artillery lively active on both sides, very little rifle or machine gun fire, a little shelling done by enemy. Company several casualties a patrol reported that 19th R.I.R. Trench were held	3 of 2nd WF
do	2			
Rest Billets	3		Battalion relieved by 1/10th R Warwicks took over Rest & Howitzer Post.	
"	4		Men were allowed to rest	
"	5		Cleaning Kit. 2nd Lieuts von Müller & Parker	
Trenches	6		The Battalion relieved the 10th R Warwicks in L Gravel Pit. Remainder went	
Lumsmay & Pit	7		[to] front line trench where we	
Trenches	8			
"	9		The Battalion relieved by 9th Kings own in the trenches	
			Owing to bright moonlight it was impossible to mount our artillery in daylight. Letters on both sides. Workings on trench at	
	10		out-worked carried on, working our RE's a friendship relieving our dying out. Lot. 2 battle planes brought down. Palmer	
	11		Artillery very active Lot work was being done to divine Lewis Artillery very active trenches to billets at Aveluy. Bath	
Rest Billets	12		Working parties of 100 men supplied. Cleaning of kit, gumboots & overcoats	
"	13		inspection. Route march & arms drill	
"	14		Working parties of 390 men found for working party R.E.'s	
"	15		The Battalion relieved the French Sappers in the trenches	
"	16			
"	17			

SECRET

Army Form C. 2118

Instructions regarding War Diaries and Intelligence Summaries are contained in F.S. Regs., Part II. and the Staff Manual respectively. Title Pages will be prepared in manuscript.

WAR DIARY
or
INTELLIGENCE SUMMARY
(Erase heading not required.)

10th (S) Bn Worcestershire Regt

Place	Date	Hour	Summary of Events and Information	Remarks and references to Appendices
TRENCHES	1916 Nov 18		On the night of the 17/18, 1 Coy joined the 8th N. Staffs to act as a clearing up party. 2 Coys joined 10 R. Warwicks & 1 Bn joined 8th Glos also to act as cleaning up parties in the attack. Our Coy R Warwicks were kept in reserve. The Brigade attacked at 6.10 AM &. Somewhat surprising the enemy, cleaned up parties followed up the various battalions & the brigade's cleaning out all dug outs & the old trenches but did not meet with any great resistance. After doing this job they remained in shell holes or old trenches suffering strong sniper & at same shrapnel & began to return to Batt HQ. An Enemy counter-attack with heavy shelling 41 wounded, YSO missing (OR) officers casualties 1 killed 1 unwounded 2 missing, believed killed & missing. During the morning the Brigade came to a Coy were ordered to go up as reinforcements to the front line & were also without casualties. The Brigade left the trenches the [illegible] of AVELUY	
"	19		cleaning clothing & equipment. Baths.	
AVELUY WARLOY	20 21		The Battalion moved from huts at AVELUY to huts at WARLOY the next 440 strong	
"	22		cleaning & fitting kit.	
ROBEMPRE	23		The battalion moved from WARLOY to billets at RUBEMPRE. It has steady one drill day. Some route marching	
MONTRELET	24		The Battalion moved from billets at RUBEMPRE to billets at MONTRELET. The battalion marching & shooting.	

WAR DIARY

INTELLIGENCE SUMMARY 10t. (S) Bage Worcestershire Reg.t

Army Form C. 2118

SECRET

Instructions regarding War Diaries and Intelligence Summaries are contained in F.S. Regs., Part II. and the Staff Manual respectively. Title Pages will be prepared in manuscript.

(Erase heading not required.)

Place	Date 15/16	Hour	Summary of Events and Information	Remarks and references to Appendices
FRANZVILLE	Nov. 25		The battalion moved from billets at MONTRELET to billets at FRANZVEVILLE. The battalion weather nothing.	
BERNAVILLE	26		Morning. Inspection of Kit, arms etc. The battalion moved at 3 p.m. from billets at FRANZVEVILLE to billets at BERNAVILLE. The battalion remained nothing.	
GEZAINCOURT	27		The battalion moved from billets at BERNAVILLE to billets at GEZAINCOURT. The battalion remained nothing.	
"	28		Cleaning of billets. Inspection of arms, gas helmets, Bainets, ammunition refilling.	
"	29	9.12-30	Squad drill without arms. Physical drill etc. The Battalion supplied 2 working parties for Rifle Ranges and 2 to Army.	
"	30	9-12-30	Squad drill with rifles without arms. The battalion provides two working parties and 2 to Army. 9.1-3 p.m. Afternoon, Football match, Drafts O.R. receiving special clothing without arms 9-12.30. Three Companies supplied to the match Parties.	
"	31		Morning Parades 9-10, 10-10.15, 10.30-1, 1.30-2.30 Q ludicrous Parties, book parties supplied from Companies Ranges Bag. Drafts 3 of O.R. received Illness 22.	

E.M.Shurt, Capt.
for O.C. 10t. Worcestershire Reg.t

WAR DIARY
INTELLIGENCE SUMMARY

Vol 19 10th (S) Bn Leicestershire Regt.

Place	Date 1917 JAN	Hour	Summary of Events and Information	Remarks and references to Appendices
GEZAINCOURT	1		Remained building party 250 O.R. 7 Offrs. Working party 50 O.R. diggng party 20 O.R. Remainder on training programme.	
	2		Working party of 10 Officers & 850 O.R. & 2 parties of 20 O.R. on building. Remainder on the training programme.	
	3		Two working parties of 20 O.R. on building. Reinforcements 1 man Cpl. Bracebridge & party for training programme.	
	4		Two working parties of 20 O.R. on building + party working parties of 1 Officer + 50 O.R. Training carries on helde. Very heavy rain.	
	5		Two working parties of 20 O.R. on building. Training carries on training programme.	
	6		Two " " " " 55 O.R. " " " " "	
	7		Two " " " " 20 O.R. " " " " "	
	8		Working party of 20 O.R. on building & working party of 1 Offr + 55 O.R. Training on programme in morning. Cleaning up billets + kits in afternoon.	

19D

WAR DIARY or INTELLIGENCE SUMMARY

Army Form C. 2118.

SECRET 10th (S) Bn Worcestershire Regt

Place	Date 1917 JAN	Hour	Summary of Events and Information	Remarks and references to Appendices
GEZAINCOURT	9		The Battalion moved from billets at GEZAINCOURT to AMPLIER	
AMPLIER TRENCHES HEBUTERNE AREA	10		The Battalion moved from billets at AMPLIER & relieved the 18th D.L.I. relief completed by 11.40 PM	
	11		Our own artillery was active all day especially in the early morning. The enemy retaliated heavily on HEBUTERNE between 9-11 am & 2 to 3 PM. Casualties 2 killed + 12 wounded. Work done entrenching a little revetting & entraining approaches & widening firesteps. All the front enemy patrols were active on the night of 11/12. One important patrol of the enemy's was at K47 and has been considerably damaged by artillery & had to beat a hasty retreat. Patrol encountered about	
"	12		Artillery fire normal. Enemy had 2 working parties of 40 O.R. forms of workmen in K.E.'s	
"	13		Artillery on both sides not very active. A patrol went out & reported two enemy at K4C27 & K4C17. Footfalls were red with enemy from K4C01 carrying out towards our line but only weak [illeg] about 75 yds on the enemy side. 2 working parties of 40 O.R. found for work of K34.7b, K34.85, K34.95. Chained parapet & improved firesteps & built small shell bombproofs. Artillery on both sides fairly quiet.	
"	14		2 enemy grenades sent over to SAILLY au BoiS. Rifle grens were occasionally sent at HEBUTERNE. A machine gun was seen firing from Gommecourt Park. Two enemy locators were not formed. An observing officer at our listening TEiling [?] everything along the night. Several messages[?] reported that they could hear the enemy talking, coughing & giving orders (words seg.) Working parties (40 men carried on for work near R.E.T. details. No hostile wire from K4C8B K4C8L4 in good condition Report from K3C87 & K3C09½5 shown to pieces.	
"	15		Enemy located at. Artillery below normal. Bn relieved by 8 Gloucester & occupied	
"	16		billets at BAYENCOURT	

Army Form C. 2118.

WAR DIARY or INTELLIGENCE SUMMARY

(Erase heading not required.)

SECRET 10th (S) Bn Worcestershire Regt

Place	Date 1917 JAN	Hour	Summary of Events and Information	Remarks and references to Appendices
BAYENCOURT	17		Baths for Battn. remainder cleaning up trenches. 3 NCOs + 3 OR work under Town Major	
	18		Baths for Remainder of Battn. General cleaning up of equipment etc. 3NCO + 3 OR working for Town Major. Lewis Gun Course carries out in each Coy.	
	19		Lewis Gun course continues. Cleaning up. inspection of Rifles guns &c Lewis gun ammunition etc. Hand working party for town major.	
	20		Lewis gun course continues. Coy practising to attack.	
BERTRANCOURT	21		Battalion were relieved by the 7th Bn S. Staffs Regt. removed to Billets at BERTRANCOURT + LOUVENCOURT.	
	22		Two Coys at workshops for built the R.E. 4 Coys at workshops 4th Bn R.E.	
	23		" " " " " " " " "	
	24		1 Coy working on platform layers equipment for workshop employment. 1 NCO + 2 men found 2 Platoons working with R.E's. C no Coy moved from Louvencourt to hut at Bus.	
	25		Coy at platoon of Coy commanders for practising to attack. 2 platoons working with R.E.'s working party INCO 2 men	
	26		Battalion practising attack. 2 platoons working with R.E.'s working party 1 NCO + 9 men	
	27		Battalion practising platoons attack " " " " " 1 " 9 "	
	28		1 platoon working for line train + hut building " " " " " 1 " 9 " Church parade. C no Coy moved from Bus to BERTRANCOURT	

Army Form C. 2118.

WAR DIARY
or
INTELLIGENCE SUMMARY

(Erase heading not required.) 10th (S) Bn Worcestershire Regt

SECRET

Place	Date	Hour	Summary of Events and Information	Remarks and references to Appendices
BERTRANCOURT	1917 JAN 28th 29th 30th 31st		Whole garrison of 1 NCO & 3 men formed. Rendezvous Bath Scheme. Cleaning up lines & Camp of old takes. Inter-pan in afternoon. Semi Final. Whole garrison of 1 NCO & 9 men formed " " " " " " Cup. Inter-pan Company went out to fire Army Course.	

1/2/17

J.G. Jerome Eisenway
Lt Col (S) Bn Worcestershire Regt

WAR DIARY or INTELLIGENCE SUMMARY

Army Form C. 2118.

10 Worcester

10th/16 November

Vol 20

Place	Date	Hour	Summary of Events and Information	Remarks and references to Appendices
Retrenchment	1917 1st		[illegible]	
TRENCHES	2		The Battalion relieved the 16th Sussex. Tour in the trenches Artillery fairly active. Post saw nothing to report. Snipers artillery fairly active. Enemy of 8th trenches.	
	3			
	4		The Boche [illegible] a fairly heavy barrage on our front line at 11-35, retaliation was called for & the enemy quickly stopped abruptly afterwards. Our [illegible] shot down a plane about opposite A post [illegible] at [illegible] shelled sporadically in and around for K 29 F 3.5 6 h 9 hours	
	5		Our own artillery fairly active during day & night. Artillery fired [illegible] during the night. [illegible] [illegible] caused by 2. Patrol went out during the night. [illegible] [illegible] very light moonlight were deployed at 4pm going 700 yards [illegible] [illegible] 10 battalion was relieved by 11th Glos Regt. Battalion [illegible] Cleaning up. Baths were detailed [illegible] [illegible] not available (no water)	LB
	6		2 coys of Battalions working parties. 1 coy? Platoons training for attack [illegible] from 9-11.30 coys of [illegible] in the R6 sector	
	7		Battalion relieved the 8th Glos in the R6 sector. Artillery very active from 7.30 to 8.30 PM. Our artillery [illegible] a barrage air 11pm [illegible] enemy [illegible] to the Batt Hqs. Batt with stretchers[?] [illegible] reported that he [illegible] at K 29 b 3 7½	
	8		[illegible] Comp Hqs very strongly. No patrols [illegible] were heavily fired on	
	9		during daylight	
	10		Artillery [illegible] on both sides [illegible] [illegible] Regt Roy detailed trenches [illegible] [illegible] [illegible] captd. A fatigue [illegible] afternoon to [illegible] [illegible] by our artillery if possible. Artillery activities [illegible] from K 29, 24 F 29 yds [illegible] [illegible] been [illegible]	20 D
	11			

WAR DIARY or INTELLIGENCE SUMMARY

Army Form C. 2118.

SECRET

19/5 19th Bn Worcestershire Regt

Place	Date	Hour	Summary of Events and Information	Remarks and references to Appendices
TRENCHES	12		11th coys attacked the evening 12th Dec. Line from K.3.q.4.3.5. to K.3.q.4.3.5. at 11.15 P.M. (map sheet 11/H) at 12th In the morning flares were perfect, it was preluced with an [artillery ?] salvo when about 150 yds we were fired upon by a [gun ?] from a farm at K.2.9.b.1/4.2.9/4 which felled the centre of a little before we got to the top the first line of the garrison [ran back ?] & were killed by our rifle fire. We then [advanced ?] to the 2nd line where the [enemy ?] heavily opened on our rifle. From [our] left front & centre, but [the ?] 2nd line was taken with ease but it was not held. From left front [dugouts ?] were searched but no [men?] were seen. Two prisoners were taken. Our casualties amounted to 4 other ranks killed & 52 wounded missing (39 W. 13 M.) Capt. Stout & 2/Lt. Bass & Raine wounded, 2/Lt. Johnston wounded. From this attack it was found that neither the [men ?] & [officers ?] were held up except by [MG ?]. The Batt was relieved by R.6 coy late by 9th Bn N.Glos. Regt. Artillery of both sides [were ?] active during the night.	
	13th		[illegible lines]	
	14th 15		2 coys working parties, remainder in [position ?] ahead. Training [illegible]	
	16		" "	
	17		Batt [with ?] 2½ coys. Batt relieved the 8th Glos in the Trenches. Owing to mist observation very difficult. Artillery of both sides quiet 2 night.	
	18		Coys relieved by 2 coys 10th R.WARW. Working parties of 6 platoons from [illegible] all very tired. Working parties of [illegible platoons ?] very little artillery activity	
	19		2 platoons went out with working parties [illegible] [illegible]	
	20		Relieved by our 2 coys. 3 platoons working parties. 2 coys 10th R.WARW.	

Army Form C. 2118.

WAR DIARY
or
INTELLIGENCE SUMMARY
(Erase heading not required.)

SECRET 10th (S) Bn Worcestershire Regt

Place	Date	Hour	Summary of Events and Information	Remarks and references to Appendices
TRENCHES	21		The Batt. was relieved in the line by the 8th Gloss Regt. marching from [?] H Platoon and Coys to working at night. Stringing up	
COURCELLES	22		O.C. Coys working parties. 25 men working under R.E. Put wire in	
"	23		A Coy + 1 Platoon to working parties wire netting	
"	24			
"	25		Two Coys on working party. 1160 + 20 men extending front.	
"	26		The [?] companies to be taken at EUSTON Dump.	
EUSTON Dump	27		2 Coys moved up to the front line at PUISIEUX + were now its commenced of B.C.10th R.WARW.	
"	28		2 Coys to supply men to dig outs in support line R&B Bay.	
"	28		Another move to relieve the in RAILWAY AVENUE. The two Coys were O.C. to R.WARW. relieved by 4th wave.	

4/3/17

J. E. [Shonels] Lieut
Adjt 10th Worcs.

WAR DIARY or INTELLIGENCE SUMMARY

Army Form C. 2118.

SECRET

10th (S)/5th Howitzer Regt.

Nov 21

Place	Date	Hour	Summary of Events and Information	Remarks and references to Appendices
TRENCHES	1		The Bat surrendered in the trenches by the 1st Cheshire Regt marched back to SAILLY BUS.	
	2		Bat. entrained for Long to ARQUÈVES	
ARQUÈVES	3		Cleaning up at rifle inspection etc.	
	4		Platoon drill Bayonet fighting practised in various 9.30 to 12.30 Voluntary R.C. & C of E services. Baths	
" Bay	5		The Battalion marched from ARQUÈVES to Bus.	
	6		1 Coy working in reinforcements / Fontaine. Platoon drill Bayonet Balk training Bayonet fighting Exercises various Bombing.	
"	7		Route march.	
"	8		The Battalion marched from Bus to LOUVENCOURT	
LOUVENCOURT	9		" LOUVENCOURT to GEZAINCOURT	
GEZAINCOURT	10		" GEZAINCOURT to BONNIÈRES	
BONNIÈRES	11		General cleaning up	
	12		The Battalion marched from BONNIÈRES to CROIX	
	13		" CROIX to TANGRY	
	14		General cleaning up	
	15		The Battalion marched from TANGRY to EQUEDECQUES	
	16		" EQUEDECQUES to BOESEGHEM	
	17		" BOESEGHEM to Concentration Area MERRIS	
	18		General cleaning up. Inoculation	
	19		Battalion act as battalion Brigade football	
	20			
21		The Battalion moved to METEREN	

Army Form C. 2118.

WAR DIARY
or
INTELLIGENCE SUMMARY

(Erase heading not required.)   10th (S) Bn Worcestershire Regt.

SECRET

Place	Date 1917 MARCH	Hour	Summary of Events and Information	Remarks and references to Appendices
	22		The Battalion proceeded from METEREN to RIDGE WOOD & relieved the 2/7 R.F.	
	23		250 O.R. Working Parties	
	24		280 O.R. Working Parties	
	25		306 D.R " "	
	26		306 O.R " "	
	27			
	28		The Battalion relieved the 8th Bn Glos Regt. in the line (Rt Subsect.) DIEPENDAAL SECTOR) Hostile artillery action most of the day. Mostar artillery very active & our artillery fairly active. Left our line & frontage chopman very important, but a working party about 30 strong in recent Phess line were seen to chop wood on top of parapet (in front of Shores bomb) at the covering party which accounted for a number of the his. M.G. fire prevented Hostile proceeding further, a great deal of movement of troops in UNIEZ TRENCH	
	29		Our artillery very active. Hostile shelling normal. T.N's fairly active. Hostile practice dropping the crater on 6 very Wester trenches in center. An officer's patrol entered the Hun line at NOTSNOSE term to enemy a working party was again seen behind the front line. The hostile officer & Sergeant N.C.O. met with in twenty yards which officer dropped on the advance of the patrol. Saw a lot of movement in the neighbourhood. Enemy firing very active between the ?: : : Back line & Back line & ...? during officers patrols went out & between the lines throughout the night. A.C. Lorenton & twenty artillery shoronement. Enemy very active between ??? ??? lines but slackened by morning. A.C. Lorenton & twenty OTHER RANKS	
	30			
	31		The Battalion was relieved by the 9th Bn Cheshire Regt. then moved back to CURRAGH CAMP P.6 c.R.2.	

J.B. ??????
Lt Col. 10th W.R.

1/4/17

Army Form C. 2118.

WAR DIARY
or
INTELLIGENCE SUMMARY

(Erase heading not required.)

SECRET 10th (S)Bn Worcestershire Regt

G.W. 22 D

Place	Date 1919	Hour	Summary of Events and Information	Remarks and references to Appendices
	Apl 1		The Battalion moved from Curragh Camp to Croix Rouge (Caestre Area)	
	2		" " " Caestre Area to Hazebrouck Area	
	3		" " " Hazebrouck Area to Arques	
	4		" " " Arques to Acquin	
	5			
Acquin	6		General cleaning up. Kit inspections etc	
	7		Squad drill 7-7.30am Platoon training 9-12.30	
	8		Coy drill 7.30am Squad drill 9-12.30	
	9		Coy dance 9-12.30 Squad drill 9-12.30 inspection by Commanding Officer Platoon	
	10		Coy. log jumping PT&BF 2.15 - 3.15am Musketry S.G. on range	
	11		Musketry & log jumping Platoon training S.G. on range	
	12		Battalion in attack before the Company Commander	
	13		Squad drill Platoon in the attack by a will PT+BF Coy in 2 coy attack	
	14		Bombing	
	15		Squad drill PT&BF Platoon in the attack 2 coy musketry by Commanding Officer	
	16		Voluntary Holy Communion R.C. Church Parade Non-conformist church parade	
	17		Cross country run Bathed & racing	
	18		Squad drill attack Squad 2/2 range Platoon training	
	19		The battalion moved from Acquin to Arques	
	20		" " " Arques to Hazebrouck	
Lacre	21		" " " Hazebrouck to Curragh Camp Lacre	
	22		Cleaning up etc	
	23		Working parties of 250 o.r. +5 officers found cleaning hutments, cleaning officials	

Army Form C. 2118.

WAR DIARY
or
INTELLIGENCE SUMMARY.

(Erase heading not required.)

10th (S) Bn. the Worcestershire Regt.

Place	Date	Hour	Summary of Events and Information	Remarks and references to Appendices
CURRAGH CAMP				
LOCRE	24		Working parties of 5 Officers & 260 O.R. found. Class of instruction for N.C.Os. Training & chicadvise	
	25		" "	
	26		Draft of 12 other Ranks. Return strength of battalion 41 Officers & 887 other ranks. Detached to Sheffield 1 RES for bath returned	
	27		Working parties of 5 Officers & 250 O.R. found. Class of instruction for junior N.C.Os. fighting strength 701	
	28		Working parties as above. fighting strength 702. draft of 4 Other ranks received	
	29		" " " Winter clothing & 2nd blanket returned to channel	
	30		Battn. Battalion moved from CURRAGH CAMP LOCRE to Sr. Lawrence Camp. near POPERINGHE	

5/9/17

J.G. Shoulsbrary Lt. Col.
10th (S) Bn. the Worcestershire Regt

Army Form C. 2118.

Vol 23

10th (S) Bn. The Yorkshire Regt.

WAR DIARY
or
INTELLIGENCE SUMMARY.
(Erase heading not required.)

Place	Date 1915	Hour	Summary of Events and Information	Remarks and references to Appendices
ST AUBREUX CAMP POPERINGHE	1		10 Officers & 43 other ranks attached for duty with the 1st Australian Tunnelling Coy.	
TRENCHES YPRES SALIENT	2		The Battalion relieved the 8th KOYLI in the CENTRE subsector of the HILL 60 sector — YPRES SALIENT Relief quiet.	
	3		Artillery very quiet. Patrols were out to examine craters & where possible were re-occupied.	
	4	9.30pm	Heavy bombardment of our lines lasting for 1 hour. Enemy Trench Mortars opened fire & 10.30pm. HQ relieved during the night into D.13. Howitzer aeroplane range from above LARCH WOOD.	
	5		Quiet day.	
	6		The Battalion was relieved by the 8th Batt. G.H.L. Regt. and went into the Brigade reserve to the Bunds & Railway Dugouts.	
	7	9.30am	Railway Dugouts twenty immediate with 1, 2 & 5g for munitions & extras of Wounded. Working Parties of 230 O.R. and 5 officers carrying & building up Dugouts.	
	8		Batts. allotted to Bn. at Transport farm from 9.30 – 12.30 – 2.30 – 4.30.	

WAR DIARY
or
INTELLIGENCE SUMMARY.
(Erase heading not required.)

Army Form C. 2118.

Place	Date	Hour	Summary of Events and Information	Remarks and references to Appendices
Trenches Ypres Salient	8		Working Parties of 8 Officers + 380 O.R. various duties carrying Dugouts and burying cable.	
	9		Working Parties as above.	
—	10	12 MN	Batt was relieved by the 11th N.F. The Batt: entrained at Ypres and went to St Lawrence Camp	
SCHERPENBERG	11th	2.45	The Batt: marched to Canarvon Camp SCHERPENBERG.	
	12		Coy at disposal of 6C Corp for cleaning up etc	
	13		Coys training Programme. Section training. Platoon in the attack taking of strong points. Bombing. Lewis Gunners firing on range.	
	—		Working party of 3 Officers + 150 O.R. 4 Officers + 160 O.R. working party attached unloading ammunition.	
	14		As above, one additional working party of 2 Officers + 100 O.R. Draft of 4 + 20 R joined Batt	
	15		do	
	16		Working parties of 3 officers + 150 OR, 4 Officers + 160 OR, 2 Officers + 100 OR. Draft of 45 OR joined Batt	
	17		Coy training Programme as for 13th do	

WAR DIARY
or
INTELLIGENCE SUMMARY.

Army Form C. 2118.

(Erase heading not required.)

Place	Date	Hour	Summary of Events and Information	Remarks and references to Appendices
	18		Working Parties as for 17th Coy training Programme. Section training Platoon in the attack taking of strong Points. Rapid training Aiming & Fire control.	
	19		As above	
	20		Draft of 11 O.R. joined Batt	
	21		The Battalion relieved the 7th E.LANCS in the right subsector of the Hebuterne sector. Our artillery somewhat active, enemy artillery active, 2	Casualties
	22	11pm	Officers patrol reconn. enemy wire & lines in front of BOIS QUARANTE, found it unoccupied. Patrol of 1 O.R. reconn. NAG'S NOSE & found no trace of movement.	4 Casualties
		11pm	Our artillery very active. Enemy fairly quiet. Patrol came in for 2½ hrs	
	23	8.15pm	Bef. dawn stand a hot down during the day. Work including up of post's outpost line. Relief cy relief. Patrols brought in later enemy from GHRU. Our artillery very active. Army mil. Draft 17 other ranks.	
	24	12.30am	Officers patrol reported enemy working in NAG'S NOSE. examined a Listen officer patrol reported a suspicious box of the enemy wire 30 yds in front of our lines in tr of our sector. Another officers patrol reported built a trench in front of BOIS QUARANTE. Another officers patrol reported OBJECT TRENCH unoccupied.	

WAR DIARY
or
INTELLIGENCE SUMMARY.
(Erase heading not required.)

Army Form C. 2118.

Place	Date	Hour	Summary of Events and Information	Remarks and references to Appendices
Trenches	25		Our artillery very active. Enemy practically nil. Aircraft 24 O.R.	
	26	6am	Our artillery very active. Enemy heavy shelling behind RIDGE WOOD.	
		12.45am	Two raiding parties under 2/Lt. Bateman & 2/Lt. Taggart each of 11 O.R. without NCOs on either side of the crater. The crater was rushed, two prisoners were taken & one man of the two was bayoneted in attempting to escape. Raiders returned at 1am with the prisoners to our trenches. About 2am enemy opened a heavy rifle & machine gun fire on our trenches. Our artillery very active. Enemy shells bursting behind RIDGE WOOD. Our artillery very active.	
	27	pm	Relieved by 1st 4th Cheshires & moved to CURRAGH CAMP. Relief complete 9.45 pm.	
CURRAGH CAMP LOCRE	28		Cleaning up. Kit inspections etc. Fighting strength 814.	
	29	7-9.40 am	Adjutants parade Steady drill. 9am-12.30pm Musketry. Rifle Inspec. 2-3.30 pm Musketry.	Lt. B. J. Celis wounded, unluckily 10 officers 75 O.R. to battalions from CURRAGH CAMP & ROSA CAMP WESTOUTRE
	30	7-9.40 am	Adjutants parade 9-12 Musketry for Coldn.	
	31		Musketry section drill. Training "Specialists" 9-9.40am Adjutants parade Steadydrill. 9-12.30 Practice "Battalion in the attack"	J.F. Bowen Lieut. Colonel Comdg. 10th (S.) Bn. THE WORCESTERSHIRE REGT

WAR DIARY
INTELLIGENCE SUMMARY
(Erase heading not required.)

Army Form C. 2118.

57/19
1st Worcestershire Regt.

Place	Date	Hour	Summary of Events and Information	Remarks and references to Appendices
EPSOM CAMP	1.6.17		Adjutants parade 7-7.40 A.M. Coy's smoke attack on Battalion Training Ground 9-10.30 P.M. Musketry 2-4 P.M. Congratulated by Corps Commander on recent raid 25/26th May.	
	2.6.17	9 am	Inspection by Divisional Commander & practice attack	
	3.6.17		Practice attack by Brigade.	
	4.6.17		Practice attack by Brigade	
	5.6.17		Cleaning up, preparing for trenches etc	
	6.6.17		The Battalion moves off to MURROMBIDGE playing area, ready to proceed to the attack on the MESSINES – WYTSCHAETE ridge.	
	7.6.17		Zero hour 3.20 am. The Battalion went forward & captured their objective. Casualties Capt. E.W. Butler & 2nd Lieut. J.H. Glee wounded. Other ranks Killed 9. Wounded 56. Missing 4 (of whom 3 have since rejoined & have been traced to Field Ambulance) wounded	
	8.6.17		Consolidating & digging new trenches in captured ground	
	9.6.17		Consolidating & digging in captured ground	
	10.6.17		In reserve trenches behind MESSINES – WYTSCHAETE Ridge	
	11.6.17		Same place	
	12.6.17		Relieved by 4th Co. Lanc. Regt & proceeded to MURROMBIDGE Camp.	

Army Form C. 2118.

WAR DIARY
or
INTELLIGENCE SUMMARY.
(Erase heading not required.)

Instructions regarding War Diaries and Intelligence Summaries are contained in F. S. Regs., Part II. and the Staff Manual respectively. Title pages will be prepared in manuscript.

Place	Date	Hour	Summary of Events and Information	Remarks and references to Appendices
MURROMBIDGEE	13/6/17	9.30am	The Battalion moved to GARDEN CAMP near LA CLYTTE	
GARDEN CAMP	14/6/17		Resting & cleaning up. 2nd Lieut H J Suckman granted Military Cross	
"	15/6/17		Battalion relieved 4th R. Sussex Regt in front line trenches.	
"	16/6/17		Consolidating new front line.	
Trenches	17/6/17		Casualties Other ranks:- Killed 5 Wounded 22	
"	18/6/17			
"	19/6/17		Battalion relieved by & proceeded to GARDEN CAMP	
GARDEN CAMP	20/6/17		Moved to CORUNNA Camp near WESTOUTRE	
CORUNNA CAMP	21/6/17		Resting	
"	22/6/17		Resting	
"	23/6/17	9.30am	Inspection by Divisional Commander	
"	24/6/17		Church Parade. Remainder of day resting & cleaning	
"	25/6/17		Adjutants parade 9-9.30 am: 9-12.30 Section & platoon training Afternoon Musketry & lectures. Games	
"	26/6/17		As for 25th	
"	27/6/17		As for 26th	

Army Form C. 2118.

WAR DIARY
or
INTELLIGENCE SUMMARY.
(Erase heading not required.)

Place	Date	Hour	Summary of Events and Information	Remarks and references to Appendices
CORINDA CAMP	28/6/17		As for yesterday. A Coy supplied working party 100 O.R. for Corps School Scheme (practice) Battalion in the attack	
	29/6/17			
	30/6/17		As for 29ᵗʰ	

R.W. Dudley Lieut.
for Lieut Col
Commdg 10ᵗʰ (S) Bn "The Worcestershire Regt.

Army Form C. 2118.

5 Bde 19 Divn

Vol 25

WAR DIARY
or
INTELLIGENCE SUMMARY.
(Erase heading not required.)

10th S. Worcestn Regt.

Place	Date	Hour	Summary of Events and Information	Remarks and references to Appendices
CORUNNA CAMP	1/4/17		Battalion moved to ~~Dickebusch~~ IRISH HOUSE N.23.C.88 Sheet 28 SW in Divisional Reserve	
GARDEN CAMP	2/4/17 to		Battalion moved into line OOSTAVERNE. 4th Bn took part in operations which were never	
TRENCHES	10/4/17		-s lightly retrieving our line.	
			Casualties Capt E. Coon, killed. 2/Lieut of Haigstone + 2/Lieut Dellow & 2/Lieut HJ Turberville wounded. Others ranks	Killed 12 wounded 36
IRISH HOUSE	11/4/17		Divisional reserve, cleaning up etc.	
	12/4/17		Working party 3 Officers + 100 O.R. covering party	
	13/4/17		Working parties 4 officers 200 O.R – 2/Lieut P. Lucovich wounded. Others ranks 11 killed 11 wounded	
	14/4/17		Working parties	
	15/4/17		Under Coy Commanders, drill etc	
	16/4/17		" " "	
	17/4/17		" " "	
	18/4/17			
	19/4/17		Battalion inspected by 2/O.C 5th Infy Brigade	
	20/4/17		Under Coy Commanders	
	21/4/17			
	22/4/17		Battalion moved into line B+C Coy in front line. A Coy in support in old front line in ROSE WOOD, D Coy in reserve in house E of GODEZONE FARM	

WAR DIARY
or
INTELLIGENCE SUMMARY.
(Erase heading not required.)

Army Form C. 2118.

Place	Date	Hour	Summary of Events and Information	Remarks and references to Appendices
COFUNDA CAMP	1/1/14		Battalion moved to ~~IRISH HOUSE~~ IRISH HOUSE N.23.c.88 Sheet 28 S.W. in Divisional Reserve	
GARDEN CAMP	2/4/14 to		Battalion moved into line ~~Battn~~ OOSTAVERNE. "B" Coy took part in operations which necessitated	
TRENCHES	10/4/14		3 entry showing extent	Killed 19
			Casualties. Capt. J. Gaer, +Lieut C.S. Nairy Grey + 2/Lieut Dellow +2/Lieut N.J. Lustman wounded. Other ranks wounded 36	
IRISH HOUSE	11/4/14		Divisional reserve, cleaning up etc.	
	12/4/14		Working party 3 Officers 4100 O.R. as carrying party	
	13/4/14		Working parties 4 Officers 200 O.R. +Lieut F. Lucovich Wounded. Other ranks 4 killed 11 wounded.	Killed 12 Wounded
"	14/4/17		Working parties.	
"	15/4/17		Under Coy Commanders, drill etc	
"	16/4/17		" " " " "	
"	17/4/17		" " " " "	
"	18/4/17		Battalion inspected by G.O.C. 57th Infy. Brigade	
"	19/4/17		Under Coy Commanders	
"	20/4/17		" " "	
"	1/5/17		Battalion moved into line. B+C Coy in front line. A Coy in support in old front line in	
ROSE WOOD	2/5/17		ROSE WOOD, D Coy in reserve, in trench E of GODEZONE FARM	
	30/4/17			

Army Form C. 2118.

WAR DIARY
or
INTELLIGENCE SUMMARY.
(Erase heading not required.)

Place	Date	Hour	Summary of Events and Information	Remarks and references to Appendices
Trenches	29/4/17 to 30/4/17		Trench warfare. Casualties 2Lieut L.Cox N.I.N.N. Wounded 11 Killed, 30 wounded fighting strength 19 Officers. 653 other ranks. Battalion relieved in line & moved back to KEMMEL SHELTERS	
KEMMEL SHELTERS	30/4/17		Resting.	
	3/4/17		Resting.	

W.W.Betts,
LIEUT. COLONEL,
WORCESTERSHIRE REGT.

Army Form C. 2118.

WAR DIARY
or
INTELLIGENCE SUMMARY.
(Erase heading not required)

Instructions regarding War Diaries and Intelligence Summaries are contained in F. S. Regs., Part II. and the Staff Manual respectively. Title pages will be prepared in manuscript.

Place	Date	Hour	Summary of Events and Information	Remarks and references to Appendices
Kinver	28/4/17 6/4/17		Trench warfare. Casualties Lieut L. Cox N.Z.D.N. Otherranks 11 killed, 35 wounded fighting strength 19 Officers. 659 Otherranks. Battalion relieved in line & moved back to KEMMEL SHELTERS	
KEMMEL SHELTERS	30/4/17 3/1/17		Resting. Resting.	

MMobs.

Army Form C. 2118.

WAR DIARY
or
INTELLIGENCE SUMMARY.

10th (S) (Erased heading not required) Duke of Wellington's Regt.

Vol 26

Instructions regarding War Diaries and Intelligence Summaries are contained in F. S. Regs., Part II. and the Staff Manual respectively. Title pages will be prepared in manuscript.

Place	Date 1917	Hour	Summary of Events and Information	Remarks and references to Appendices
KEMMEL SHELTERS	Aug 1st		Cleaning up, etc.	
"	2nd		Cleaning up etc	
"	3rd		Physical training, Squad drill, Steady drill. All N.C.O's under the Adjt & R.S.M. Major A.S. Barlow (West Riding Regt) joined Bn. as 2nd in Command. 2/Lieut H.M. Hales joined	
TRENCHES H.Q. in DENYS WOOD	4th		Battalion proceeded to trenches with Headquarters in ROSE WOOD	
"			Headquarters moved to DENYS WOOD. Casualties during day 1 O.R. Wounded	
SUPPORT LINE	5		Battalion moved back to old support line. S.P. 12 Casualties D/Rer ranks killed	
			3, wounded 6. 2/Lieut O.J. Short joined Battalion	
	6		Casualties Officers wounded, Capt. B.M. Riblett & 2/Lt H.M. Hales (at duty).	
	7		Other ranks, wounded 3.	
	8		Still in support	
	9		Battalion moved to CORONNA CAMP WESTOUTRE	
CORONNA CAMP	10		Cleaning up, saluting, handling of arms	
	11		Battalion moved by train to NIELLES-LES-BLEQUIN, entraining at BAILLEUL & detraining at WIZERNESS.	

Army Form C. 2118.

WAR DIARY
or
INTELLIGENCE SUMMARY.
(Erase heading not required.)

Instructions regarding War Diaries and Intelligence Summaries are contained in F. S. Regs., Part II. and the Staff Manual respectively. Title pages will be prepared in manuscript.

Place	Date	Hour	Summary of Events and Information	Remarks and references to Appendices
MELLES-LEZ BLEQUIN	12		Saluting drill, Handling of arms & cleaning up	
	13		The Battalion was inspected by the Second Army Commander at HARLETTES	
			2/Lieut C.G.Y Dalley & 2/Lieut E.G.H Formby joined Battalion	
	14		Handling of Arms. Physical training, kit inspection. Afternoon Games	
	15		Bayonet fighting, Handling of arms & Musketry	
	16		" "	
	17		" "	
	18		The Battalion was inspected by the Divisional Commander at HARLETTES	
	19		Church parade. Brigade sports. 2/Lieut E.C. Coxwell joined Battalion	
	20		Physical training, A & B Coys on range, Steady drill, musketry.	
			Afternoon Divisional Sports	
	21		Battalion parade under Adjt 4-4.40am Remainder of day, Physical training Musketry,	
			Handling of arms, C & D Coys on range. Afternoon Divisional point to	
			point races. 2/Lieut J.B Stuart joined Battalion	
	22		The Battalion moved to billets at ESCOUELLES and SURQUES	
ESCOUELLES	23		Physical training, musketry Handling of arms, section & platoon training	

WAR DIARY
or
INTELLIGENCE SUMMARY.

(Erase heading not required.)

Army Form C. 2118.

Place	Date 1917 August	Hour	Summary of Events and Information	Remarks and references to Appendices
ESCOVELLES	24		Steady drill, Physical training, arms drill, musketry, section & platoon training	
			A + B Coy on range	
	25		Do	
	26		The Battalion proceeded to bathe near BOULOGNE & were conveyed there in motor lorries.	
	27		Steady drill, Physical training, arms drill, musketry, section & platoon training	
			All Coys on range at various times. C Coy won Brigade firing competition	
	28		The Battalion moved to WALLON-CAPPEL area by motor lorries.	
			Headquarters near HONDEGHEM	
HONDEGHEM	29		The Battalion moved to STRAZELLE area with billets near METEREN	
MOOLENACHER	30		Cleaning up, refitting	
	31		Steady drill, Physical training, musketry, adjutants parade.	
			In the field	
			1.9.17	

A.W.Bell
LIEUT. COLONEL
COMDG. 10TH (S.) Bn. THE WORCESTERSHIRE REGT.

WAR DIARY or INTELLIGENCE SUMMARY.

Army Form C. 2118.

10 Worcesters

Place	Date	Hour	Summary of Events and Information	Remarks and references to Appendices
MOOLENACKER	1st Sept		Physical training, musketry. Coy in the attack. Adjutants parade. Inspection of C Coy by Commanding Officer.	
	2		Church Sunday. Afternoon Games.	
	3		Brigade Scheme attacking over Shell hole area. Inspection of Gas helmets by Divisional Gas Officer. Afternoon Football Bath. v. 8th Glouc Regt Result 1–0	
	4		Physical training. "Battalion in the attack" over Shell hole area, platoon & section training. Afternoon Games.	
	5		Physical training. "Battalion in the attack" over Shell hole area, platoon & section training. Football match Bath. v. 8 Glouc Regt Result 3–1 21st-8/15 Devs. 2 hours Cross Country Run	
	6		The Battalion moved to "CORUNNA" camp near WESTOUTRE	
CORUNNA CAMP	7		The Battalion carried out a practice attack over an imaginary Shell hole area. Afternoon training of sections. Night work:– A & B Coys	
	8		Rapid firing practice. Adjutants Parade 4-4:45 P.M. Practice attack as yesterday, by Battalion. Draft 1 Officer 2/Lieut P.J. Smith + 21 other ranks arrived.	27D
	9		Brigade Scheme Marine attack. Draft of 25 other ranks joined	

Army Form C. 2118.

WAR DIARY
or
INTELLIGENCE SUMMARY.
(Erase heading not required.)

Place	Date	Hour	Summary of Events and Information	Remarks and references to Appendices
CORUNNA CAMP	10		The Battalion moved to a camp at N.9.d.8.5 (Sheet 28)	
Camp at N.9.d.8.5	Sept. 11		The Battalion proceeded to the trenches in front of BATTLE WOOD taking over from 1st Brigade 10th K.N. Lancs. Enemy shelled Imperial Communication Trench with tear gas shells. Casualties Officers wounded 2 (1 at duty 1 at light). Draft 44 O.R.	
Trenches	12		Still in trenches. Ordinary trench routine.	
"	13		A & B Coys were relieved in front line & Bull Ridge support by C Coy & E. Lan Regt.	
"	14		A & B Coys moved to reserve trenches behind sector, near BATTLE WOOD. Bn wounded 1 O.R. Battalion was relieved by Casualties Officer wounded 1 Lieut. H. Moorhouse	
Camp at N.9.d.8.5	15		Cleaning up etc. & inspection of new drafts by Commanding Officer. Draft of 1 Officer 2/Lieut W.E. Woodcock & 35 other ranks joined	
"	16		Practice attack by Battalion. Only men taking part in forthcoming operations Paraded. Draft of 54 others ranks arrived. Working party of 25 O.R. obstructing [illegible]	
	17		Practice attack.	
	18		Battalion moved forward to assembly area around SPOIL BANK (A. B. & C. Coys)	

WAR DIARY
or
INTELLIGENCE SUMMARY.
(Erase heading not required.)

Army Form C. 2118.

Place	Date	Hour	Summary of Events and Information	Remarks and references to Appendices
	18/9/17		D Coy remaining at Camp (H.9.d.8.5) One platoon B Coy moved up to front line between J.36.d.6.60 & J.31.a.15.00 (Sheets 28 NW & NE) with one platoon in reserve. Battalion moved up by bus to ST ELOI	
	19/9/17		2 platoons of B Coy, A & C Coys & Battn H.Q. moved up to assembly area for attack at ZERO. D Coy moved from Camp at N.9.d.8.5. to support trenches other having moved up	
	20/9/17		Battalion attacked on a front between J.36.d.80.60 & J.31.a.15.00 (Sheet 28 N.W. & N.E.) with Zero hour at 5.40.a.m. 3 Coys (A.B. & C) in front. Two leading platoons of each Coy (each platoon forming one wave) advanced under barrage to the GREEN LINE & paused for 35 minutes. The two rear platoons (with two waves) leap-frogged through & advanced under barrage to BLUE LINE. D Coy moved up to OLD BRITISH FRONT LINE at ZERO + 29 minutes. The GREEN LINE was consolidated by the leading platoon of each Coy & the BLUE LINE by 3rd platoons. All objectives were taken. Casualties Officers killed 2/Lieut P Jones. Wounded 2/Lieuts H Thompson, H.H. Hale, F Thogatt, E. G. Carroll, L.A. Brett, 2/Lieut H J Lucknow M.C. (at duty). Other ranks. Killed 20 Wounded 95 Missing 38.	
	21/9/17		Consolidating new line & establishing strong posts. Casualties Officers Wounded	

WAR DIARY
or
INTELLIGENCE SUMMARY.
(Erase heading not required.)

Army Form C. 2118.

Instructions regarding War Diaries and Intelligence Summaries are contained in F. S. Regs., Part II. and the Staff Manual respectively. Title pages will be prepared in manuscript.

Place	Date	Hour	Summary of Events and Information	Remarks and references to Appendices
	21/9		2nd Lieut J.B. Hunt (on duty) Officers route Killed 10 Wounded 19 Missing 5. The Battalion was relieved during the night of 21/22/9 by 4th E Lancs	
	22/9		& moved to Staging area camp at N.9 d.8.5. for the night. Thence to camp at FERMOY FARM at LOOS E. Arriving there about noon. Resting & cleaning up during the day	
	23/9		Cleaning up etc. 3 Officers Lieut Q + O Churchs & Lieuts IG Cromwells + 2nd Lt Salmon rejoined battalion.	
	24/9		Physical training. Adjutants parade. Baths. Cleaning up their various platoons	
	25/9		Physical training. Adjutant parade. NCO's parade under R.S.M. Park.	
	26/9		Physical training. Adjutants parade. Battalion moved to a camp at N.6.c.3.3 (Sheet 28 SW)	
	27/9		Battalion moved to line relieving the 6TH BEDFORD Regt in support H.Q. at LARCH WOOD Casualties Officers nawks 1 Killed 1 Wounded	
	28/9		Still in support, in dug outs ere Still 6b Casualties 1 Killed 1 Wounded (Offrs route)	
	29/9		Still in support	
	30/9		Still in support	

A.W. Colver Major.
Comdg 10th (S) Battalion The Worcestershire Regiment.

WAR DIARY

INTELLIGENCE SUMMARY.

1st (Busy heading not required) Bn. Worcestershire Regiment

Army Form C. 2118.

Place	Date	Hour	Summary of Events and Information	Remarks and references to Appendices
HILL 60	1/10/17		Battalion in support. 1 O.R. wounded	
	2/10/17		Battalion moved to line relieving 9th Glos Regt with HQ and RofTower Hamlets	
			Major D.A. Bowen & 3 O.R. joined Battalion.	
	3/10/17		Still in line. 2 O.R. wounded	
	4/10		Still in line. Casualties Other ranks Killed 3 Wounded 12 Draft 4 O.R.	
	5/10		Battalion was relieved by a Battalion of the 56th Bde & moved out to ROSSIGNOL CAMP. Casualties Officers wounded 2/Lieut E & H Tomby Other ranks Wounded Two	
ROSSIGNOL CAMP	6/10		Cleaning up.	
"	7/10		Working parties 115 O.R. Remainder of Battalion fit inspections cleaning	
"	8/10		Boys reorganising cleaning up huts dug-outs	
"	9/10		Adjutants Parade, Bayonet fighting Musketry in the morning. Platoon training in the afternoon. 2 Officers 2/Lieut A.J. Andrews & G. Rice attached to Battalion from 10th RWar Regt	
	10/10		Adjutant's Parade Bayonet fighting Musketry in the morning. Platoon training in the afternoon. 2/Lieut 1 O.R. also attached to Bn from 10th R War Regt	

WAR DIARY
or
INTELLIGENCE SUMMARY.

(Erase heading not required.)

Army Form C. 2118.

Instructions regarding War Diaries and Intelligence Summaries are contained in F. S. Regs., Part II. and the Staff Manual respectively. Title pages will be prepared in manuscript.

Place	Date	Hour	Summary of Events and Information	Remarks and references to Appendices
ROSSIGNOL CAMP	11/10		Battalion proceeded to Support line SPOIL BANK, relieving the 6th Wilts Regt	
SUPPORT LINE	12/10		Working Parties of 210 O Ranks. Cleaning up tunnels etc.	
"	13/10		Working Parties of 210 O Ranks cleaning up etc. Draft 1 O.R.	
LINE	14/10		The 5th Bde took over the 19th Bde front. The Battalion relieved the 10th R War Regt & 8th Glos Regt, 3 Coys in front line, 1 Coy in IMPERFECT COPSE. Battalion HQ at I.36.c.3.1. Right subsector, Boundary line PRINCE'S HOUSE – I.36 central – I.35 central – I.34 central. Reference HOLLEBEKE Sheet 1/10000.	
"	15/10		Battalion in line. Draft 1 O.R.	
"	16/10		Battalion in line. Enemy shelled D Coy HQ & Bn HQ with gas shells. Casualties. Officers Wounded 2/Lieut J.W. Starr. Other ranks Wounded 9.	
"	17/10		Battalion relieved by 8 Glos Regt in line & moved to SPOIL BANK. Casualties Officers Wounded 2/Lieut Bree 10th R War Regt, attached. Other ranks Wounded 5. Draft Officers 2/Lieut J.C. & Brake	
SUPPORT	18/10		Working parties of 200 Other ranks	
	19/10		Battalion relieved by 6th Wilts Regt & proceeded to BOIS CONFLUEN	

Army Form C. 2118.

WAR DIARY
or
INTELLIGENCE SUMMARY.
(Erase heading not required.)

Instructions regarding War Diaries and Intelligence Summaries are contained in F. S. Regs., Part II. and the Staff Manual respectively. Title pages will be prepared in manuscript.

Place	Date	Hour	Summary of Events and Information	Remarks and references to Appendices
	19/10 Contd		Relieving Kings Own R Lancaster Regt in NORTON CAMP	
NORTON CAMP	20/10		Cleaning up & working in camp	
	21/10		Working Parties 250 O.R. Remainder of Battalion working in camp duck boarding, building drying rooms etc. 2/Lieut T Bishop & 9/Yorks Regt joined Bn.	
	22/10		Same as 21st	
	23/10		Same as 22nd	
	24/10		Physical Training, Arms Drill, Saluting. Working Parties 300 O.R. New draft joined. Other ranks 9	
	25		Physical Training, Arms drill, Saluting, musketry. Working parties 300 O.R.	
	26		Same as for 25th	
	27.		Battalion moved to billets at KEMMEL SHELTERs relieving Kings own R Lancaster Regt.	
KEMMEL SHELTERs	28		Cleaning up Kit inspections etc	
	29th		Church Parade	
	30th		Route March. Afternoon Adjutants Parade	
	31st		Adjutant Parade, Platoon Training, Saluting, Steady drill	

Army Form C. 2118.

WAR DIARY
or
INTELLIGENCE SUMMARY.

(Erase heading not required.)

Instructions regarding War Diaries and Intelligence Summaries are contained in F. S. Regs., Part II. and the Staff Manual respectively. Title pages will be prepared in manuscript.

Place	Date	Hour	Summary of Events and Information	Remarks and references to Appendices
KEMMEL SHELTERS	31/10		Cleaning camp. Lewis Gunners on range.	

B.M. Potter
LIEUT. COLO...
CMDG. 10th (S.) Bn. THE WORCESTERSHIRE REGT.

Headquarters
57th Brigade

Herewith "War Diary" for
November 1917.

[Stamp: 10TH (S) BATTALION, THE WORCESTERSHIRE REGIMENT. No. A272 Date: 2-12-17]

1/12/17

Dubbs
LIEUT. COLONEL,
COMDG. 10th (S.) Bn. THE WORCESTERSHIRE REGT.

Army Form C. 2118.

10 Worcesters / 29

WAR DIARY or INTELLIGENCE SUMMARY.
(Erase heading not required.)

Place	Date	Hour	Summary of Events and Information	Remarks and references to Appendices
KEMMEL SHELTERS	1/6/17		Adjutants Parade 9.15 to 10.15 am	
			Presentation of Medals Ribbons by G.O.C. 19th Division to the following, except those otherwise marked	
			MILITARY CROSS — Capt. A.E. Owens (not available), Capt. J.G. Sharper R.A.M.C.	
			D.C.M. 12424 Sgt Calder E.J., 15630 Sgt Barker A.,	
			M.M. 14221 Cpl Moran H.S., 18428 Cpl Yarranton W., 16013 Pte Butler A.N. (Killed in action)	
			16929 Cpl Helton A., 15662 Pte Yeates J., 15625 Pte Whitmore J., 8608 Pte Griffiths B.	
			14335 Pte Osborne J., 15353 Pte East H., 48458 Pte Howard C., 15551 Pte Green C.	
			36880 Pte Vievers A., 15619 Pte Jones A. (Wounded), 29859 Pte Matthews J.	
			19382 Pte Slater A., 33459 Pte Dalton E., 24461 Pte Carter A., 40915 Sgt Wakeley S.	
			24429 Sgt Millard A.,	
"	2nd		Battalion Training	
"	3rd		" " Draft Officer, 2/Lieut J.C. Scriber	
"	4th		The Battalion proceeded to trenches, relieving the 1/2 S. Staffs Regt in the line	
			Right sub sector PRINCES H.Q. — 1.36 central — 1.35 central — 1.34 central Reference	
			HOLLEBEEKE sheet 1/10000. Headquarters at 1.36.c.3.1.	
			The Battalion were conveyed as far as ST ELOI by bus	

29 D

Army Form C. 2118.

WAR DIARY
or
INTELLIGENCE SUMMARY.
(Erase heading not required.)

Instructions regarding War Diaries and Intelligence Summaries are contained in F. S. Regs., Part II. and the Staff Manual respectively. Title pages will be prepared in manuscript.

Place	Date	Hour	Summary of Events and Information	Remarks and references to Appendices
TRENCHES	5th		Battalion in line. Casualties - Other ranks Killed 1 Wounded 2	
	6th		Battalion in line. Working parties 50 O.R. Draft 3 O.R.	
	7th		The Battalion were relieved in the line by the 8th Glos Regt & proceeded to SPOIL BANK.	
SPOIL BANK	8th		Working parties of 200 Other ranks. Casualties 1 Other rank wounded	
"	9th		The Battalion moved to BOIS CONFLUENT relieving the 4th N. Lancs Regt	
BOIS CONFLUENT	10th		The Battalion moved by bus to the MERRIS AREA with Headquarters MOOL- MOOLENACKER.	
MOOLENACKER	11th		Cleaning up etc. Draft Officers 2/Lieut J E Davies Other ranks 26	
"	12th		The Battalion moved to BLARINGHEM entraining at CAESTRE Station	
"			detraining at EBLINGHEM, thence by march route	
BLARINGHEM	13th		Cleaning up, Kit inspections etc. Draft 16. O.R.	
	14th		Steady drill etc. Training. Draft Officers 2/Lieut L J Smith	
	15th		Training. Draft Officers 2/Lieut C A Underwood Other ranks 3	
	16th		Training. Draft Officers 2/Lieut R B Jarrott	
	17th		Training	

WAR DIARY
or
INTELLIGENCE SUMMARY.

(Erase heading not required.)

Army Form C. 2118.

Place	Date	Hour	Summary of Events and Information	Remarks and references to Appendices
BLARINGHEM	18th		Training	
	19th		Training	
	20th		Training	
	21st		Training	
	22nd		Training. Afternoon Football Match Officers v Sgts. Result Officers 0 Sergeants 4	
	23rd		Training	
	24th		Training. Draft Officers Lieut G E Grove	
	25th		Training	
	26th		Training	
	27th		Training. Afternoon Football Match. Battn v Bde H.Q. Result Battn 2 Bde Nil	
			Tug of War Battn v 8th N. Staff Regt. Battn won	
	28th		Battalion proceeded to CORMETTE for the purpose of firing on TILQUES Ranges	
TILQUES	29th		Ranges	
	30th		Ranges. Battalion proceeded to new billets at LE RONS, SABLONIERE &	
COURONNE				

Dukes
LIEUT. COL.
COMDG. 10th (S.) Bn. THE WORCESTERSHIRE REGT.

Army Form C. 2118.

WAR DIARY or INTELLIGENCE SUMMARY.
(Erase heading not required.)

Vol 30

10th (S) Battalion The Worcestershire Regt

Place	Date	Hour	Summary of Events and Information	Remarks and references to Appendices
LE SARTONNE	1/9/17		Battalion cleaning up etc	
"	2/17		Inspection of all Coy fighting order	
"	3/17		Battalion training. 2nd Lieut W Clifford joined Battalion	
"	4/17		Training	
"	5/17		Platoon training. Special intense training. Football match Battalion v 6th R.N. Staffs Regt. Final in Bde. Championship Football competition. Result Battalion 3. N Staffs Nil. Results of shooting on Musketry Course collected. 8 Silver Bugles presented to the Battalion by MISS HEAP. These bugles are to be presented to the line Battalions upon demobilization of the Battalion 16 to 1st, 2nd, 3rd and 4th Battalions. Training	
"	6/17		Training	
"	7/17		The Battalion moved by bus + march route to BERLES. Entraining at SOMER Station at 5.10 pm and detraining at MONDICOURT at 7.30 PM. Thence by march route	
"	8/17		The Battalion moved to staging camp at ETRICOURT.	

30 D

WAR DIARY
or
INTELLIGENCE SUMMARY.
(Erase heading not required.)

Army Form C. 2118.

Place	Date	Hour	Summary of Events and Information	Remarks and references to Appendices
ETRICOURT	10/12		The Battalion moved to Brigade Reserve in the HINDENBURG LINE Map Reference L.31.C. Sheet M.A.R.O. taking over from 1st Bn Buffs. Casualties Other ranks 2 Killed 5 Wounded	
	11/12		Proceeded to front line, 3 Coys in front, 1 in support, taking over from 11th Essex Regt	
	12/12		Battalion in line	
	13/12		Battalion in line	
	14/12		Battalion in line. Reinforcement. Officers Capt E.W Butler & 2/Lieut P.G Wilson & P.G Thompson	
	15/12		The Battalion was relieved by 1st S. Staffs Regt & proceeded to Brigade Reserve HINDENBURG LINE taking over from 1/4 S. Staffs Regt. Casualties Other ranks 2 Killed & 3 Wounded	
	16/12		Brigade reserve	
	17/12		Brigade reserve	
	18/12		Battalion proceeded to Camp at HAIRINCOURT WOOD	
HAIRINCOURT WOOD	19/12		Cleaning up. Reinforcement Officers 2/Lieut N. Bryant & 2/Lt Guest taking over from 10th Essex Regt	
	20/12		Battalion proceeded to Bde Reserve taking over from 10th R. War Regt	

Army Form C. 2118.

WAR DIARY
or
INTELLIGENCE SUMMARY.
(Erase heading not required.)

Instructions regarding War Diaries and Intelligence Summaries are contained in F. S. Regs., Part II. and the Staff Manual respectively. Title pages will be prepared in manuscript.

Place	Date	Hour	Summary of Events and Information	Remarks and references to Appendices
Ribemont	21/12		Code Reserve	
Front Line	22/12		Battalion proceeded to front line. Casualties Other ranks 2 wounded	
	-.-		Took over from the 9th Welsh Regiment Left Sub Section Brigade front	
	23/12		4 rows line	
	24/12		— do —	
	25/12		— do —	
	26/12		— do —	
	27/12		— do —	
Support	28/12		Relieved by the 1st Queens Regt. Proceeded to Brigade Support.	
	29/12		Still in Support.	
	30/12		— do —	
	31/12		Relieved the 8th N Staffs in the Right Sub Section of the Brigade front	

D. Watts
Lt. Col Commdg.
10th (S) Bn Worcestershire Regt.

Army Form C. 2118.

WAR DIARY
or
INTELLIGENCE SUMMARY.

(Erase heading not required.)

1st Battalion (S) Pn the Worcesters Pure Regt

Place	Date	Hour	Summary of Events and Information	Remarks and references to Appendices
Flesh Subsector Sh 57 D.N.W.	1/1/18	10.K(S)	Trenches	
	2/1/18		"	
	3/1/18		"	
	4/1/18		Bhatt. to O.R	
	5/1/18		Battalion moved to HAWES CAMP HAVRINCOURT WOOD in Brigade reserve	
Reserve	6/1/18		Cleaning up etc	
	7/1/18		Cleaning up etc	
	8/1/18		Cleaning up, refitting etc	
	9/1/18		Cleaning up etc	
	10/1/18		Route Marching	
	11/1/18		Training. Battalion proceeded to trenches in Tt Subsector relieving 4th (K.O) R Lanc Regt. Casualties O.Ranks Wounded 1	
	12/1/18		Improving Posts. Trenches waterlogged	
Trenches	13/1/18		Improving building up trenches. Casualties Officers wounded 2/Lieut T Bishop Other Ranks wounded 1	
	14/1/18		Improving & building up. Diett 1 O.R. Casualties O.R Killed 1	3/D

Army Form C. 2118.

WAR DIARY
or
INTELLIGENCE SUMMARY.
(Erase heading not required.)

Instructions regarding War Diaries and Intelligence Summaries are contained in F. S. Regs., Part II. and the Staff Manual respectively. Title pages will be prepared in manuscript.

Place	Date	Hour	Summary of Events and Information	Remarks and references to Appendices
Trenches	15/1/18		Battalion was relieved by 13th (R) W. Yor Regt & proceeded to support line	
	16/1/18		In support. Working parties. Draft Officers 2/Lieuts 2. Coleman & 2. Drake, J.H. Sharpe, W.G. Franklin	
	17/1/18		Battalion proceeded to line in relief of 2/K.Y.L.I. Regt. Casualties O.R. (Wounded 1)	
Trenches	18/1/18		Clearing & building up trenches	
	19/1/18		" Casualties O.R. ranks killed 2 wounded 2	
			" Draft joined O.R. ranks 5	
	20/1/18		Improving trenches. One prisoner pioneer Batt. 50th Reserve Division captured. Casualties O.R. ranks wounded 1	
	21/1/18		Battalion was relieved in the trenches by 9th Berkshire Regt. & proceeded to VALULART CAMP nr. YPRES. Casualties O.R. ranks Wounded 1	
VALULART CAMP	22/1/18		Cleaning up etc.	
	23/1/18		Battalion proceeded to Right subsector in support relieving the 8th Glos. Regt. Draft Officers 2/Lieut 2. J.B. Harrison & T. Colbeck	
	24/1/18		Support. Wounded O.R. 2	

WAR DIARY or INTELLIGENCE SUMMARY

Army Form C. 2118.

(Erase heading not required.)

Place	Date	Hour	Summary of Events and Information	Remarks and references to Appendices
Support	26/1/18		Battalion proceeded to line Right Subsector relieving 6th Wilts Regt. Casualties Officers to hand Wounded 2	
	27/1/18		Trench routine. Casualties Wounded 2/Lieut L. Drake since died of wounds. 2/Lieut S. Davis Other ranks Wounded 1	
	28/1/18		Working on line communication trenches boarded trenches in very muddy waterlogged state Front line Casualties Other rank Wounded 1	
	29/1/18		Battalion were relieved in front line by 6th Bn Wilts Regt & proceeded to EASTWOOD CAMP HAVRINCOURT WOOD	
	30/1/18		Cleaning up Bath forned Officers ranks &	
	31/1/18		Cleaning up Working parties etc Ration strength Officers 20 Other ranks 351	

C Carlson MAJOR
COMDG. 10th (S.) Bn. THE WORCESTERSHIRE REGT.

WAR DIARY or INTELLIGENCE SUMMARY

Army Form C. 2118.

Place	Date 1916	Hour	Summary of Events and Information	Remarks and references to Appendices
BASTWOOD CAMP	1/7		Cleaning up. Building round Ret. veterans etc. Return strength Officers 20 Other Ranks 346	
HAVRINCOURT WOOD	2/7		Battalion proceeded to line taking over from 4th S. Lancs Regt on the left subsector. Cleaning up etc.	
	3/7			
	4/7		Our enemy fighting patrol attempted to reach C Coy No 1 Post at L 34 a. 43.58 at about 3 AM this morning. We opened rapid fire for about 5 rounds, sending up 8 very lights. The enemy patrol appeared to extend & approach the post on both sides. Upon our opening fire, he apparently withdrew. We succeeded in wounding two of the enemy. A party of 6 was immediately sent out but failed to find any trace of the enemy patrol. Sergt J.C. Davies accidentally injured. One O.R. wounded.	
	5		The enemy again attempted to enter post at L 34 a 43.58 but was driven off.	
	6		Widening + deepening trenches. Battalion was relieved in front line on night of 6/7th by 10th R War Regt & moved to Intermediate line.	

Army Form C. 2118.

WAR DIARY
or
INTELLIGENCE SUMMARY.
(Erase heading not required.)

Instructions regarding War Diaries and Intelligence Summaries are contained in F. S. Regs., Part II. and the Staff Manual respectively. Title pages will be prepared in manuscript.

Place	Date 1916	Hour	Summary of Events and Information	Remarks and references to Appendices
	7/2		In Intermediate line	
	8/2		"	
	9/2		Proceeded to front line relieving to R War Regt.	
	10/2		In front line. Draft joined 11 Officers & 54 Other ranks out of a draft of 15 Officers & 300 O.R. posted from 3/4th Batln. the Worcestershire Regt. Officers – 2/Lieut W.A. Beaman M.C., 2/Lieut A. Elford, 2/Lieut L.J. Lisick, 2/Lieut E.L. Griffiths, Lieut W.J.Y. Heape, A/Capt R.S. Hemmingway, 2/Lieut J.J. Roy, 2/Lieut C.J. Bullio, 2/Lieut P.J.B. Ward, 2/Lieut J.A. Cumberland, 2/Lieut E. Stainton. 1 Officer joined from 4 N Sans Regt 2/Lieut W Sheppard	
	11/2		In front line	
	12/2		"	
	13/2		Batn was relieved in front line by the Artists Rifles, & proceeded to hut at ASSAYE Camp BEAULENCOURT	
	14/2		Cleaning up. 2/Lt W Schoales joined Bn from 4/ N Sans Regt	
	15/2		Training	
	16/2		Training. Noted for information. the two silver bugles presented by	

(A7853) Wt. W809/M1672 350,000 4/17 Sch. 82a. Forms/C/2118/14 B. D. & L., London, E.C.

WAR DIARY
or
INTELLIGENCE SUMMARY

(Erase heading not required.)

Place	Date	Hour	Summary of Events and Information	Remarks and references to Appendices
	16/2		Brigadier General T Astley Cubitt. C.M.G., D.S.O. to the Battalion for the best shooting team in the Brigade, are to be given to the 5th & 6th (Reserve) Battalions of the Worcestershire Regiment, upon the demobilization of this Batln.	
	17/2		Training. 1 Officer joined from 2/4th Bn. 2/Lieut D.P. Drake	
	18/2		Training	
	19/2		Training	
	20/2		Training	
	21/2		Training	
	22/2		Training	
	23/2		Training. Ration Strength Officers 33 Other ranks 642	
			" " " 31 " " 642	
	24/2		Training. Draft 1 Capt & 6 Subalterns joined from 4/N Lancs Regt	
			Ration Strength Officers 30 Other ranks 636.	
	25/2		" " " 30 " " 631	Training
	26/2		" " " 30 " " 632	Training
	27/2		" " " 29 " " 632	Training
	28/2		" " " 30 " " 638	Training

Army Form C. 2118.

WAR DIARY
or
INTELLIGENCE SUMMARY.
(Erase heading not required.)

Instructions regarding War Diaries and Intelligence Summaries are contained in F. S. Regs., Part II. and the Staff Manual respectively. Title pages will be prepared in manuscript.

Place	Date	Hour	Summary of Events and Information	Remarks and references to Appendices
Hallowt	1915			
	28/2		Shewing Ration Strength Officers 29 Otherranks 630.	

Wee Sole
LIEUT. COLONEL,
COMDG. 10th (S.) Bn. THE WORCESTERSHIRE REGT.

19TH DIVISION
57TH INFY BDE

57TH MACHINE GUN COY.
FEB 1916 - JAN 1918

19

57th M.G. Coy.
Vol I

Feb '16
Jan '18

Army Form C. 2118

WAR DIARY
or
INTELLIGENCE SUMMARY
(Erase heading not required.)

No. 57 Company
M. G. Corps

Instructions regarding War Diaries and Intelligence Summaries are contained in F. S. Regs., Part II. and the Staff Manual respectively. Title Pages will be prepared in manuscript.

Place	Date Feb.	Hour	Summary of Events and Information	Remarks and references to Appendices
GRANTHAM	8th	8 a.m	The Company left by train for Southampton	P.K.U.
	9th		Arrived at Southampton SOUTHAMPTON	P.K.U.
HAVRE	10th		Arrived at HAVRE and went to No. 5 REST CAMP	P.K.U.
"	11th		In rest camp	P.K.U.
"	12th		do	P.K.U.
"	13th		do	P.K.U.
	14th	a.m.	Left by train for MERVILLE to join 57th Inf. Bde 19th DIV.	P.K.U.
ROBECQ	15th		Marched from MERVILLE to billets at ROBECQ arriving 7 a.m.	P.K.U.
"	16th		Inspected by Brigadier General TWYFORD commanding 57th Inf Bde	P.K.U
ROBECQ	17th		Route march	P.K.U.
"	18th		In billets	P.K.U.
"	19th		do	P.K.U.
			57 Bde moved up from rest billets into Divisional reserve BHQ at LA GORGUE	P.K.U.
PURESBEC-QUES	20	10.30 a.m.	M.G Company marched to billets at PURESBECQUES	P.K.U.
"	21		In Divisional Reserve at PURESBECQUES. One mule died of Colic	P.K.U.
"	22		do	P.K.U.
"	23		do Heavy Snow Storm	P.K.U.
	24		Four M.G's with two Officers moved to PONT DU HEM and took over M.G's in 4 Keeps behind front line from No. 58 M.G. Coy. Remainder of Coy moved to PONT DU HEM and relieved the remainder of No. 58 M.G. Coy taking over H.Q. at K.A. BASSE ROAD point MPK.6.0 guns another billets as follows—	P.K.U. P.K.U.

1875 W.t.W593/326 1,000,000 9/15 J.B.&A. A.Dis. S./Forms/C.2118.

WAR DIARY or INTELLIGENCE SUMMARY

Army Form C. 2118

N° 57 Company M. G. Corps

Place	Date	Hour	Summary of Events and Information	Remarks and references to Appendices
PONT DU HEM.	Feb. 24		Six guns in front line N°s 1, 3, 5, 7, 9. Four guns in Keeps, 7 guns at C.H.Q. Gun positions 2, 4, 6, 8, to hill by terra firma. On the establishment of the company men not permitted to move guns being mounted. Brigade front guns SIGN POST LANE to ERITH POST. 5 men and 1 N.C.O. on each front line gun and 1 N.C.O. on each gun in Keeps. Two on ground and Gran. front.	M
do	25		Night foggy. Owing to difficulty in obtaining glycerine trouble was experienced with 6 waterjackets.	M
do	26		One Sergt. and 6 men of 10 Warwicks attached to Coy. Next continued.	M
do	27		Thaw set in and trench have become rather muddy.	a
do	28		2nd Lt Hatch and Sergt. A. Smith sent to Divisional School of Instruction at MERVILLE.	M
do	29		A fair amount of aircraft activity. Gun was mounted behind our Trench & was used for overhead fire.	PKW

Army Form C. 2118

WAR DIARY
or
INTELLIGENCE SUMMARY

(Erase heading not required.)

No 57 Coy M.G. Corps.

Instructions regarding War Diaries and Intelligence Summaries are contained in F.S. Regs, Part II. and the Staff Manual respectively. Title Pages will be prepared in manuscript.

Place	Date	Hour	Summary of Events and Information	Remarks and references to Appendices
PONT DU HEM	March 1.		a M.G. was placed behind our trenches & was used for overhead fire.	P.K.V.
do	" 2		Sergt Litton 10th Worcester Regt attached to Coy Transport, Lt Wells the Transport Officer owing to Brigade Orders made a Sec: Commander.	P.K.V.
do	" 3		1 N.C.O. killed 1 man wounded, a M.G was mounted behind our trenches near SUNKEN ROAD for overhead fire.	P.K.V.
do	" 4		Zepps seen flying in a S.W. direction	P.K.V.
do	" 5		Our M.Gs assisted in a demonstration by our Artillery & T.M	P.K.V.
do	" 6		M Gs in front lines changed, a gun was mounted behind our trenches & fired at AUBERS, after the first burst a red parachute rocket was sent up near the village, then red bengal rockets followed at about four minutes intervals	P.K.V.
do	" 7.		Artillery activity on both sides, at night between 8 & 9 pm a starlight played on our parapet.	P.K.V.
do	" 8.		Weather very bad, all very quiet	P.K.V.
do	" 9		Weather cold, our Siege Batteries very active also the Field Batteries fired salvos at intervals in conjunction with the T.M.s & M.Gs	P.K.V.

WAR DIARY
or
INTELLIGENCE SUMMARY
(Erase heading not required.)

Army Form C. 2118

No 57 Coy M.G.C.

Place	Date	Hour	Summary of Events and Information	Remarks and references to Appendices
PONT DU HEM.	Nov: 10.		Quiet day, a flight of 31 aeroplanes seen flying in a N.E. direction	P.K.V.
do	11.		Very quiet all day.	P.K.V.
do	12.		Fine day, aircraft & artillery very active	P.K.V.
do	13.		All very quiet, weather fine	P.K.V.
do	14.		1 Officer wounded 1 N.C.O. killed 1 N.C.O. wounded 1 man killed. The enemy sprung a mine under THE DUCKS BILL, not a great deal of damage was done, aeroplanes active, the 57th Coy temporarily attached to the 106th Brigade, the weather fine	P.K.V.
do	15.		Artillery active, weather unsettled	P.K.V.
do	16		Our artillery active during morning, weather cold & dull.	P.K.V.
do	17.		1 man wounded.	P.K.V.
do	18		1 man wounded & 1 N.C.O. very slightly wounded. An attack was made by the enemy on THE DUCKS BILL crater but was checked by bombs and nose fire of M.G.s	P.K.V.
do	19.		Aircraft & artillery activity	P.K.V.

Army Form C. 2118

WAR DIARY
or
INTELLIGENCE SUMMARY

(Erase heading not required.)

N:57 Coy M.G.C.

Instructions regarding War Diaries and Intelligence Summaries are contained in F.S. Regs., Part II. and the Staff Manual respectively. Title Pages will be prepared in manuscript.

Place	Date	Hour	Summary of Events and Information	Remarks and references to Appendices
PONT DU HEM.	Mar. 20.		All very quiet nothing to report.	P.K.V.
do	21.		" " " during the day, at night we successfully exploded 5" mines, two M.Gs mounted behind our lines did good work.	P.K.V.
do	22.		Snowing hard, between 9 & 10 a.m. the enemy artillery shelled our front line heavily doing a good deal of damage	P.K.V.
do	23.		A quiet day, a M.G. was mounted close behind the front line with the object of catching the German relief, after about 1,000 rds the Germans started shelling & sent about 10 Whizz Bangs over	P.K.V.
do	24.		Nothing to report hardly any activity whatever	P.K.V.
do	25.		Snow & rain a defensive mine was exploded very little damage was done.	P.K.V.
do	26.		Snow cleared but weather very unsettled, enemy very very active during the whole day. 1 N.C.O wounded 1 man slightly wounded.	P.K.V.
do	27.		Very quiet nothing to report, had a draught of 9 men arriving in the evening	P.K.V.
do	28.		" " " " " " " " " "	P.K.V.

WAR DIARY
or
INTELLIGENCE SUMMARY

(Erase heading not required.)

No 61 Coy M.G.C.

Army Form C. 2118

Place	Date	Hour	Summary of Events and Information	Remarks and references to Appendices
PONT DU HEM.	Mar. 29.		Very quiet all day & night.	P.K.V.
do	30.		Very quiet day, rather more activity at night than there has been for the last few days, 1 Officer 2nd Lt Davis slightly wounded.	P.K.V.
do	31.		Weather very fine, the 54th Coy M.G.C were relieved by the 118th Coy M.G.C. the 54th Coy left for billets at Merville arriving there about 7.30 p.m.	P.K.V.

WAR DIARY or INTELLIGENCE SUMMARY

Army Form C. 2118

No 5Y Coy Machine Gun Corps

Vol 3

Place	Date	Hour	Summary of Events and Information	Remarks and references to Appendices
PURESBECQUES MERVILLE	1/4/16		The day was spent in overhauling, cleaning & re-organising Guns, Stores & Equipment used in trenches. Fine warm day.	P.K.O
do	2/4/16	10 a.m to 2 p.m	Yesterdays programme was continued. Fine warm day.	P.K.O
do		9 a.m to 10 a.m	Coy parade for drill	
		11 a.m to 12 noon	Drivers parade for drill.	
do	3/4/16	9 a.m	Coy parade for drill & physical training	
		10 a.m	Drivers parade for drill & physical training	
		10.15 a.m	Sections parade for washing limbers &c	P.K.O
		2.15 p.m	Coy parade for drill	
		5.30 p.m	Inter Coy football match	
do	4/4/16	9 a.m to 1 p.m	Yesterdays programme continued	
		3 p.m	Football match	
		5.30 p.m	Grand Concert.	P.K.O
do	5/4/16	—	Quiet day. Inspections & packing of wagons.	P.K.O
do	6/4/16		Moved forward to PONT-DU-HEM and took over Billets, Kreps & timned	P.K.O

WAR DIARY or INTELLIGENCE SUMMARY

Army Form C. 2118

No 57 Coy Machine Gun Corps

Place	Date	Hour	Summary of Events and Information	Remarks and references to Appendices
PUBESBECQUES	6/10/16		Positions from 118th Battn. Machine Gun Coy	P.T.O.
PONT-DU-HEM	7/10/16		Dispositions etc. 1, 3, 5 Guns Right Sub-Sector, 8 & 9 " Left Sub-Sector, Keeps Grouse Post, Tilleroy North, Signpost Lane, Suprise East, Tilleroy South	P.T.O.
do	8/10/16		do	P.T.O.
do	9/10/16		do — Cpl. England wounded — fine warm day	P.T.O.
do	10/10/16		do — Front line Gun Teams relieved. Pte Fatchem wounded	P.T.O.
do	11/10/16		do — Dull, wet, sunny weather	P.T.O.
do	12/10/16		do	P.T.O.
do	13/10/16		do	P.T.O.
do	14/10/16		do — Front line teams relieved, very stormy weather	P.T.O.
do	15/10/16		do — Cold wet day	P.T.O.
do	16/10/16		do — fine warm day	P.T.O.
do	17/10/16		do — Relieved during afternoon & evening in trenches & Keeps by the 113th Battn. Machine Gun Coy. Billeted at Cheltenham Rd.) for night	P.T.O.

WAR DIARY
or
INTELLIGENCE SUMMARY

No. 57 Coy Machine Gun Corps

Army Form C. 2118

(Erase heading not required.)

Place	Date	Hour	Summary of Events and Information	Remarks and references to Appendices
ROBECQ	19/4/16	10.a.m	Parade, all present, and marched via LA-GORGUE, MERVILLE, to ROBECQ & billeted at MARQUOIS. Very wet cold day.	S.M.
do	20/4/16		The day was spent in cleaning, overhauling & unpacking Guns & Limbers. Inspections of Equipment & personnel	S.M.
HAM	20/4/16	9.a.m	Marched from Billets & took part in Brigade march to new area and billeted at HAM near AIRE. Weather showery	S.M.
do	21/4/16	8.a.m	Coy parade in Marching Order & paraded to 10th Worcesters for antigas training	S.M.
do	22/4/16	8.a.m	Coy parade & marched to ranges near St JULIAN and carried out a programme of Section firing, results were very good. Very wet day.	S.M.
do	23/4/16		Easter Sunday, no training. Very fine & warm.	S.M.
do	24/4/16	8.30am	Coy parade & marched to 10th Worcesters for training	S.M.
do		9.a.m	Limbers were paraded & marched to training ground & carried out drill	S.M.
do		12 noon	Coy assembled at EQUINEGATTE and carried out field movements &c.	S.M.
do		2.30pm	Marched back to billets. Very hot day	S.M.
do	25/4/16	8.30am	Coy all present, paraded & marched to training ground and carried out an extensive programme. Very hot day.	S.M.

WAR DIARY
or
INTELLIGENCE SUMMARY   No. 57 Coy. Machine Gun Corps

Army Form C. 2118

(Erase heading not required.)

Instructions regarding War Diaries and Intelligence Summaries are contained in F. S. Regs., Part II. and the Staff Manual respectively. Title Pages will be prepared in manuscript.

Place	Date	Hour	Summary of Events and Information	Remarks and references to Appendices
PONT-DU-HEM	26/4/16	6.30	The same programme was carried out as yesterday — Weather very hot	9PP
do	27/4/16	8.30	———— do ———— Preliminary events for Coy Sports ———— do ————	PP
do	28/4/16	9 a.m.	Coy parade & marched to range near St. JULIEN & carried out a programme of field firing	PP
do	29/4/16	9 a.m.	Parade by S/C; for equipment fitting & washing bunkers etc.	
		9 p.m.	Parade for night operations in conjunction with the Brigade & returned to Billets at 6.30 a.m. — 30/4/16 — Weather still very hot	PP
do	30/4/16		Transport entered in two events at Divisional Horse & Mule Show one team being successful in getting into the final. Coy. Sports were held in the afternoon & was a great success. Forty men were attached — so to no far duty. Weather very hot.	9PP

Army Form C. 2118

X IX Vol 4

WAR DIARY
or
INTELLIGENCE SUMMARY

No 57 M.G. Coy

(Erase heading not required.)

Instructions regarding War Diaries and Intelligence Summaries are contained in F.S. Regs., Part II. and the Staff Manual respectively. Title Pages will be prepared in manuscript.

Place	Date	Hour	Summary of Events and Information	Remarks and references to Appendices
Nau.	May 1st to 6th		The Company took part in Divisional Training under somewhat trying conditions, the weather being very hot the atmosphere close.	S.D.
	2nd		Our men arrived as reinforcement, having been sent to No 58 M.G. Coy by mistake from here in reply to reinforcements from the Base Depôt.	S.D. S.D.
	7th 8th		The Company marched to Arsi returning. Detraining at Hein Aurand & marched out about 12 miles to Nignacourt.	S.D.
	9th - 19th		Training under Company arrangements.	S.D.
	20th		Company took part in a Brigade Scheme of Attack.	S.D
	22nd		The Company marched to a range about 7 miles out. Transport Sergeant left in the Base Depôt is a Corporal from the 10th Hussars arrived to take over the transport. 2 men arrived from the Base Depôt on appointment.	S.D.
	23rd		Our "Changes" arrived for use 7 transport Sergeant, 8 men, reinforcements from Base Depôt.	S.D.
	26th		The officers of the Company took part in a Tactical Scheme under the G.O.C.	S.D.
	27th		Divisional Sports took place at Hamelles. Our Section of the M.G. Company consisting of was disqualified on a Technical point by one Judge. This section is in the 28 seconds quicker on 7 actions than any other.	S.D.
	29th		The Judge who had disqualified our Section on the value of the final Mys. glued by the Division! was to have won then the Sports Shield by 60 faces which!	S.D.
	30th		The Company marched with the Brigade to Sr Reisier, the Hanavie Area.	S.D
	25th		Four Men reinforcements, repeats ten arrived from the Base Depôt.	S.D.

Army Form C. 2118
June 1916
57 M.G.B.a.

WAR DIARY
or
INTELLIGENCE SUMMARY
(Erase heading not required.)

Instructions regarding War Diaries and Intelligence Summaries are contained in F.S. Regs., Part II. and the Staff Manual respectively. Title Pages will be prepared in manuscript.

XIX

Vol 12

Place	Date	Hour	Summary of Events and Information	Remarks and references to Appendices
ST FUSCIEN	1st		Brigade Training	
"	2nd		Battalion Training	
"	3rd		Brigade Training	
"	4th		Sunday. Rest. A.M. G. Coy officers + B.C. recce a Tactical Scheme in morning	
"	5th		Battalion Training	
"	6th		Brigade Training (very wet)	
"	7th		Battalion Training	
"	8th		Brigade Training. Orders issued for move to VIGNACOURT 10/6	APP I
"	9th		D.W. Training. Army + Corps Commander present	
"	10th		Marched to VIGNACOURT where Brigade was billetted in the old Billets left St RIQUIER at 8 am, Brigade in billets VIGNACOURT 3 pm.	
"	11th		Sunday. Rest. 101st War. R + Det. of 2 off. 120 O.R. 8th M staff marched to forward area.	APP II
"	12th		Company Training. Orders issued for 101st R. War. R. + 815 M. Staff to proceed to forward area	APP III
"	13th		101st R. War. R + 8th N Staff moved to the forward area. 8th G.me. + 8th Yorks Memorial service to late Lord Kitchener 11am gas demonstration 2.30 pm	
"	14th		8th G.me. Coy Training	
"	15th		8th G.me. R. Training	
"	16th		B.G. L.Q. 24 G.me. R. M. G. Coy + T.M. Battery in work training fighting. Orders issued for move to RAINNEVILLE. Bry. for C.C.	
RAINNEVILLE	17th		Brig. Gen. Taylor having assumed command, evening took over command of the Brigade Gellow C.M.G. having arrived earlier in the evening of 17. G.O.C XIth visited 1st 10th R. War. 17. 10th Warc E.Q.N. Staff in the forward area	APP IV
"	18th		Conference at D.H.S.	
"	19th		G.O.C + B.M visited forward area	
"	20th		8th G.m. R. M. G. Coy + T.M.B.s Training	

Army Form C. 2118

WAR DIARY
or
INTELLIGENCE SUMMARY
(Erase heading not required.)

Place	Date	Hour	Summary of Events and Information	Remarks and references to Appendices
RAINNEVILLE	June 21st		Conference of C.O.'s at B.H.Q.	APP IV
"	22nd		Training. Div. Indrs No. 51 issued	
"	23rd		Presentation of Medals by Div. Commander to Major Henderson, 10th R.War.R., 2nd G.B. Bird 10th R.War.R. Pte. W. Tolley 10th R.War.R. Sgt. Major T.Ryan 10th Wor.R. D.C.M. L/Sgt. W.G. Bennett 8th Glo.R. D.C.M. 19th Div. operation orders received.	APP V
"	24th		Training. B'de operation orders issued, including orders to move to forward area. 8th N. Staffords and 10th Royal War.R. move to BRESLE, from ALBERT and the surrounding district. — 24th B'de Orders No. 13 issued	
"	25th		Sunday rest.	
"	26th		Training. Further B'de Orders No. 14 issued. 8th Glo. Regt move off at 7.20 p.m. from RAINNEVILLE. Head of column reach BEHENCOURT at 9.45 p.m. at 11 p.m. the Batt. is in Bivouacs in FRANVILLERS WOOD. B'de inders No. 14 issued.	APP VI
"	27th		Very wet. Despatch received at 1.20 A.M. hastening move for 48 hours.	
BEHENCOURT	28th		Training	
"	29th			
"	30th		Special order of the day to the 19th Div. by Major General BRIDGES published to the troops. — The 8th Glo. Regt leave FRANVILLERS WOOD at 8.20 p.m. Head of Column reaches MILLENCOURT at 11.15 p.m. The remainder of the Bn. B'de also tram through MILLENCOURT at 11 p.m. At 12.30 a.m. the 6.7th B be's in the trenches. V.24.d. — 30.b.d. (TYLER'S REDOUBT)	APP V

WAR DIARY or INTELLIGENCE SUMMARY

(Erase heading not required.)

Army Form C. 2118

REGISTRY
MACHINE GUN CORPS
24 JUL 1916
RECORD OFFICE
No. 66/251

(130)

Place	Date	Hour	Summary of Events and Information	Remarks and references to Appendices
WEST?	1916		Preparations were being made to harass area of St RIQUIER.	
	2		Heavy fire. Letter at Brigade HQ MONACOURT to harassing area of St RIQUIER	
			Relief being made for	
			Coy went out in New Scheme. 2nd Lt Bennett attached to attend Divisional School	
SAINT RIQUIER	3		Instruction	
	4		Wrote field day with Brigade another fine	
	5		Nothing to report, weather	
	6		Brigade carried out a tactical scheme in which the Coy took part	
	7		The return from the scheme made from the Coy was moved to the afternoon	
	8		Brigade manoeuvres and strenuous night attack orders the Coy took part	
	9		Preparations made for a trip with Army orders to the billets at MONACOURT	
	10		The 9th Bn moved from harassing area at St RIQUIER to its Billets at MONACOURT. The Coy finished movement of yesterday. Brigade at MONACOURT except Coy which was not ready for troops at MONACOURT at Billets about 10 miles further on across	

WAR DIARY
or
INTELLIGENCE SUMMARY

Army Form C. 2118

(131)

Place	Date	Hour	Summary of Events and Information	Remarks and references to Appendices
		10.30 a.m	The Coy Paraded for Divine Service the remainder of day was	
	12		given over to the cleaning themselves up & writing	
			home. Church Parade services were conducted for other then Catholics	
	13		Capt. S. M. E. Bingham & 2/Lt. Davis proceed on a course of instruction to the	
			Kenchs for two weeks. 2/Lt. Denton left on command [B.H.Q] or worked	
			in a clothes of funds the Cook Kitchens were opened at [B.H.Q]	
			& more morning parades in the afternoon the Coy marched to a pt 3½	
			miles from MERICOURT were a lecture was given by the Chairman	
	14		Armoures M.C.O. [ ] from Bev. H.G. Salvat.	
			Weather very cold wet to Coy Paraded at 8.30 a.m. for school	
			Until the Coy was warned that the Demers in France in accordance	
			with recent orders of French Gov. that the time would be advanced 60 min.	
			Cap. E. Alinc[?] & 2/Lt. Davis returned from the Kenchs weather very cold	
			not settled.	
	15		The Coy all ranks paraded at 7.15 a.m & moved off at 7.30 a.m	
			behind 7th Gloucesters. to 9½ miles to new billets at RAINNERVILLE,	
			on arrival spirits and falling rain on the ground. weather fine	

Army Form C. 2118

WAR DIARY
or
INTELLIGENCE SUMMARY

57th O.F.C. Mechanical Trans. Coy

(132)

Place	Date	Hour	Summary of Events and Information	Remarks and references to Appendices
	17		Weather much improved, first the Coy paraded at 9 a.m. all harness was refurbished & washed. Lt R.S. Greaves L Hanson proceeded on a visit of inspection to the trenches.	A
do	18		The Coy paraded for Divine Service at 9.30. Lt Elanders returned from leave, weather fine.	A
do	19		Coy paraded 9.30 a.m. for Gen Stewart Bull which was carried on until 1 p.m. weather very unsettled.	A
do	20		2 L.D. Horses, 1 L.D. Mule & 2 Riding Horses were handed over to G.S.G.O. weather fair.	A
do	21		Parade at 9.30 a.m. for Route March under Lt E Elanders, weather warm & fine.	A
do	22		Testing rifles & kit &c, weather fine.	A
do	23		Coy paraded with Gen inspection at 9 a.m. for Gen Stewart Bull. Shower of rain dry, heavy thunder storm in the afternoon.	A
do	24		Coy paraded for Route March at 9 a.m. under Lt E Elanders in the afternoon the Coy was paid	A
do	25		Coy paraded for Divine Service at 10.30 a.m. weather fine.	A
do	26		Coy attended inspection by Cap Ellington & the Coy followed by an address.	A

C. Shelton Capt.

Army Form C. 2118

WAR DIARY
or
INTELLIGENCE SUMMARY   2nd Div Machine Gun Coy

(Erase heading not required.)

(133)

Place	Date	Hour	Summary of Events and Information	Remarks and references to Appendices
	July 3	11	The Coy left RAINNEVILLE 1.30 p.m. for FRANVILLERS WOOD. arrived at WOOD about 11 p.m. bivouacked weather showing	A9
FRANVILLERS WOOD	"	15	They bivouaced about 24 hours not men to "stand fast" for 48 hours instead of marching 6 day	A9
"	"	4	Remained in bivouac. Ill day weather showery 2nd Lt. Durrant returned from Divisional School.	A9
"	"	5	Coy left FRANVILLERS WOOD at 8.15 arriving at MERRICOURT about 11 a.m. weather very unsettled.	A9

57th Inf.Bde.
19th Div.

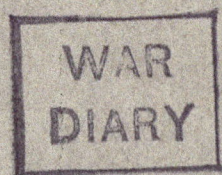

57th MACHINE GUN COMPANY.

J U L Y

1 9 1 6

INTELLIGENCE SUMMARY

57th Bde Machine Gun Coy

Vol 6

Place	Date	Hour	Summary of Events and Information	Remarks and references to Appendices
MILLENCOURT	July 1/16		Bivouac at MILLENCOURT. Time very hot. The Company is told off as follows:—	

Each Section
- 1 Officer
- 4 N.C.O.s
- 24 Gunners
- 1 Batman

Coy H.Q.
- C.O.
- C.S.M.
- 2 Signallers
- 1 Orderly
- 1 Batman

1 Officer Lt. ELDRIDGE (2 in Command) is attached to Bde H.Q. as Liaison Officer.

1 Officer 2nd Lt. VERE is in charge of the limbers & supplies.

All the remainder are in reserve.

Officers commanding Sections as follows:—

No 1 Sec. 2nd Lt. H.D. PHILLIPS
" 2 " 2nd Lt. H.D. HANSON
" 3 " 2nd Lt. H.B.W. HATCH
" 4 " 2nd Lt. R. RAMSBOTTOM

INTELLIGENCE SUMMARY 51st Bde Machine Gun Coy

Place	Date 1916	Hour	Summary of Events and Information	Remarks and references to Appendices
MILLENCOURT	July 1	5.30 pm	Recvd orders to move to W.29a (Junct E of ALBERT) move up west 12 lorries & bivouac in a field. Reserves, transport, & Officers stables stay with Bde. Transport in MILLENCOURT.	GM
		8.0 pm	The C.O. reports to Bde. H.Q. of USNA REDOUBT & receives orders to mount 2 guns about X.7.c.95 to fire between OVILLERS & LA BOISELLE. 2 guns of No. 2 Sec. under 2nd Lt HANSON are sent for & are brought up on hand cart arriving after dark. The trenches are unknown & no guides are available & the guns & lobes that may & return to Bde H.Q. 1.30 a.m. 1.45 a.m. they set out again via ST ANDREWS AVENUE but owing to block in trenches etc. do not get into position until 5 a.m. meantime projected bombing attack in LA BOISELLE has been cancelled.	
ALBERT	2		2 Guns of No. 1 Section under 2nd Lt PHILLIPS are sent up to relieve No. 2 Sec: who are pretty well exhausted. The guns are mounted in the left Division point X.7.c 95 & are ordered to support bombing attack by 68th Brigade in LA BOISELLE from the S. by firing along N. edge of village. This is done.	GM
do	2	7.0 am	Attack 4 p.m. only partially successful, arrangements are made by the 51st Brigade to attack LA BOISELLE from S.W. at 3.15 a.m. 3.7.16 and the two guns in the Left Division are ordered to fire N. of BOISELLE previous to attack and to cease fire at 3.15 a.m. the time of fire to attack X.14 c. & d. This was arranged by Comdrs & Harassing dicted on tripods.	

INTELLIGENCE SUMMARY

57th Brigade Machine Gun Coy

(Erase heading not required.)

Instructions regarding War Diaries and Intelligence Summaries are contained in F.S. Regs., Part II. and the Staff Manual respectively. Title Pages will be prepared in manuscript.

Place	Date 1916	Hour	Summary of Events and Information	Remarks and references to Appendices
	July 3		The program is carried out, the trenches are heavily bombarded but no damage to guns & teams.	
		11 a.m.	The 67? Brigade attack is successful in taking LA BOISELLE. Orders received for the guns in the left Plaque to keep German trench X.8.d.9.9 & X.9.d.0.0 under fire day and night. This is arranged & carried out.	PH
		4 p.m.	Orders received to arrange M.G. fire down NASH VALLEY in case of German counter attack on LA BOISELLE. Two guns of No.3 Section under 2/Lt HATCH were sent up & mounted in Staff at Junok about X.13.c. Guns at X.7.c.9.5 fired on M.G. repelling bombing attack from LA BOISELLE. the gun disappeared.	
	4	11 a.m.	Received orders to mount two guns in X.13.c. Two guns of No.1 Sec under 2nd Lt. RAMSBOTTOM were mounted at X.13.c.4.4. but were so heavily shelled that their position was altered to support trenches about X.13.c.0.6 in the evening.	PH
		11.15 a.m.		
		2 p.m.	Received orders to send two guns to LA BOISELLE to assist in repelling anyhow No.2 counter attack. Cap ELLINGTON & 2/Lt HANSON went down to LA BOISELLE to reconnoitre, Two guns of No.2 Sec being ordered to move up to KIRCALDY AVENUE	

INTELLIGENCE SUMMARY

of 57th Brigade Machine Gun Coy.

(Erase heading not required.)

Place	Date	Hour	Summary of Events and Information	Remarks and references to Appendices
	July 4		and wait orders, reported to Lt. Col WINSOR 9th S. LANCS, and arranged gun positions.	
		7.0pm	Capt ELLINGTON returned to USNA REDOUBT and received orders to go to LA BOISELLE with four more guns. Four guns of No 4 Sec. were taken down to LA BOISELLE after dark on ALBERT-POZIERES ROAD. They arrived at LA BOISELLE 12 M.N. the two guns of No 2 Sec. owing to meet and block in communication trench did not arrive until 4.30 a.m. The guns went in supported as follows — two on N.W. side of village near south of forward trench. Three in ruins in village. One by church flanking forward trench.	SM
	5	4 am	2nd Lt DAVIS arrived in LA BOISELLE, all guns were heavily shelled this day casualties 2 killed 4 wounded.	
		2.0pm	Bombing attack was made by the 1st SHERWOODS, guns at X Y c 95 under 2nd Lt PHILLIPS observed Germans moving across gaps in communication trenches towards LA BOISELLE fire was opened and good effect obtained. One of the gaps was afterwards seen to be blocked by 2 dead bodies. The two guns at X 13 c 56 under 2nd Lt RAMSBOTTOM supported the attack by firing down MASH VALLEY.	SM
		7.30pm	Some Germans and two M.G.s from the guns at X c 95 2nd Lt PHILLIPS opened fire and at X 14 d 2.8½ from the guns at X c 96 2nd Lt PHILLIPS opened fire and possibly a third M.G. were seen	

INTELLIGENCE SUMMARY

51st Brigade Machine Gun Coy

(Erase heading not required.)

Place	Date 1916	Hour	Summary of Events and Information	Remarks and references to Appendices
	July 5		and was assisted by an Artillery observation Officer succeeded in killing two men and putting Tans gun out of action. The remainder disappeared.	AA
	6	9.0pm	Received news that No 4 M.G. Coy would relieve us to-morrow	
		9.0am	Capt ELLINGTON went to USNA REDOUBT to arrange relief.	AA
		11.0am	O.C. No 74 M.G. Coy arrived.	
		12pm	Guns at X.Y.C.95 are ordered to continue as they are not to be replaced	
		7pm	Guns in support trenches in X13c relieved.	
			The Coy went into billets at ALBERT.	
ALBERT	7.	1.30am	The guns in LA BOISELLE were relieved and came back across country. they were delayed by shelling & arrived at ALBERT at 4.30am. 2nd Lt. HANSON was hit on the Chose Coy a piece of shell, but did not penetrate but made him lame, one man was wounded. Rest of day in billets at ALBERT.	AA
MILLENCOURT	8		Ja Incomae at MILLENCOURT	AA
do	9		do	AA
do	10.	9.0am	The Coy paraded for the purpose of overhauling Guns, limbers etc.	AA
do	11.		In Incomae at MILLENCOURT	AA
do	12.		do	AA

INTELLIGENCE SUMMARY

(Erase heading not required.)

54th Coy Machine Gun Corps

Place	Date	Hour	Summary of Events and Information	Remarks and references to Appendices
MILLENCOURT	July 13		In bivouac at MILLENCOURT. The 54th Brigade was inspected by the Corps Commander.	
"	14		In bivouac at MILLENCOURT	
"	15		do	
"	16		do	
"	17		do	
"	18		do	
do	19		2nd Lt DURRANT went into Hospital (Reported later that he was suffering from Neuritis/ours) Brigade moved up & bivouacked at F.6.b.6.8. leaving MILLENCOURT 10.30 p.m. arriving Bivouac about 2 a.m.	SR
"	20		Brigade moved up to relieve 96th Brigade in Section N. of BAZENTIN-LE-PETIT village. Left bivouac at 9.30 m arrived MAMETZ WOOD 12.30 p.m. Guides limbers at X2H.2.3.4 S. of MAMETZ WOOD & sent mules back to Transport pt F.8.6.6.8 Coy H.Q. in middle of MAMETZ WOOD in old German Trench. Btn H.Q. in German Dug Out about 100 yds N of Coy H.Q. Lt ELDRIDGE relieved 2 guns in cemetery (No.3 Sec.) 2nd Lt GARDNER with remaining guns of No.3 Sec. relieved 2 guns in S.E. corner of BAZENTIN-LE-PETIT 2nd Lt HANSON relieved 4 guns (at S.E. side of BAZENTIN-LE-PETIT)	SR

INTELLIGENCE SUMMARY

(Erase heading not required.)

Place	Date	Hour	Summary of Events and Information	Remarks and references to Appendices
WOOD	July 20		Remainder in reserve at Coy. H.Q.	AW
	21.	12.30am	Capt. ELLINGTON reports to Bde. H.Q. & was told that there was a gap between WINDMILL & HIGH WOOD. He received orders to reconnoitre at daylight for gun position to cover right flank.	AW
		3.0am	Capt. ELLINGTON went out to reconnoitre. He arranged 2 guns with 2nd Lt. HANSON (behind BAZENTIN-LE-GRAND WOOD) to flank any counter attack on ground S.W. of HIGH WOOD in case of counter attack. Reconnaissance was impeded owing to fog which lasted till 6.0am; a position was selected in an old German trench between S.15.b.1.1 & S.15.d.6.2 for 4 guns. No.1 Section under 2nd Lt. DAVIS was sent up to take up this position which was in the 51st Div. front.	AW
		11.0am	LIEUT. ELDRIDGE slightly wounded, splinter in left arm, at his gun position S.8.b.8.2 he returned to position of bivouac of yesterday, and remained there. Sergt. SCHOFIELD to left in charge.	
	22	2.45am	2nd Lt. GARDNER reported one of his guns having had water jacket punctured in two places, one of No.4 Sec. Parts was sent down to him to replace same. Damaged gun returned to 1st Line Transport.	AW
		9.30am	Brigade Ord. Headquarters to S.I.H. A.5.2. Coy H.Q. remaining the day over 12 guns were supporting the Bde. as yesterday in case of counter attack	

INTELLIGENCE SUMMARY

(Erase heading not required.)

59th Coy Machine Gun Corps.

Place	Date	Hour	Summary of Events and Information	Remarks and references to Appendices
		6.30pm	O.C. again journeyed to Bn. H.Q. & reported for orders, whilst that message was received from SERGT SCHOFIELD asking O.C. to confirm orders he had received from O.C. 8th N. STAFFS. to take at dusk one of his guns from CEMETRY QUARRY to a strong point being 100+ N. of WINDMILL nr. I.S.9.4.63. O.C. ordered him to carry on with this as soon as dusk. SGT. SCHOFIELD having previously reconnoitred the position & asked for covering party of bombers.	
		9.45pm	O.C. received orders to send 4 guns to O.C. ROYAL WARWICKS and 4 guns to O.C. GLOSTERS, he obtained permission to alter the number of guns to 3 each & to report at earliest opportunity	M
		10.20pm	O.C. despatched from Coy H.Q. SGT. SCHOFIELDS gun from CEMETRY & reported with three guns on all 4 gun party with guide, with instructions to 2nd Lt GARDNER to call on R. WARWICKS (attached) with covering party with guide, with instructions to 2nd Lt GARDNER to call on O.C. GLOSTERS for night operations, this party was shelled while proceeding to 2nd Lt GARDNER the Cpl. being severely wounded the message ultimately being delivered at 3.0.a.m 23.4.16. two late to be of use the attack having been launched & proved a failure	
		11.0pm	SERGT YEO & three guns & team No 4 Section & carrying party reported to O.C. R. WARWICK REGT	
		11.30pm	C.O. moved from MAMETZ WOOD to Bde H.Q	

INTELLIGENCE SUMMARY of 54th Coy Machine Gun Corps.

(Erase heading not required.)

Place	Date	Hour	Summary of Events and Information	Remarks and references to Appendices
	July 23	5.30am	SERGT YEO reported failure of ROYAL WARWICKS attack & that he had received instructions to report to CAPTN ELLINGTON for orders. O.C. R.WARWICKS no longer requiring his assistance. He was ordered to remain with R.WARWICKS	
		5.45am	Brigade ordered an Officer to be sent up to the CEMETRY. 2 LIEUT PHILLIPS (Liaison Officer) was sent up. CAPT ELLINGTON was ordered to go to — BAZENTIN-LE-GRAND & remain there until further orders as a counter attack was expected on that flank. The Coy proceed & in the evening the Coy was relieved by 58th Coy M.G.C relief being completed 1.30 a.m returned to bivouac at F.8.6.68.	AA
	24		In Corps reserve at F.8.6.68.	AA
	25		do	AA
	26		do	AA
	27		do	AA
	28		do	AA
	29		The Coy moved up to relieve 98th Coy MACHINE GUN CORPS. By A.2 being at S.14 a 16. and guns were disposed as under 2 Guns front line Bde. Hd.Qrs. Crater. Right. 2 " " " " " " Left. 4 " in Support " 4 " in BAZENTIN-LE-GRAND WOOD at 16.00 under 2 Lt PHILLIPS.	AA

INTELLIGENCE SUMMARY

(Erase heading not required.)

Place	Date	Hour	Summary of Events and Information	Remarks and references to Appendices
	July 29.		to be used for indirect fire when the attack started. 2nd LIEUT RAMSBOTTOM and 2nd LIEUT HATCH went up with the front line and support the former being in command of the guns in the front line and support	
		6.50 p.m.	by 6.50 p.m. The guns in B.de Left Sector were placed under command of the O.C. 8th GLOUCESTER REGT & the the guns on B.de Right Sector under the O.C. 1st K.O.R.L. REGT	
		10.50 p.m.	Between 10.30 & 11.30 p.m. one of the gun positions in the Left pos line was heavily shelled with H.E. & shr. Two gunners wounded. Two N.C.O's wounded, two were working, & two were suffering slightly from shell shock. One man was wounded. One gun team from No 3 Section was sent up to replace the team which had been knocked out the previous night. One corporal in charge of one of the teams in the support line was accidentally wounded.	
	30"	11 a.m.	One of the gun positions in the right sector was shelled with H.E. shr. which the team was buried. One man was dug out only carefully was sent to the Dressing Station suffering from shock	
		3.30 p.m.	Two gun teams of No 2 Section were sent up to relieve teams of No 1 Section in the front line & shortly after another was sent up to relieve the teams in the front line who had been buried.	
		6.9 p.m.	Our Artillery started an intense bombardment, the enemy replied rather heavily. At 9.p.m. Lt PAUL proceeded to consolidate his position, 2 guns of No 2 Section in a known Enemy Machine gun in the N.W. corner of HIGH WOOD.	

INTELLIGENCE SUMMARY

(Erase heading not required.)

Instructions regarding War Diaries and Intelligence Summaries are contained in F. S. Regs., Part II. and the Staff Manual respectively. Title Pages will be prepared in manuscript.

Place	Date	Hour	Summary of Events and Information	Remarks and references to Appendices
	July 30th	6.10 pm	The Brigade attacked the German entrenched line, at the same time two of the guns under 2Lt Phillips fired on the road leading North. During this one the gun teams in the support line were heavily shelled, one man being killed, a Corporal & 3 men wounded. As a result of the attack the K.O.R.L Regt & part of the 10 R.W.R Regt succeeded in gaining their objective.	SW
		11.30pm	Acting under instructions from B.H.Q. Capt ELLINGTON took up 2 gun teams under 2 Lt HAMSON to the line which had been captured by the K.O.R.L Regt, there selected positions for the guns. During the night the whole line was subjected to a heavy bombardment, 2 on L Corporal was wounded.	SW
	31.2.		In the early morning a "Minenwerfer Bomb" which burst on the parapet at C.H.Q. seriously wounded one man & slightly wounded another. The same afternoon the Brigade was relieved & the 101st M.G. Coy returned to their unit Relief completed to Bivouacs at S.78.c.6.8	
		9 pm		

57th Brigade.
19th Division.

57th BRIGADE MACHINE GUN COMPANY

AUGUST 1 9 1 6 ::

WAR DIARY or INTELLIGENCE SUMMARY

Army Form C. 2118

57 M.G. Coy Vol 7

Place	Date	Hour	Summary of Events and Information	Remarks and references to Appendices
N. FRICOURT	August 1st	4 p.m	The Company march from bivouac near Fricourt to Bresle.	
BRESLE	2nd	3 p.m.	The Corps Commander inspects the Brigade. The Brigade First Line Transport in my C.11 at 3.30 pm to Bouchon via Allonville, bivouacing for one night at the latter place.	20
	3rd	6 a.m.	The Company march to Mericourt and entrain for Longpré-sur-Somme, arriving about midday, from by route march to bivouac near Bouchon.	
BOUCHON	5th		The Company is inspected by Brig General Tufnell	
	6th	4.30 am	Leave Bouchon & entrain at Longpré to Bailleul, arriving about 4 pm, from tea station by route march to billets close to Dranoutre.	
DRANOUTRE	7th	2.30 am	The Company moves up to take over billets from N°149 M.G. Coy at N 31 a 93. The transport remaining at Dranoutre at M 36 c 49. Six guns are sent up to the following positions, two to Shell Farm, one to Battleaxe, and to S.P. 7 Left out to Frenchman's Farm, one to Kingsway. Two other guns are sent down with teams to Divisional Reserve at M 36 c 49. The remainder trans H.Q. at N 31 a 93	
	8th		A Draft of 8 men arrive from the Base Depot at Camiers	
	9th		A Fighting Limber with 2 guns, I limit to the Divisional M.G. School at La Lovrette	
	10th		A Draft of 12 men arrive from the Base Depot at Camiers	
	11th		Gun Teams from Coy H.Q. where there is in the line	
	14th		2nd Lieut HANSON. One Sergeant leave to Camiers to attend the M.G. School. 2nd Lieut L A Brunt reports for duty from	
	15th		Company Relief takes place Base Depot	
	16th	3.30 p/m	A bombardment takes place. Our Heavy Medium T.M.s answered by 14" Dir R.F.A. bombardeous German Front line - support lines	

Army Form C. 2118

WAR DIARY
or
INTELLIGENCE SUMMARY
(Erase heading not required.)

Instructions regarding War Diaries and Intelligence Summaries are contained in F.S. Regs., Part II. and the Staff Manual respectively. Title Pages will be prepared in manuscript.

Place	Date	Hour	Summary of Events and Information	Remarks and references to Appendices
Dranoutre	Aug 16th		One Gun Team sent up to take on new position at PICCADILLY	SD
"	17th		A draft of 3 men arrive from the Base Depot. These men are sent to the Brigade for a course on Signalling.	"
"	18th		8 men are sent to the Divisional M.G. School at LA KEYETTE.	"
"	19th		Company Relief takes place.	"
"	20th		Two new Gun Teams are sent up, one to take up a position in the FRONT LINE + another at S.P.7 Right.	"
"	21st	3.30pm	Our Heavy Howitzer T.M.'s answered by the Right Group Artillery bombard the German Front Line & First Support lines.	"
"	23rd		Company Relief takes place for 7 Teams	
"	25th		2 Lieut PEACOCK reports for duty from the Base Depot.	
"	27th		Company Relief.	
"	28th		Two men are temporarily attached to the B'N STAFF R. 1 Lieut N.B. FINDLAY reports for duty from no 71 M.G. Coy as Second in Command	

VOL 8

Army Form C. 2118

WAR DIARY
or
INTELLIGENCE SUMMARY

No 59 N.G. Coy.

(Erase heading not required.)

Instructions regarding War Diaries and Intelligence Summaries are contained in F. S. Regs., Part II. and the Staff Manual respectively. Title Pages will be prepared in manuscript.

Place	Date Sept	Hour	Summary of Events and Information	Remarks and references to Appendices
DRANOUTRE	4th	9 a.m.	2 Lieut H.D. HANSON and Serjeant arrived from the M.G. School at CAMIERS	SD
ROMARIN			The Company have arrived in Billets to 109 M.G. Coy & proceed by route march to Billets at ROMARIN with the whole of the Transport Gun Teams remain in the line, except those in Divisional Reserve moving with the Company.	SD
	5th		The 109th M.G. Coy relieve the Gun Teams at FRONT LINE, BOLT COURT and CAUSEWAY. Three their Gun Jumps Gun ammunition etc at FRENCHMANS FARM, & removed by York Road to ROMARIN. Ration limber for the Trenches will be back store from FRENCHMANS FARM.	SD
	6th	1 p.m.	2 Lieut HATCH with three Gun Teams relieves No 105 M.G. Gun Teams near HYDE FARM	SD
		2 p.m.	2 Lieut HANSON & 2 Lieut PEACOCK relieve 5 Gun Teams of No 105 M.S. Coy. One Serjeant (being attached) to the party. H.Q. at the CHATEAU.	SD
DRANOUTRE		2 p.m.	Six Gun Teams of 109 M.S. Coy relieve Gun Teams at FRENCHMANS FARM, PICCADILLY, SIDING FARM, BATTIFAYE, S.P.7 REDT. LEFT these Teams proceed by route march to new Billets.	SD
ROMARIN	7th		Right Motor return to the Company from the Divisional M.G. School.	SD
	8th	9 p.m.	Gas Alarm was received in the Camp, which ultimately proved false.	SD
	9th		2 Lieut DURT and Serjeant proceed to the Divisional Course of Instruction, to form line to the Divisional M.G. Course at LA LEVOTTE	SD
	10th	11 am	2 Teams are sent up to take on new positions in the line	SD
		1 pm	Company Relief takes place for six Teams in the line	SD
		5 pm	The Company moves off and was Headquarters at LA PETITE MUNQUE Transport Remaining at the old billet	SD

1875 Wt. W.593/826 1,000,000 4/15 J.B.C. & A. A.D.S.S./Forms/C. 2118.

Army Form C. 2118

WAR DIARY
or
INTELLIGENCE SUMMARY
(Erase heading not required.)

No 57 M.G Coy.

Instructions regarding War Diaries and Intelligence Summaries are contained in F.S. Regs, Part II. and the Staff Manual respectively. Title Pages will be prepared in manuscript.

Place	Date	Hour	Summary of Events and Information	Remarks and references to Appendices
ROMARIN	May 13	6.0 A.M	Nine Surplus M.G Privates are sent to the Base Depot at CAMIERS to duty	Sd.
"	14		Our Artillery opened out of the day in retaliating with successful results. 2 Machine guns fire on the gaps during the night dispersing forced working parties.	Sd
"	15	10.30 P.M	Our Artillery opened fire on enemy front line trenches firing extremes the space of one minute, & two railway junctions to our left. The Gloucester on the left of the Minutes on the left. The later said pieces his Gloucester succeeded. One of the enemy trench mortars to fire at the Gloucester. After the enemy had been Trench. Enemy retaliates with Mt.	Sd.
"	16		Coy spent with take place day Quiet.	Sd
"	18th		The Company sense out at Billet at LA PETITE MUNQUE to Transport	Sd
"	19		Billet. The time on the line are relieved by No 91 M.G. Coy. The men estimated the night in billets.	Sd
OUTTERSTEEN	20th		The Brigade sent on by route march 7 about 3 miles to OUTTERSTEEN returned.	Sd
BURRE	21st		The Brigade turn out by route march 7 about 5/6 miles to BURRE was the Company to ride billets.	Sd
"	22		Day spent in cleaning up tackle.	Sd
"	23		2 Men Company furnish Tal: place, supply everybody Lambert, One Subaltn ammo for duty	Sd
"	24,25		Lecture on Discipline by Brig. General Jeffreys to all officers in the Brigade.	Sd
"	26		Company Training	Sd
"	27th	2.30 p.m	The Brigade is inspected by the Army Commander, who distributes medals to the Some Third	Sd

1875 Wt. W593/826 1,000,000 4/15 J.B.C. & A. A.D.S.S./Forms/C. 2118.

Army Form C. 2118.

WAR DIARY
or
INTELLIGENCE SUMMARY

(Erase heading not required.)

No 57 M.G. Coy

Instructions regarding War Diaries and Intelligence Summaries are contained in F. S. Regs., Part II. and the Staff Manual respectively. Title Pages will be prepared in manuscript.

Place	Date Sept	Hour	Summary of Events and Information	Remarks and references to Appendices
BORRE	28"		The O.R. return to the Company from the Divisional M.G. School.	50
"	29 "	10 A.M	The Transport paraded for Brigade Inspection.	50
"	30 "	9.15 A.M	The Company proceed for a Route March HAZEBROUCK – CAESTRE – STRAZEELE	50

Adam 2Lt A/Ag
No 57 M.G. Coy

2449 Wt. W14957/M90 750,000 1/16 J.B.C. & A. Forms/C.2118/12.

Army Form C. 2118.

WAR DIARY
or
INTELLIGENCE SUMMARY
(Erase heading not required.)

No 37 M.G. Coy. Vol 9

Instructions regarding War Diaries and Intelligence Summaries are contained in F.S. Regs., Part II. and the Staff Manual respectively. Title Pages will be prepared in manuscript.

Place	Date October	Hour	Summary of Events and Information	Remarks and references to Appendices
BORRE	3rd	11 a.m.	H.M. The King of the Belgians inspects the Brigade, & 37 S.W. Borderers on a field S.E. of BORRE, after which the Brigade march past H.M.	520
"	5th	7.30 a.m.	The Company proceed on a short route march.	520
BORRE	6th		The Company marched off at 4-30 A.M. to BAILLEUL where they entrained at 9 A.M. and moved off at 10.28 A.M. arriving at DOULLENS at 4 P.M. they then marched to SARTON where they stayed the night. Capt. ELLINGTON returned to his unit.	A.B.C.
SARTON	7th		Capt. KNOX-LITTLE from 115 Company took Command. The Company moved off at 1.45 P.M. and marched to ST.LEGER-LES-AUTHIE arriving there at 3-30 P.M. It rained very heavily all afternoon.	A.B.C.
ST. LEGER	8th		Raining. Gun drill etc. indoors.	A.B.C.
"	9th		As previous day.	A.B.C.
"	10th		Fine. O.C. Company and 1 Section Officers made a Reconnaissance of the line and important strong points. N.C.Officers attended a lecture on "Tanks".	A.B.C.
"	11th		Dull and showery. Company practised advancing with guns in Artillery formation, with lateral intervals of 50 yds. Infantry training remainder of time.	A.B.C.
"	12th		Still. Company had both parades from 7-30 A.M. 600 11-A.M. Infantry training remainder of time. Nos. 1's and 2's and rangefinders were on the range for rangetaking practice.	A.B.C.
"	13th		Dull. Infantry training and Gun Drill.	A.B.C.
"	14th		Fine, Cold. The Company acted as the enemy while the remainder of the Brigade attacked a line of Trenches.	A.B.C.

WAR DIARY

Army Form C. 2118.

57th M.G. Company

Place	Date 1916	Hour	Summary of Events and Information	Remarks and references to Appendices
St Leger	Oct. 15th		Showery. R.C. Church parade. Remainder of Company did Infantry drill	A.B.G.
	16th		Showery. Infantry training and advanced M.G. drill	A.B.G.
	17th		Fine but cold. The Company marched off at 9-30 a.m. and proceeded, in rear of the Brigade, across country to Warloy - Baillon arriving there at 2-30 p.m.	A.B.G.
Warloy	18th		Cleaned billets left by Canadians.	A.B.G.
	19th		Rain. Marched towards SENLIS but had to return to WARLOY. the reason for doing so was not stated.	A.B.G.
	20th		Fine, cold. The Company had a route march through VARENNES and back to Warloy.	A.B.G.
	21st		Fine, cold. The Brigade marched through SENLIS and BOZENCOURT to Camp at W27a 3.8. on the Bouzincourt - Albert road.	A.B.G.
Camp	22nd		Fine, cold. Marched to the trenches via AVELUY and NAB VALLEY and relieved the 75th M.G. Coy. who had taken the REGINA trench the previous day.	A.B.G.

WAR DIARY or INTELLIGENCE SUMMARY

Army Form C. 2118.

57th M.G. Coy.

Place	Date	Hour	Summary of Events and Information	Remarks and references to Appendices
In the Trenches	Oct. 22		2nd Lieut H.D. HANSON with a gun Travd. relieved the Travis doing Indirect Fire at R.27.C.3.8. to R.27.C.8.8. Lt. Gardner relieved the 3 Travis in HESSIAN TRENCH. 2 Lt. PHILLIPS relieved the 2 Travis in STUFF REDOUBT. The Conditions are very bad the going very heavy. During the night Indirect Fire took place on the following Targets:– R.15.Bd.2.9. to bottom of Q in CEMETERY intermittent fire from 11pm to 3am & from 3am to 5am. R.15 a 8.6. Intermittently from W.50 pm to 12.50 am & then 2.50 am to 4.30 am. Rounds fired 2,500.	S.D.
	23rd		STUMP ROAD from R.15.C.8.8. to Con Road R.15 a 8.6. intermittent. STUFF REDOUBT was heavily bombarded. During the morning the Maty POMP made a reconnaissance of REGINA TRENCH & in the afternoon O.C. Company went up from C.H.Q. to a position near 2nd Lieut DUNT 2L/PR 14LPS place 3 guns. Lt PHILLIPS guns. Difficulty was experienced in getting rations up, must up in place to so 20 in the dark & next many loads of got lost in the sunk. Impossible to bring up. At least 8 mules were required for an ordinary limber load.	S.D.
	23/24th		1st Lieut HANSON carried out Indirect Fire on the following parts of GRANDCOURT TRENCH to prevent the Enemy working (when enclosed by points R.15.C.8.4.–R16.C.8.2. R.15.Central–R.16.C.9. Bujstha enclosed by points R.15.b.0.4.–R15.b.0.2.–R16.a.85.– R.16.b.1.9. Firing done 160 rounds per hour.	S.D.
	24th		2 Lieut PHILLIPS was killed by a shell in the FRONT LINE. Lieut GARDNER handed over to 2 Lieut DUNT & went into REGINA TRENCH. The O.C. Company inspected the left hand gun in STUFF REDOUBT to HESSIAN TRENCH. Enemy Artillery non action.	S.D.
	24/25		Indirect Fire continued by day & night. 2000 rounds fired.	S.D.
	25th		O.C. - Next O.C. Company inspected the other gun from STUFF REDOUBT & the Trav returned to C.H.Q. 2 Lieut HATCH relieved Lieut GARDNER in REGINA TRENCH.	S.D.

Army Form C. 2118.

WAR DIARY
or
INTELLIGENCE SUMMARY

(Erase heading not required.)

57 M.G. Coy.

Instructions regarding War Diaries and Intelligence Summaries are contained in F.S. Regs., Part II. and the Staff Manual respectively. Title Pages will be prepared in manuscript.

Place	Date	Hour	Summary of Events and Information	Remarks and references to Appendices
In the TRENCHES	25/26 26		2nd LIEUT RAMSBOTTOM carried out the indirect firing Programme fired 6,000 During the early morning. Our artillery carried out a very heavy bombardment of the enemys front line.	SD SD
"	26/27.		Went 3.30 pm to Relief from No. 58th M.G. Coy being arrived for the guns in the front line HESSIAN TRENCH. Two gun teams started from C.H.Q at about 6 pm and have in HESSIAN TRENCH. The relief was carried out about 6 pm and have started from C.H.Q. about 5 p.m.----being heavy fire never swept SAM the next morning. This was due to the fact that the rain was very exhausted owing to the heavy ground. That is no absolute information to go up in the dark. However one Team of the Company how the men carrying out in fact only 1 Team arrived at C.H.Q. before midnight. All the men were very exhausted.	SD
"	26/27 27.		2nd Lieut HANSON carried out indirect fire as before firing about 2,000 rds.	SD
"	27/28 28.		The Company. the TRANSPORT go into Billets at AVELUY. 2nd Lieut RAMSBOTTOM carried out indirect fire. 4,500 rounds. Vist my coy.	SD SD
"	28/29 29.		Day was cold showery. Spent in cleaning guns, Tripods ek. Indirect fire carried out by 2 Lieut HATCH Coll + Mr. BECK Been cleaned tripods.	SD SD SD
"	30		The Company (7 gun Teams) relieved No 58 M.G. Coy. 3 Gun Teams going into REGINA TRENCH + 4 Teams into HESSIAN indirect fire two carried out during the night 29/30 by 2 Lieut DUNT. Day very cold wet. During this relief Pack Mules were used for carrying all Guns Tripods Ammunition so far as the Gravel Pit site. Great success. the relief was completed in good time.	SD
"	31"		Heavy rain. During night 30/31 working the Tunches dry trod. One gun in HESSIAN TRENCH was damaged by the fire.	SD

B. Davis 2nd Lieut
57 M.G. Coy

2449 Wt. W4957/M90 750,000 1/16 J.B.C. & A. Forms/C.2118/12.

Army Form C. 2118.

WAR DIARY
or
INTELLIGENCE SUMMARY

(Erase heading not required.)

No 57 M.G. Coy.

Place	Date	Hour	Summary of Events and Information	Remarks and references to Appendices
In the Trenches	1.	9.0 am	An extra Company Relief was carried out for the guns in REGINA & HESSIAN Trenches. 2Lt HATTON took over from 2Lt RAMSBOTTOM, & 2Lt GARDNER from 2Lt HANSON. During the night had with this was carried out no previously on part of GRANDCOURT Trench, about 4,000 rounds being fired. The men are still very unsettled & seem unfit to the Trenches in a very bad condition.	SD.
"	1/2			SD.
"	2nd	9.0 am	50 M.G. Company relieved the guns in the Front & Support Lines Relief completed at 2.30 pm the Company proceeded to camps bivouac at AVELUY. Indirect Fire during the night 8,500 rounds one fired. Night cold & wet.	SD.
"	2/3			SD.
AVELUY	3rd		Day spent in cleaning up details. guns & material, the Company went to the Baths. Indirect Fire during the night 4,000 rounds were fired.	SD.
"	3/4			SD.
"	4.		Day spent out on S.W. exit. Indirect Fire during the night 3,500 rounds were fired	SD.
"	4/5			SD.
"	5	10. am	The Company proceeded to Brewis Sevens at HESSIAN HUTS 2Lt RAMSBOTTOM & 2Lt D.R. proceeded to CAMIERS to the 33rd M.G. Course. Indirect Fire during the night 4,500 rounds were fired. Night very cold wet.	SD.
"	6		The Company paraded for Infantry Drill No 33 M.G. Coy relieved us for the Enemy Source Between 12.45 pm & 1.15 pm. Heavy shower during the day	SD.
"	7		Weather continued to be bad, the day was very wet & cold. Kit inspection	SD.

Army Form C. 2118

WAR DIARY
or
INTELLIGENCE SUMMARY
(Erase heading not required.)

No 57 M. G. Coy

Instructions regarding War Diaries and Intelligence Summaries are contained in F.S. Regs., Part II. and the Staff Manual respectively. Title Pages will be prepared in manuscript.

Place	Date	Hour	Summary of Events and Information	Remarks and references to Appendices
In the Trenches	8		The 57" Infantry Brigade took on the Divisional Front. Day was very showery. The Company relieved 16 Goal Trans of No 58 M.G. Coy in the following positions. RIGHT Sector 3 Trans in REGINA TRENCH, 2 Trans in HESSIAN LEFT Sector 5 Trans in STUFF TRENCH, 2 in reserve in HESSIAN, and 2 in reserve in THIEPVAL REDOUBT was in command of the guns in the right Sector. LIGHTFOOT in HATCH in command of the guns in STUFF TRENCH 2.lt HANSON in command of the reserve Trans. Most of the relief was carried out in the broad relief completed at 6 pm. Casualties 2.O.R wounded. The Trenches were all in very bad condition. Communication between the front & support lines by day was impossible. Enemy artillery was fairly active.	EA
"	9"		Weather was excellent all day. Carrying parties were employed during the day in taking up Sand bags for the purpose of making the parapets. This were especially difficult owing to the state of the Trenches any digging causing the Trenches to fall in at once. There was a great deal of aeroplane activity all day. The enemy Kite balloon were much in evidence. Night was fairly quiet.	EA
"	10"		Our Artillery started a bombardment of the enemy's lines at 5 AM from 5:30 AM to 6:0 AM fired intense. Enemy retaliated on our front line at the same time. Two new Gun Trans were sent into ZOLLERN REDOUBT in reserve. Weather fine outside afterwards from 7 am.	EA
"	11"		Our Artillery again bombarded enemy line, beginning at 5:30 am from 5:45 to 6:0 am firing intense. Afterwards from 7 am a deliberate Enemy bombardment took place. The Trans in the Right Sector was relieved by 50 M.G. Coy Relief	EA

WAR DIARY or INTELLIGENCE SUMMARY

Army Form C. 2118

57 M.G. Coy

(Erase heading not required.)

Place	Date Nov	Hour	Summary of Events and Information	Remarks and references to Appendices
In the Trenches	11		Completed at 6 o'clock. Casualties 10 R.	20
	12		During the night the front support line was shelled & our bombardment continued. Intense fire being carried out from about 5.15 am to 6 am. The trenches on the left flank was relieved by 58 M.G. Coy. Relief completed at 9.30 pm. Reinforced 2 O.R.	20
Crucifix Corner	13		The Company proceeded to Buy note at Crucifix Corner. Day spent in cleaning Guns & personal effects etc.	20
	14		Company paraded & inspection was held thoroughly overhauled.	20
	15		Day very cold. The Company prepared to relieve No 110 M.G. Coy. The O.C. went up to St Pierre Divion where had been captures the previous day the to under the necessary arrangements for this relief. In the afternoon the orders were cancelled. The Company standing by.	20
	16	3pm	Frost severe the night. The Company marched up to relieve 110 M.G. Coy Cox on arriving at Beta Pos there was but back to billets.	20
	17		The Company returned and set out on line to support the attack which was to take place in the early morning. 4 guns were placed under 2/Lt Hanson in Muff Trench between Stump Road & O.9.1 & other guns under 2/Lt Hatch were also placed on New Trench to follow up the attacking troops. 2 guns under 2/Lt Dunt were placed between Lucky May the Left Brigade Boundary. 2 guns under Lt Gardner were placed between O.9.1 Lucky May	20

WAR DIARY or INTELLIGENCE SUMMARY

No 57 M. G. Coy.

Army Form C. 2118

Place	Date Nov.	Hour	Summary of Events and Information	Remarks and references to Appendices
IN THE TRENCHES	17		The night was very quiet. The two guns, No 1 & 11 HATCH men to follow the left of the 8th N. Staff R. when the attack started. Take up positions about R.15. c.5. 95. The remained in the guns were placed with a view to covering the attack by covered fire. The two remaining guns for any counter attack. Remaining guns were at Battle Hqrs at R.26.b.13.	20 20
	18	6 am	Morning was very quiet. Zero hour was 6.10 AM. The two guns opened such a heavy fire (accurate) the Staff & men on the Tp's. they immediately came under machine gun fire suffered a few casualties only on the .... but within about 50 yards of the first enemy trench. though the did not come abreast of they were heavily bombed & received very T.L. the S.M. Staff & started to come back 2nd Lt HATCH whilst lying along the parapet & the team were struck by a bomb & killed. The No 2 of our was knocked out. The remaining team in a state of confusion fell back to but the gun was put out of action. The staff of confusion fell back to but pl bo ... to one that the Infantry were killed. 1.O.R. King. 1.O.R. Mansley. 1.O.R wounded including & Pte R .... Prendergast. all the Guns matured in lost. The remaining guns in the line were moved to fire at all, many to the units the conditions of the ground.	80
	19		No 50 M G Coy relieved the Company at Sunset & the other Company went back with supports at CRUCIFIX CORNER.	
CRUCIFIX CORNER	to		Day spent in cleaning & rest etc	20

WAR DIARY
or
INTELLIGENCE SUMMARY

Army Form C. 2118

No 57 th. F. Coy

(Erase heading not required.)

Place	Date	Hour	Summary of Events and Information	Remarks and references to Appendices
CRUCIFIX CORNER	21.		The Company proceeded by route march to follow in MARLOY. Transport followed thro' Brigade.	
MARLOY	22.		Company remained in billets. Day spent in preparing numbers at to cheval de frise, ravine shafts, and dumps. Drew blankets and to carried about et 8 O.R. arrived as reinforcement from 5th Base Depot.	
RUBEMPRÉ	23.		The Company proceeded by route march via HERISSART & RUBEMPRÉ to billets	
CAMPLES	24.		The Company proceeded by route march via TALMAT - HANGMISE - HAVERNAS to CAMPLES. Day very hot.	
FRANQUEVILLE	25.		The Company proceeded by route march via HALLOY - SIEGER - DOMART en POITIEU to FRANQUEVILLE. Day very hot. 2 O/R RAMSBOTTOM + C.A. joined from M.S. Depot.	
BERNAVILLE	26.		The Company proceeded by route march via BARLETTE - RIBEAUCOURT to BERNAVILLE.	
LONGUEVILLETTE	27.		The Company moved to post billets via FIENVILLERS to LONGUEVILLETTE.	
"	28.		Day spent in cleaning up billets which not very July cleaning Guns & limbers.	
"	29.		Guns trained overhauled.	
"	30.		Limbers, Guns, Spare parts & belts cleaned.	

1st Lieut. J.H. May
No 57 M.S. Coy

Army Form C. 2118

WAR DIARY
or
INTELLIGENCE SUMMARY
(Erase heading not required.)

Vol XI

Confidential.

WAR DIARY
57th Coy. Machine Gun Corps.
December 1916.

WAR DIARY or INTELLIGENCE SUMMARY

Army Form C. 2118

No 57 M. T. Coy.

(Erase heading not required.)

Place	Date Dec	Hour	Summary of Events and Information	Remarks and references to Appendices
LONGUEVILLETTE	1.		Weather was very cold with sharp frost. All Beds were thoroughly overhauled & repaired. And used into stove round arrangements with the O.N. Diff. R.	SAS
	2.		Training under Company arrangements.	SAS
	3.		The Company less transport went to the Baths at CANDAS. The transport was allotted to billets in the afternoon, but the men carrelled round soon ordered suddenly arriving, the Company was ordered to HEM.	SAS
HEM.	4.		Day spent in cleaning up billets & fetching stores et where ordered up to CANDAS to HEM. the previous Day. that first	SAS
	5.		Rain during the night. The Company paraded for Inspection & Head Dress. Afterwards deficiencies checked. Is was cleaned etc.	SAS
BEAUVAL	6.		The Company moved by Route March to BEAUVAL went into Billets. Lorries were parked on the road outside.	SAS
	7.		Billets cleaned. Trunks repaired. Coothouse built	SAS
	8.		Company Training. Coothouse built	SAS
	9.		Route March.	SAS
	11.		Company Training.	SAS
	12.		Snow.	10
BEAUVAL	13.		The Company moved by route march to BEAUVAL to billets	SAS
	14.		Guns and Front cleaned. Lorries mounted repacked. Billets cleaned	SAS
BEAUVAL	15.		The Company returned to the same billets at BEAUVAL.	SAS
	16.		Company Training.	SAS

Army Form C. 2118

WAR DIARY
or
INTELLIGENCE SUMMARY

No. 57 No. 8 Coy

(Erase heading not required.)

Place	Date	Hour	Summary of Events and Information	Remarks and references to Appendices
BEAUVAL	17		Roman Catholic Service in BEAUVAL Church.	
"	18		Water my own on sharp frost. Company Training	
"	19		" equipment done to billets.	
"	20		"	
"	21		Day was wet	No 1 Section to range. No 2 "
"	22		Company Training	Too hot for No 3 Section true Range
"	23		"	No 3 Section to Range
"	24	9.30	Church of England Service at Mairie, BEAUVAL	
"	"	9.	Roman Catholic Service in BEAUVAL Church	
"	25	9.	Roman Catholic Service in BEAUVAL Church	
"	"	11.30	Church of England Service at Mairie BEAUVAL	
"	"	2pm	57th Coy. had a Christmas sit down dinner & timber etc.	
"	26		Company Training. 2nd Lt DUNT & Pte WRIGHT - left for M.G. Course at Camiers	
"	27		Company Training - No 4 Section to Range	
"	28		Company Training - Nos 1 & 2 Sections Carried to Range	
"	29		A New draft of reinforcements arrived, 7 M.G. gunners & 1 GHQ store	
"	30		Company Training - Nos 3 & 4 Sections Carried & Range	
"	31	11.30	Route march. Training the boots have been much hampered by rain. Voluntary Church Service at the Mairie BEAUVAL	

W. Knox Little Capt.
O.C. No. 57 COY.
M.G. CORPS

WAR DIARY
INTELLIGENCE SUMMARY

No 57 M.G. Coy

Army Form C. 2118

Vol 12

Place	Date	Hour	Summary of Events and Information	Remarks and references to Appendices
BEAUVAL	1/1/17		Company Training. Reinforcement of 1 Sergeant arrived from Base Depot.	
"	2/1/17		Company Training. Nos II-VIII Sections to Range to fire 61 shoots	
"	3/1/17		Company Training.	
"	4/1/17		Company Training. Nos I-IV Sections to Range to fire Stoppages. Bath at Beauval allotted to the Company.	
"	5/1/17		Company Training	
"	6/1/17		No I & II Section to Range at Gezaincourt	
"	7/1/17		No III & IV Section to Range at Gezaincourt.	
AUTHEULE	8/1/17	9.15	The Company moved and by route march to huts at AUTHEULE	28
"	9/1/17	9.15	The Company moved by bus via SARTON-AUTHIE-COIGNEUX-BAYENCOURT. Remainder packing limbers and made Brigade arrangements. Coy Hqrs. BAYENCOURT. The Transport	20
BAYENCOURT			Twelve gun Teams went into the Line to relieve No 95 M.G. Coy. Guns being placed as follows:-	10
			No 1 Gun at K36. 85. 50 ⎫ MOUSE TRAP.
			No 1a " " K34. 10. 40 ⎭
			No 2 " " K46. 44. 87. YUSSIE
			No 3 " " K95. 70. 61. YOUNG
			No 4 " " K96. 81. 29. YIDDISH

WAR DIARY or INTELLIGENCE SUMMARY

No 57 M.G. Coy

Place	Date	Hour	Summary of Events and Information	Remarks and references to Appendices
AUTHUILLE	10.		Position of M.G.'s cont? No 5 Gun at K 10 c. 65. 95. YANKEE. No 6 Gun at K 10 d. 36. 62. WOMAN. No 7 Gun at K 10 c. 78. 22. CROSS ST. No 8 Gun at K 10 d. 57. 24. WELCOME. KEEP. K 9 a. 57. 22 / K 9 a. 61. 22. KELLERMAN. K 3 c. 20. 30.	SD
HEBUTERNE			Advance HQ K9 c. 90.00 HEBUTERNE. The night was fine but misty. Activity very quiet until 6 a.m. when our Artillery commenced a bombardment. Reply weak. Late in the Day the Enemy shelled the following points, HEBUTERNE. the whole of what was shelled, the K. R. Line, the 5 Gun Round around the Major Elms Gun was damaged by shell fire at No 2 position by O.P. was killed. No 7 Emplacement was damaged by shell fire.	
"	11.		Night was very cold with some snow. Activity very quiet.	SD
"	12.		Day was misty but fine. Various Evening No 7 Emplacement sited with stop range night very quiet	SD
"	13.		Morning fine, afternoon rain, late Evening to dawn shorts, slight intermittent shelling throughout the day. 1 R.C.C. O S men. (Sappers) attached to the Company for work on Emplacements for MG	SD
"	14.		Weather cold & dull, night quiet. Activity. Enemy suspect small group (Enemy) out on a par by our artillery at night at about 11.30 pm.	SD

Army Form C. 2118

WAR DIARY
or
INTELLIGENCE SUMMARY
(Erase heading not required.)   No 57 H.F. Coy.

Instructions regarding War Diaries and Intelligence Summaries are contained in F.S. Regs., Part II. and the Staff Manual respectively. Title Pages will be prepared in manuscript.

Place	Date Jan	Hour	Summary of Events and Information	Remarks and references to Appendices
HEBUTERNE	15		Weather cold & dull. Visited my Tank. First towards morning. Activity Quiet. HEBUTERNE — SAILLY road shelled intermittently. Ridges of HEBUTERNE shelled in 3 bursts between 8pm & 10pm. N.C.O. in charge of No 6 Gun reported 2 men challenged approaching his Gun Pits, who stopped that sentry fired. Nothing was seen later on. Prisoners no reported by the R. War. R.	20
"	16		Heavy snowfall. Activity Quiet. Locality by No 1914 shelled.	20
"	17		Weather cold. Village of HEBUTERNE shelled intermittently, increasing somewhat about 11pm. YANKEE ST entrance was blocked by shell fire from front of the Boys & front at night.	20
"	18		Activity Very Quiet. No 7 Gun was relieved, & two Guns from No 58 H.G. Coy, one at REVEL, the other PELISSIER, taken on.	20
"	19		Fine Weather with hard frost at night. Activity Very Quiet.	20
"	20		Weather cold with hard frost at night. Activity No 2 Gun position somewhat heavily shelled between 10am & 11am also at 1.30pm. Within cow frosty.	20
"	21		Activity our Artillery was actively replied vigorously to enemy from Lad Wood, shelled, & good number of Gun Shells being employed. Sally Road & HEBUTERNE were as per usual attention. About 7.30pm there 40 rounds Burst again. Found Shells came into BAYENCOURT.	20

Army Form C. 2118

WAR DIARY
or
INTELLIGENCE SUMMARY   57 M.G. Coy

(Erase heading not required.)

Instructions regarding War Diaries and Intelligence Summaries are contained in F.S. Regs., Part II. and the Staff Manual respectively. Title Pages will be prepared in manuscript.

Place	Date	Hour	Summary of Events and Information	Remarks and references to Appendices
BAYENCOURT.	Jan. 22		No 57 M.G. Coy relieved the Guns Teams in the line. Relief completed at 7.30 p.m. During the first in the line all were one happened with Gun Posts in charge. I took over respired, this enabled two teams to keep their Post in Good condition. Only two Expert ever 2 French Post were reported there was owing to the fact that 9 mm Boots were not available.	S.D.
COURCELLE.	23.		The Company moved out huts at COURCELLE. My had Post in the night. Day time but cold. The Company was Employed in clearing Guns etc all of which were frozen in spite of sterrine being used. Shell proof revised trenches also took place.	S.D.
"	24.		Very hard frost again. Bolt Boxes, spare parts etc cleaned & work maintle - 2 proms taken place as previous day.	S.D.
"	25.		The Company provided a route march through Sailly - BAYENCOURT. All used as a bit Inspection took place. Frost continued	S.D.
"	26.		The Company marched out along the COURCELLE - BAYENCOURT road & Exp Inspector a point where trenches were dug for the purpose of a Brigade manoeuvre. Hard frost continued	S.D.
"	27.		Battle at SAILLY DELL was started to the Company, but owing to the frost no one could be made of them.	S.D.
"	28.	1 p.m.	The Company moved out Hutments, nearly occupied by the 10th M.R. a. to the Bus - ST LEGER Road. at T.19.B.6.A. Frost continued.	S.D. S.D.

Army Form C. 2118

WAR DIARY
or
INTELLIGENCE SUMMARY

(Erase heading not required.)

N° 577 ␣. ␣. Coy

Instructions regarding War Diaries and Intelligence Summaries are contained in F. S. Regs., Part II. and the Staff Manual respectively. Title Pages will be prepared in manuscript.

Place	Date	Hour	Summary of Events and Information	Remarks and references to Appendices
Bus	29.		The Company Took part in a Brigade Tactical Exercise. Weather fine but frosty & a very cold wind.	Sd.
"	30.		The Company Took part in a Brigade Tactical Exercise. Some rain in the night. Weather slightly warmer.	Sd.
"	31.		The Company Took part in a Brigade Tactical Exercise before the Army Commander.	Sd.

13 Dawn U
57 Ind Coy

Army Form C. 2118

WAR DIARY
or
INTELLIGENCE SUMMARY

(Erase heading not required.)

57 M.G. Coy.

Place	Date	Hour	Summary of Events and Information	Remarks and references to Appendices
BUS COURCELLES	1st 2nd		The Company moved back again to the same billets at COURCELLES. C.C. Coy was a few of the line occupied by 58 M.G. Coy. & 95 M.G. Coy (preparatory to taking over.) Coy gains fresh but cold. Lt TUDOR & 2 Lt RANGERTON were sent up to obtain found of 98 M.G. Coy. Your guns sends positions as follows:— 2 guns (as in action) at K.23, B.5,9. R.3 (WATERLOO BRIDGE) 1 " " K.28 d 5.1 M.G.S. (Beaumont) 1 " " K.29 b.8.2 M.G.6. (Campion)	20.
			Known on guns was relieved by Coy. Day out at war found the night day that the position Could be fairly reached by Coy. Snowed at battery activity. Two guns transferred Lt HANSON & 2 Lt BOYLE ordered a similar arrangement to guns of 98 M.G. Coy. Positions as follows:	20.
"	2/3 3rd		1 gun at K.23 a.14 12 BAPOUT 1 " K.23 c.6. 4 MAIN 1 " K.22 b.4. 2 TRAM BART 1 " K.22 d.23 5.2 FORT DONI 1 " K.21 d.4. 2 ROLLAND	20.
"	3/4		CoW + gentry. M Sector. Activity normal. About 11 pm an intense bombardment opened on the night L SECTOR. Enemy activity attn. as usual our batteries otherwise quiet	20.
"	4/5		Weather cold & wet. Visibility poor. Enemy short return. 11 pm burden was staled. Into function of BUNHOW + FLAG AVENUE	20.
			LEFT SECTOR Listening Post pushing on into WUSS Bur Invest into TRAM WAY & FORT BRIGGS still under bombardment.	20.

WAR DIARY or INTELLIGENCE SUMMARY

Army Form C. 2118.

57 M.G. Coy

(Erase heading not required.)

Place	Date	Hour	Summary of Events and Information	Remarks and references to Appendices
COURCELLES	5/6.		Weather cold & frosty. Visibility low. Right Sector Enemy quiet. Heavy bombardment took place on the Right Sector about 9.10 pm. Left Sector activity normal.	800.
	6/7.		Cold weather continued. Right Sector Hostile Trench Mortars. RAILWAY AVENUE, HOOK TRENCH + Trenches near MATTON COPSE and OBSERVATION WOOD were shelled by 77M SOUTHERN AVENUE received some attention. Aircraft was active & a plane was seen to fall in his Enemy lines. Left Sector Very quiet except for a few rifle & Lewis gun bursts. A Tramway position was moved forward to a more advantageous position.	801
	7		Sub-company relief carried out 10 pm to 2 am on the line (Front Line Quiet)	30
	7/8		Weather cold & quiet. Right Sector Quiet. Some H.E. + Gas shells in YELLOW LINE. Heavy shelling on night between 11 pm + 2 am. Enemy aircraft active. An flying flag on no mans land – EASTERN DUMP received some Gas Shells. Left Sector 9 pm 7 pm & am. Front line very quiet.	30
	8/9.		Weather cold but bright. R.Sector Warfield fired at FLAG AVENUE. Res. Roy. Junction, + RAILWAY AVENUE & 11 pm to 3 pm + TANK'N TRENCH. SOUTHERN AVENUE was shelled with H.E. & Gas Field Guns continued firing front line from 12.10 pm to 12.30 pm. Left Sector Quiet with a few shells near HOLLAND + HOME TRENCHES. Casualties 1.o.R. wounded	30
			Front continued.	
	9/10.		R.Sector Quiet until 6.30pm. From 6.30pm to 10.30pm & on bombardment on left Enemy trenches & without immediate result on our front supported their German front line trenches. FLAG AVENUE received a good deal of attention. Our Field Guns fired rapid at 7.20pm in Enemy Front Line. Left Sector Quiet except for usual fire on & off. Casualties 2.o.R. wounded.	30

WAR DIARY or INTELLIGENCE SUMMARY

Army Form C. 2118.

7/7 M.G. Coy

Place	Date	Hour	Summary of Events and Information	Remarks and references to Appendices
COURCELLES	13/11		Misty. Slightly warmer.	
			R.S.Fox. Our aeroplanes flying at times. Sent K.33 Bomp toind on Cabin Corp. Front in deep zonds. Heavy shelling on Dist & Flag Avenue com in front strum between Gispa moonlight.	
	11°		L.Bty. No.2 M.Gpostns received some hits.	
			In 7a Lay until took place on the German lines (a) font line from K.29 d.1.9½. The 10th Inf R. carried out a raid at K.29.6.3.3. (b) German 2nd line from K.29.6.35.0 to K.29.6.57.3. The company was detailed to place a barrage of H.G. fire on the following points:	
			(a) Serre trench from K.30.c.1.8 to K.30.a.2.3½ with 3 guns.	
			(b) C.T. from K.29.b.9.5 to K.30a.2.3½ with 1 gun.	
			(c) C.T. from K.29.d.0.6.6 to K.30.c.1.8 with 1 gun.	
			The 5ith M.G. went west during the day for the purpose.	
			The Barrage on Serre trench was carried out from position in Tripier Trench.	
			R1. — K.33.b.60.56.	
			R2. — K.33.b.63.71.	
			R3. — K.33.b.55.94.	
			To carry out the enfilade of trench K.29.d.62.6. — K.30.c.1.8. 1 gun was placed in position at K.33.b.90.46.	
			To bring enfilade fire on C.T. K.29.b.9.5 — K.30.a.2.3½, 1 gun was placed in position at Fort Briggs.	
			Zero hour 11:15 p.m. at which time an intense bombardment was opened H.G. The tick fired some difficult no hoperious orris of the con, but with the exception of 1 gun a good rate of fire was maintained. Reward: first in all 5.300, Enemy curfing was very suitt, only a fath hombardment was put after reply	

Army Form C. 2118.

WAR DIARY
or
INTELLIGENCE SUMMARY.

(Erase heading not required.)

57 H.S. Coy

Place	Date Feb.	Hour	Summary of Events and Information	Remarks and references to Appendices
GINCHY	12/13		Right & Left Sector. There was a light snow in the right of a general thaw. Fairly quiet what 7 PM shells fell in the vicinity of the SUGAR REFINERY. Our artillery was normal.	SD
	13/14.		Left Sector. Very quiet. Morning misty, rest of day frost. Sharp frost. Right Sector. Enemy appear to be a certain amount of registration, directed the Sack area including GLM Camp. Left Sector. Very quiet from noon. On the part of the enemy. Bright, cold & snow except.	SD
	14/15		Right Sector. Activity normal till evening. About 6:57 PM enemy bombarded our line FLAG AVENUE, FACTORY ST, DURHAM ST, front line all receiving attention. Our artillery replied vigorously.	SD
	15		Left Sector. About 3 am Minnie Trench & Trap Bay mined on Ridge F.A. & Trench in the West battalion H.S. placed at COLD Camp to evade duty.	SD
	15/16.		Quiet. Clear to the front all night.	SD
			Sector. Front 24 9/am enemy shelled Hood 7 of EATON DUMP. Left Sector. Enemy shelling with Trench Mortars. Our artillery a Tm at night. Rest of night. Very quiet.	SD
	16/17.		R. Sector. Ray front by british the afternoon, front support but trench shelled also neighbourhood of RED COTTAGE. Left Sector. Our artillery firing active. Enemy quiet.	SD

A 5834. Wt. W4973/M687. 750,000 8/16. D. D. & L. Ltd. Forms/C.2118/13.

WAR DIARY
or
INTELLIGENCE SUMMARY

Army Form C. 2118.

57 F.C. Coy.

(Erase heading not required.)

Place	Date	Hour	Summary of Events and Information	Remarks and references to Appendices
COURCELLES	17.		S.D.M.G. Sy relieved the Coy in the left sub sector. Coy paid recon'd from Forward Flare Coy H.Q. Took me H.Q. 9/97 by bus in POPERINGHE.	A6
"	18/19		Rifle & Stn. activity. Quiet. Taking H.Q. man and O.O. T.R.3 (WATERLOO) The team were - T. R. Ques. mt. Itch'r call outs used much.	20
"	19/19		Returning wire details FLAG AVENUE. MATERIAL DUMP. Gas activity. Quiet. Relief carried out for 2 mount in the last	20
"	"		Water fine. No days throughout the day. This went out west Enemy activity much. Here Below wounded. The batteries fired directing guns more active until Wound'd. Gas activity normal.	20
"	20/21		Rain all day. Tank went at rapid fire considerable shelling my bad. Enemy activity. No shelling throughout the day. Gas activity. Below wounded.	20
"	2/22		O Dont relieved to RAMSBOTTOM in the field. Water. Bull party. Activity. Point firing the day at sight Enemy shelled at intervals went from FULTON DUMP to PRESTON trench went to QUARRY & FLAG AVENUE.	20
"	22/23		Weather Dull. Enemy Artillery active between 10.1.2.0 from At 10 am a faint bombardment attack accompanied by a bombardment took place. No reply from Enemy.	20
"	23/24		Dull Misty Day my quiet. Our artillery very active on SPREE TAC. FARM and in the Enemy lines. No M.G. SIEPPA li. Company Relief for old Tennand in the land.	20

WAR DIARY
or
INTELLIGENCE SUMMARY

Army Form C. 2118.

Place	Date	Hour	Summary of Events and Information	Remarks and references to Appendices
COURCELLES	24	11.30pm	Orders were received for the Company to carry out the following the Enemy having Evacuated part (1) to take on the N.E. front.	
	25		In accordance with Corps Operation Order O.2807 with 2 Teams at their base, was instructed to report to C.O.C. 5th R. for issue instructions on to survive the Guns forward. Remainder of Coy wanted for COURCELLES at 8.30 am arriving at Buxton Dump & 6.30 pm. First Series was placed in Taylor Trench & march in POZIÈRE, Mining & list post main & steam guns returns 3.30pm - 6.30pm when on England ragtime. Also May Leo on the gas Screen Front Line.	
			Orders received to send 4 guns forward to Keep Infantry LOCS N1 front line of Cpls. Paul, Miss Stemel (2) Snipe (2) Robin (3) Presented (4) GROUSE to ROBICHON W. HAMLETS must found with task Sums, positions being secured by 10pm. Consisting of the winning firm, reference about mentioned Burning this covered and to ROB ROY & BARON WOOD. Orders to supply Enemy Works to W on FIELD TRENCHES. U POINTS Trees returned to Manual H.Q. about 3 am.	
	26/27		Protection for guns midnight (200) Stores but inhaling belts by trench out the day fire was sent by the Enemy R Unit R afforded Than attacked OPEN HOME taken & No extra information received of all.	20
	27/28		Weather fine during midday. Sent some men shelled at entrance the FLAG AVENUE H.S. position murdered The Company will return by SOM.S. Co	20

M.B. Allen (H.D.)
to O.C.57 M.C.C.

Army Form C. 2118.

WAR DIARY
or
INTELLIGENCE SUMMARY.
(Erase heading not required.)

57 M.G. Coy

Place	Date March	Hour	Summary of Events and Information	Remarks and references to Appendices
COURCELLES	1.		The Company moved into Nissen Huts at Bus. Great difficulty was experienced with transport owing to the state of the roads.	SD
BUS.	2.		Huts cleaned. Petrol wagon reserved.	SD
	3.		All guns except from 3 gun material cleaned & overhauled.	SD
	4.		The Company marched to LOUVENCOURT for Divine Service. Have had rug out.	SD
	5.		Heavy snow during the night	SD
	6.		The Company proceeded on a route march. Company Training.	SD
	7.		Pack mule drill was carried out	SD
	8.		The Company proceeded on a route march. During the afternoon lumbers were packed ready for a journey.	SD
MORE	9.		The Company moved by road march to VAUCHELLES and went into billets at LONGVILLETTE.	SD
	10.		The Company moved to billets at BOUQUE MAISON.	SD
	11.		The Company moved into billets.	SD
	12.		Coy rearranged in billets	SD
	13.		The Coy moved to billets at VAUCHIN	SD
	14.		The Coy moved to billets at PRESSY LES PERNES	SD
	15.		Coy remained in billets	SD
	16.		The Coy moved to billets at ST HILAIRE	SD
	17.		The Coy moved to billets at HOUDAIN	SD

Army Form C. 2118.

WAR DIARY
or
INTELLIGENCE SUMMARY.
(Erase heading not required.)

57 H 9 C3

Place	Date	Hour	Summary of Events and Information	Remarks and references to Appendices
	18		The Company moved to billets at BLEU near VIEUX BERQUIN	2.
	19		The Coy. remained in billets. Band, Horse, part & Kit Inspections	2D
	20		O.C. Coy proceeded to DICKEBUSH Schl to reconnoitre positions in the line then preparatory to taking over from No 1224 M.S. Coy	2D
LA CLYTTE	21		Two Sections under Lt Hanson & 2Lt Thornton (West) proceeded by motor lorry into B Camp & Messe No 1224 M.S Coy in the line. The remainder of the Company with transport proceeded by route march to H.Q. in huts at LA CLYTTE. Relief was completed by 2.45pm. Rear positions taken over in the following positions:—	2D
			Front line (New River Trench) (1) ABEERLY Post N. 11. c. 6½. 3. (2) GRANTHAM Post. N. 11. b. 4¼. ¾. (3) WOOLLEY Post. N. 12. a. 5⅜. 4. (4) SOUTHERN REDOUBT. N. 12. b. 2½. 3¾. (5) GODDEN Post. O. 1. c. 3. ½. O.W. Reserve Trench (6) Mc DONALD Post. N. 11. b. 7. 4½. (7) HAWTHORPE Post. N. 6. c. 6. 4. (8) BEGGARS REST N. 6 d. 9½. 6½.	
	2/22		Day fine but cloudy. Night dark with much rain. Activity slight. Boss CARRE receiving some attention. Owing to Coy. new arrival important the support Hd DONALD Post +BESSMAP Post into dugouts for in Mess were not(worked). Works coy. into huts at night.	2.
	2/23			2D

Army Form C. 2118.

WAR DIARY
or
INTELLIGENCE SUMMARY.

57 M.G. Coy

(Erase heading not required.)

Instructions regarding War Diaries and Intelligence Summaries are contained in F.S. Regs., Part II. and the Staff Manual respectively. Title pages will be prepared in manuscript.

Place	Date March	Hour	Summary of Events and Information	Remarks and references to Appendices
LA CLYTTE	22/23		VEERSTRAAT. RIDGE WOOD were both shelled during the night also BASS CARRE. M.G.s active during night. BASS CARRE was shelled during the day, one M/G falling in CHICORY LANE	SD
	23/24		The night was calm except Front lines guns firing slightly. Hostile R.G.i active as usual. Ridge Wood was shelled intermittent by trenchmortar fire & got H.E. shrapnel, also BRIGERIE FARM	SD
	24/25		The night was cold spent a slight frost. Ridge Wood was shelled during the night. Enormous everything was very quiet including hostile M.G.s. Heavy firing took place on our left during the day & for abt ½ hour snipers at the New Reserve line abt foot of ZILLEBEKE RD in T.M.i active	SD
	25/26		The night not extraordinary with a quiet noon. Day night Quiet MM3 & Bopers. The morning line at BASS CARRE was shelled slightly from some enemy T.M. activity of night between RS & Rifle action was considerable during day. Artillery Early morning VEERSTRAAT was shelled considerable during day from 2	SD
	26/27		Field Guns. On 7 the big actions against VANDEBERGEN. Night fine clear growly Day fine Artillery quiet. RIDGE WOOD shelled abt 7.30 pm. In reply enemy McDonnell Post received some shells abt 15-20 light Bangs falling on the vicinity Hostile T.M.s were active against our front line	SD
	27/28		Night mist with Heavy rain early morning. Night quiet except for some M.G. fire towards dawn. The NEW RESERVE line was very heavily shelled	SD

WAR DIARY or INTELLIGENCE SUMMARY.

Army Form C. 2118.

57 M.S. Coy

Place	Date	Hour	Summary of Events and Information	Remarks and references to Appendices
LA CLYTTE	29/30		Night fine till about 2.0 a.m. then rain began. Mostly fine with light wind.	SO
			Enemy M.G. activity during the night usual. The front was put in near HAZING. Capt POPPY & Lieut HARTLEY became 2nd Lieuts being passed.	
	30		The Company tin huts at LA CLYTTE were packed by Lorry & sent to CHIPPEWA The Transport late starting also signal L.S.P.H.S. Coy delayed. The Coy whole had moved up.	SO
	31		The Coy been entrained on this line by 5.P.M. S. Coy Relief completed 10.30 am. The Transport moved to CURRAGH Camp for the night.	SO

P.S. Dean H-M
to O.C. S Bulls

Army Form C. 2118.

WAR DIARY
or
INTELLIGENCE SUMMARY.

57 M.G. Coy.

(Erase heading not required.)

Instructions regarding War Diaries and Intelligence Summaries are contained in F.S. Regs., Part II. and the Staff Manual respectively. Title pages will be prepared in manuscript.

Vol 75

Place	Date April	Hour	Summary of Events and Information	Remarks and references to Appendices
CAESTRE AREA.	1.		The half Coy at CURRAGH CAMP moved up to the CAESTRE area joined the remainder of the Coy near FLETRE.	AD
HAZEBROUCK.	2.		The Coy, with Transport, moved by route march to billets in the HAZEBROUCK area. Day was wet.	AD.
WIZERNES.	3.		Heavy rain. H.33 and which rendered marching very difficult. The Coy moved to WIZERNE area	AD.
Val d'Aquin.	4.		The Coy moved to its Training Area at VAL D'AQUIN.	AD
"	5.		Coy Training, guns shoots been cleaned.	AD.
"	6.		Coy Training	AD
"	7.		" "	AD
"	8.		Divine Service paraded for Roman Catholics.	AD
"	9 & 10		Coy Training.	AD.
"	13.		On the 14th a Brigade Transport Competition took place at OVER CAMP.	AD.
"	14.		Washing Packing & brushes preparatory to a move.	AD.
"	17.		The Coy moved by route march to WIZERNES	AD.
"	18.		The Coy moved by route march to the HAZEBROUCK area.	
"	19.		The Coy, less section 4 guns, moved up in close support to SCHERPENBERG. One section, under Lt TUDOR, 2H WEST. proceeded to CAESTRE to act as an anti-	AD
			aircraft Gun Guard on CAESTRE DUMP.	AD
"	20.		Coy Training. Guns spare parts all overhauled.	AD.

WAR DIARY
or
INTELLIGENCE SUMMARY.

Army Form C. 2118.

59 M.G. Coy.

(Erase heading not required.)

Place	Date April	Hour	Summary of Events and Information	Remarks and references to Appendices
SCHERPENBERG	21		1 M.G.O. W.O.R. were attached to the R.E's at HALLEBAST CORNER & employed in loading ammunition stores. 20 men employed in various returning preparing Rwk. D. Smith & Officer & 20 men employed in returning & preparing Rwk. D. Smith & 20 men attack about M19c.91. a.b (Sheet 28), Ewing at the WESTOUTRE-YPRES ROAD about M17a. 1.9. Remainder of the Coy. employed in parading, returning & training.	20
"	22		Spent in former way	20
"	23		" " "	20
"	24"		O.C. Coy. Visit officer i/c R.C.O.'s proceeded by Bus to reconnoitre the line in the HOOGE-HILL SIXTY SECTOR. Preparatory to relieving 70 M.G. Coy.	
"	30"		The Remainder of the Coy. moved up by motor march to the OUDERDOM Area into Huts.	

R.H.Davis U/Lt
for O.C. 59 MGC.

WAR DIARY or INTELLIGENCE SUMMARY.

57 M.G. Coy

Army Form C. 2118.

Place	Date May.	Hour	Summary of Events and Information	Remarks and references to Appendices
HILL SIXTY-HOOGE SECTOR.	1/2nd		The Company relieved No 70 M.G. Coy in The Hill Sixty-Hooge Sector (Ypres Salient). The Relief was completed at 1.15AM. Coy H.Q. & Gun positions were taken on as follows :- Reference ZILLEBEKE TRENCH MAP 1/10,000.	80.
			1. COMPANY H.QRS. RAILWAY DUG-OUTS. I 20.b.10.20.	
			2. VERBRANDENMOLEN SECTOR	
			SECTION H.QRS. Sunken Road I 28d 20.30.	
			1 GUN AT L.10. VERBRANDENMOLEN I 28d 54.40. ANTI AIRCRAFT POSITION	
			1 GUN AT C.6. GRAND FLEET STREET I 34.b. 54. 92	
			2 GUNS IN RESERVE AT COY H.QRS.	
			3. DUMP SECTOR	
			SECTION H.QRS DUMP I 29 C 20.30.	
			1 GUN AT L.11 LARCH WOOD. I 29.C. 16.89. ANTI AIRCRAFT POSITION.	
			1 GUN AT L.2 DUMP I 29 C 18.32 (A Bombing Post of 5	
			1 GUN AT L.4 DUMP I 29 C 28.32) Infantry is attached)	
			1 GUN AT L.1 INFANTRY TUNNEL I 29 C. 42 41.	
			4. FOSSE WAY SECTOR	
			SECTION H.QRS. FOSSE WAY. I 23 c. 30.20.	
			1 GUN AT L.3. METROPOLITAN LEFT I 29 a. 70. 20.	
			1 GUN AT L.7 KNOLL FARM. I 29 a. 71. 78.	
			1 GUN AT L.13 FOSSE WAY I 23 C. 20.08. ANTI AIRCRAFT POSITION.	
			1 GUN AT MANOR FARM IN RESERVE	

Army Form C. 2118.

WAR DIARY
or
INTELLIGENCE SUMMARY.

57 M.G. Coy.

(Erase heading not required.)

Place	Date May	Hour	Summary of Events and Information	Remarks and references to Appendices
HILL SIXTY-HOOGE SECTOR			5: MANOR FARM SECTOR	50.
			SECTION H.QRS. MANOR FARM I 22 c 70. 48	
			1 GUN AT L 12 STRONG POINT 10 I 28 b. 50. 58.	
			1 GUN AT L 14. VERBRANDEN ROAD I 28 a. 24. 83.	
			1 GUN AT L 15 THE HALT I 22 c. 65. 26.	
			1 GUN AT L 16. THE HALT I 22 c. 72. 28.	
	1/2		Weather. Night calm + clear. Day. Bright. Sunny + warm.	
			Activity. Hostile M.G. fire was kept up intermittently throughout the night. Artillery on the whole very quiet. During the night the Sq. Inf. Bde relieved the 70th Inf. Bde. The following places were shelled during the day. The vicinity of RENNIE'S FARM, bunch of shrapnel on I 28 central between T.M's at the DUMP where a range of the HALT and MANOR FARM. YPRES was heavily shelled throughout the Day. Transport H.Q was established near BUSSEBOOM. G15d.3.3. (Sheet 28 1/40,000)	50.
	2/3"		Weather. Night fair + clear. Day. Bright + sunny. Visibility good.	
			Activity. During the night the 57 Inf. Bde relieved the 70 Inf Bde. Artillery was very quiet throughout the night. At about 10.0 pm. Garrison Horn were sounded 'a gas alarm given N of M.G position L.10. Our Artillery opened fire. Enemy sustained same. It was reported that the alarm came from a neighbouring Division. Activity increased during the day, one shell falling close to M.G.L.15. (I 22 c. 65. 26).	50.

Army Form C. 2118.

WAR DIARY
or
INTELLIGENCE SUMMARY.
(Erase heading not required.)

57 M.G. Coy.

Place	Date MAY	Hour	Summary of Events and Information	Remarks and references to Appendices
HILL SIXTY - HOOGE SECTOR	3/5		Weather. Night fine & clear. Bright morning. Visibility good. Strong Breeze.	20.
			Activity. During the usual artillery was very quiet. H.Q. fire was normal on the front. Hostile firing directed against the DUMP & a few rifle grenades sent over. During the day rather fire on both sides below normal. Enemy dropped 10 shells 50 yards to the right of L.14 Central the afternoon. (12.0p.m. 23.) No damage near Dump. Shrapnel fell around L.10 (12.0 d 5h.40) Between 5.30 & 6.0 pm. Some T.N.T. fell on the DUMP.	
"	4/5		Weather. Night fine. Day Sunny. Visibility fair.	20.
			Activity. Hostile artillery was slightly more active during the night. VERBRANDEN-MOLEN HILL 60 & the H.Q. & the 10. R. WA R. The ground between 5.9s. A fair amount of hostile H.B. fire took place during the night. An enemy plane flew over our lines at 9. P.20 pm. Our anti-aircraft H.Q. in FOSSE WAY (I.23.E. 20.08) fired about 130 rounds & at L.23 it very soon after the gun position was started. At 6.0 pm there was an aerial battle between 6 of our planes & two enemy. One Enemy machine was brought down at L.29 a.5.0. in flames. It was not clear which M.G. Coy fired him in an enemy shell. 58 M.G. Coy. observed him at FOSSE WAY L.29 a. 20.08.	20.
"	5/5		Weather. Night cloudy. Day cloudy & cold in morning, improving till in the afternoon, when visibility became good.	20.

WAR DIARY or INTELLIGENCE SUMMARY

Army Form C. 2118.

37 M.G. Coy.

Place	Date May	Hour	Summary of Events and Information	Remarks and references to Appendices
HILL SIXTY - HOOGE SECTOR	5/6		Enemy Artillery opened Rifled track fire with shells of about and night fire was opened heavily on SUPPORT & RESERVE LINES also on this area. H.E. whizzbangs were used. Our M.G. front were around the DUMP received a lot of attention. This continued until a few later, rather subdued, but to day-break. Day was fairly quiet.	20
"	6/7		Weather fine. Visibility good. Activity. There was increased Artillery activity during the night our Front / workshop, however opened retaliating fire. Shortly after the Heavies were dropping my shorts some fell on the FRONT LINE between arrival of the DUMP. Le Sars Tramway dugout at I.29.c.18.92 was pierced, as also was part of the Tunnel leading from H.Q at I.29.c.20.50. the DUMP. FRONT LINE & LARCH WOOD were badly shelled. One of our guns (I.29.c.20.92) was slightly damaged by shell fire the anti-aircraft position at I.29.c.16.89 was damaged. Ten pole tripod from was fired. During the morning & afternoon Bn. H.Q. & RAILWAY Dug-outs were very heavily shelled, a considerable number of dugouts being blown in as far down as (an enemy aircraft Canadian camp) Gun 1A. Sun at I.28.d.5h.40. fired 500 rounds at an enemy plane.	20
"	7/8		Weather. Night misty Dark. Day slight rain early morning, clearing later. Activity. In retaliation for troops shelling of RAILWAY Dug-outs we carried out a 5 minute intense trench bombardment at 9.45 p.m., also at 11.15 p.m.	20

WAR DIARY
or
INTELLIGENCE SUMMARY

Army Form C. 2118.

67 M.G. Coy.

Place	Date May	Hour	Summary of Events and Information	Remarks and references to Appendices
HILL SECTOR - HOOGE SECTOR	7/8:		The Enemy replied vigorously to our first bombardment, the ground around the Wood, the VERBRANDEN MOLEN SECTOR & KNOLL FARM all received attention. There was very little reply to our second bombardment. A few rifle grenades fell near RAVINE WOOD. During the afternoon a good number of "Minnies" fell around the DUMP, RIGHT BATTN H.QRS. & L10 Gun (I 28d. 5A.10.). We had 1 Casualty. 1 man firing privately wounded.	(A)
"	8/9:		Night bright. Day fine, visibility fair. Night was exceptionally quiet. VERBRANDEN MOLEN RIDGE was shelled with Activity. H.E. about 6.45 a.m. The DUMP, as usual, received a good many T.M's. YPRES was shelled throughout the day. There was a good deal of aerial activity and an Enemy plane engaged a British gunner, shots - it of. During it was forced to descend, later, but out of our friends, shortly after descent smoke continued from where in rear of BEDFORD HOUSE. About 7.0 pm rather sister aim & pm Notes standard flew low on our stars enemy Trenches.	(B)
"	9/10:		Weather. Dark at first. Haze at times Day. Bright clear. The early part of the night was fairly quiet. A warning was received of the likely hood of a raid at all gun teams were duly warned. About 9.30 p.m. the enemy opened a heavy bombardment of this sector, which was immediately replied to by our Artillery & H. C.s L5 Gun (I 29a. 70. 20) at once opened fire on the S.O.S. lines & German Support lines, keeping up a steady fire (1,000 rounds fired.)	(D)

Army Form C. 2118.

WAR DIARY
or
INTELLIGENCE SUMMARY.
(Erase heading not required.)

57 M.G. Coy

Place	Date MAY	Hour	Summary of Events and Information	Remarks and references to Appendices
HILL SIXTY-HOOGE SECTOR	9/10		Our LARCH WOOD Guns also fired on the German Support lines from I.34.a.80.88 to I.35.a.35.10. Rounds fired 1106. It is known was the Enemy opened to have the Trenches. The Remainder of the night was quiet until 5.40 am when the Enemy again opened an outburst from bad wind. The LS Guns again opened fire, about 750 rounds were fired. KNOLL FARM Guns (I.29.a.71.73) also opened fire (1000 yds.) The Enemy succeeded in capturing an advanced Post of the 10th R. WAR R (6 men). Afterwards he did not succeed in reaching our line at any point. Casualties were not heavy. This Coy had 1 man slightly wounded. Remainder of the day was quiet.	S.O.
	10/11		Intense night bark, but first day Burst. During the night the 68th Inf Bde (23rd Div) relieved the 57 Inf Bde in the M.G. Coy & T.M.Bs. The night was very quiet save in the morning the Enemy shelled TRANSPORT FARM, RAILWAY Dug-outs the battered in the vicinity My heavily until about 1.0 p.m. Considerable damage was done some Guns knocked out. The 69th M.G. Coy relieved this Company. Relief completed at 1.0 A.M.	Do
SCHERPENBERG AREA	11/12		On completion of relief the Company marched via St RAPHEL CORNER. CAFÉ BELGE – LA CLYTTE to the SCHERPENBERG AREA. The Transport arrived to our new field near SCHERPENBERG CAMP. The Coy reached billets at 5.0 A.M.	S.O.
	13th		1 Officer & 30 O.R. reported for duty at I.S.21.a.a.a. (near BELLE-EUE) HECTOR BELGIUM, FRANCE. This party was employed for unloading Ammunition at a dump, returned at dawn. The dump.	S.O.
	14th		1 N.C.O. & 20 O.R. reported to 136 Co. R.E. at BOESCHEPE for duty (water supply). Remainder of Coy employed in cleaning up &c. Since open parts etc.	S.O.

A334 (It. W14973 M687 750,000 8/16 D.D.& L. Ltd Forms/C.2118/13.

Army Form C. 2118.

WAR DIARY
or
INTELLIGENCE SUMMARY.
(Erase heading not required.)

57 M.G. Coy

Place	Date May	Hour	Summary of Events and Information	Remarks and references to Appendices
SCHERPENBERG AREA	15.		Coy Training with the few remaining men not employed on Working Parties.	—
"	16.		Beds cleaned. M used a Working Party of 1 N.C.O. + 20 men as supplied for car loading. T.M. Gun unsern. Party returned 4.0 a.m.	—
"	17.		No Work Parties owing to no water, also no available men.	—
"	18.		Coy Training.	—
"	19.		Coy Training. Working Party from Brigade returned for duty.	—
"	20.		On the night of the 20/21st. The 57. Inf Bde. Rec 57 M.S. Coy relieved the 56 Inf Bde in the DIEPENDAAL SECTOR. Working Party from BERTHEN returned to duty.	—
LA CLYTTE	21st		The Company relieved 58 M.G. Coy on the same date, being carried out with the aid of Park Motors.	—
"			The remainder of the Company carried up to Huts at LA CLYTTE, occupying the transport. Relay complete 4.15 p.m.	
			Four Teams with men to the following positions:-	
			(1) HARROWBY POST N.11.C. 6¼.3.)) 1 Offr. Major Cipse
			GRANTHAM POST N.11.B. 4¼.¼.)
			MORRISON POST N.12.A. 2.3) 2/Lt Rogerson
			(2) SOUTHERN REDOUBT N.12.B. 2¼. 3¾.) H.Q.v. TELFORD POST
			S.P.7. O.7.a. 2½. 8.)
			GORDON POST O.1.C. 3.½.) 2/Lt Thornton.

Army Form C. 2118.

WAR DIARY
or
INTELLIGENCE SUMMARY.

(Erase heading not required.)

57 M.G. Coy

Place	Date May.	Hour	Summary of Events and Information	Remarks and references to Appendices
LA CLYTTE	21.		BEGG M.G. REST 6d 3½ 6½ MANTHORPE POST N.6.c.6.4 HORT. MANTHORPE POST. N.11.b.7.4½ MacDONALD 2 Lt WEST. The remainder of the Company were employed mostly in working improvements to various fire positions from about N.11.6.9.7 to N.12.a.1.4½. (References WYTSCHAETE 28.S.W.2 Ed.5.A.) Day wet misty cloudy. Hot in the afternoon. Our Artillery fairly active.	(a)
	21/22		Being given a heavy bombardment at 9.5 p.m. except 10.35 a.m. in region of BOIS CARRÉ near mostly S.93. NEW RESERVE LINE also shelled.	20.
	22/23		Visibility fair. Hostile artillery very quiet except for a few shells into BOIS CARRÉ. Our artillery very active interrupting work. Spent one of our wounded brought down. A.A. Shoot. one of our machines brought down. On M.G. of MacDONALD MANTHORPE POST fired about 1200 rds at gaps in enemy wire but was greatly hampered by patrols.	(a)
	23/24.		Slight rain about 2.30 a.m. otherwise fine. BOIS CARRÉ - ROSE WOOD shelled otherwise little activity. Our artillery very active. Great Enemy activity on our front. 2 of our planes brought down. MacDONALD POST fired 2000 rds at gaps in wire. MANTHORPE " 1500 "	(a)

Army Form C. 2118.

WAR DIARY
or
INTELLIGENCE SUMMARY.

57 M.G. Coy.

(Erase heading not required.)

Instructions regarding War Diaries and Intelligence Summaries are contained in F.S. Regs., Part II. and the Staff Manual respectively. Title pages will be prepared in manuscript.

Place	Date MAY	Hour	Summary of Events and Information	Remarks and references to Appendices
LA CLYTTE	24/25		Fine. Visibility good. 10.30 p.m. there was a heavy bombardment on our right by the enemy replied fiercely on NEW RESERVE LINE in the vicinity of S.P.7 and GORDON POST (heavily strafed). Guns firing died down and rifles opening again for a short time and bright. 2 a.m. our batteries in rear of RIDGE opened were slated. MacDonald Post fired 1000 rds at gaps in wire Monthorpe Post " 1500 " " " " The Transport mule to a field at H.M.D. 2.4. One Officer & 1 C.Q.M.S. reported for duty with the Coy.	(2)
"	25/26		Weather fine. Visibility good. Hostile aeroplanes very active. Artillery confined to Artillery & Rifle fire & Stokes bombs	(2)
"	26/27		Weather fine. Visibility good. Our Artillery very active. Hostile Artillery quiet. Hostile M.G. fire on RIDGE in front of RESERVE REST	(2)
"	27/28		Weather. Hostile Artillery more active. 9 p.m. NEW RESERVE LINE Bus CRAFT POPPY LANE were shelled. GORDON POST S.P.7 shelled. The situation quieter at MORNING. Post MORVEN. 10 p.m. The bombardment died down. Our M.G.s co-operated with Artillery firing 13 or 15 on gaps in wire.	(2)
"	28/29		Weather. Clear. Calm. RIDGE was much shelled. Our POPPY LANE & MORVEN LANE Our Artillery active. H.G.s co-operated again with Artillery.	(2)

Army Form C. 2118.

WAR DIARY
or
INTELLIGENCE SUMMARY.

37 M.G. Coy

(Erase heading not required.)

Place	Date May	Hour	Summary of Events and Information	Remarks and references to Appendices
La CLYTTE	25.		37 M.G. Coy 68 M.G. Coy moved into the huts. The Coy moved to a Camp under canvas near WESTOUTRE. (M.14.b.7.9).	40.
"	26.		Draft ammunition obtained.	41.
"	27.		Coy Training.	

Signed [illegible]
J.O.C. 37 M.G. Coy

Army Form C. 2118.

WAR DIARY
or
INTELLIGENCE SUMMARY.
(Erase heading not required.)

57 M.G. Coy.

Place	Date June	Hour	Summary of Events and Information	Remarks and references to Appendices
WESTOUTRE	1st		Company Training. S.A.A. shot off at night - to prepared Barrage Gun positions	
"	2nd		Company Training	
"	3rd		The Company took part in a Brigade Scheme of Attack in the morning. Brigade Scheme of Attack repeated in the afternoon.	
"	4th		All Guns prepared for action. All Teams given full notes on the plan of attack & objectives.	
"	5th		The Company Section Officers & O.R.'s went up to the assembly area at LA CLYTTE to HARRUM BRIDGE CAMP. Transport remained at WESTOUTRE.	App. A
"	6th	11 p.m.	The Company moved up to its assembly position - 2 Sections to the OLD RESERVE LINE and N12.a.6.9½ - and 2 Sections to the barrage positions about N.12.a.0.3.	R/28/Jun 2
In Action	7th	2.15 a.m.	The B.S.F. Guns and D. HANSON & 2/Lt THORNTON were in position and commenced firing the stay for barrage guns.	
		3.10 a.m.	Zero hour. Artillery, Machine Guns fired just the M.G's Coy's Barrage just fired then fire in accordance with the Artillery program as always firing 250-300 in front of the Artillery barrage.	
		5.50 a.m.	Infantry of 57th Bdr. moved forward according to orders the 8 Team of this Coy followed up immediately in pursuit. Each team was supplied with 2 carriers from the Infantry. Each team taking up 3 Belt Boxes of ammunition on a Yukon Pack.	App A
		7.0 a.m.	The above Teams arrived at the BLUE LINE.	

WAR DIARY or INTELLIGENCE SUMMARY

Army Form C. 2118.

57 M.G. Coy.

Place	Date	Hour	Summary of Events and Information	Remarks and references to Appendices
In action	June 7th	6.10 a.m.	The Barrage Machine Guns ceased fire followed by the 1st 8 Guns or quickly as possible, arriving at the BLUE LINE at 7.30 a.m.	App A
		7.30 a.m.	The Infantry advanced to the GREEN LINE just 8 guns following closely. The 2nd Barrage guns arrived at the GREEN LINE about 7.45 a.m.	
		7.50 a.m.	The Infantry attacked the final objective the BLACK LINE (about O.20.a.55.9) - OOSTAVERNE TRENCH - O.15.a.4.15) by 10 a.m. 12 m. g's were distributed along this line accordingly (As A.5.2?). The Infantry were not immediately met on the 2nd objective to MAUVE LINE (about O.21.c.8 P - O.15.c.55.93.)	
		11.25 a.m.	The four remaining M.G's under 2/Lt LAWSON & 2/Lt THORNTON moved forward to the above line, immediately OOSTAVERNE WOOD was reported cleared of the Enemy.	
		1.30 p.m.	By this hour were substituting positions had been selected for the defence of the BLACK & MAUVE LINES and the presence of his own made known. Coy. H.Q.u was established at SOMER FARM (O.14.c.9.2.) Communication on the right, (a.) from Battalions Head Qrs were kept best. Stretcher bearers supplied with hot food. M.G. casualties killed 1. O.R. wounded 2 O.R.	
		3.45 p.m.	O.C. Coy was informed by one of the Motor Commanders that an Artillery Barrage would open again at 3.10 p.m. the Brigade would make a further attack, advancing the line to ODONTO TRENCH.	

WAR DIARY or INTELLIGENCE SUMMARY

Army Form C. 2118.

57 M.G. Coy.

(Erase heading not required.)

Instructions regarding War Diaries and Intelligence Summaries are contained in F.S. Regs., Part II. and the Staff Manual respectively. Title pages will be prepared in manuscript.

Place	Date	Hour	Summary of Events and Information	Remarks and references to Appendices
La Bissée	June 7	2.05 p.m.	Orders were at once given for 2 guns to follow up this attack to take up positions as soon as possible for the protection of the last objective. 8 guns were kept back for the defence of the Black & Mauve Lines.	
		3.40 p.m.	Orders were received for all guns to move forward, the Ostermann in Y. Graue wand ref. to this new objective. Positions were taken up but had to be constantly moved owing to our guns moving to shelling. Night Quiet.	
	8.	1.45 a.m.	The Infantry commenced to take up a line about O.22 a.1.3. – O.16.a.d.2. O.15.d. 9.2.	Rl 22 S W 2
		7/8 a.m.	The 16 guns of the Coy. were placed in this line — 2 on right flank, 2 on strong point about O.22.a.2.45, 10 distributed along the line (in front near the Ostermann Sapp.), 2 forming strong point on left flank.	
		7.30 a.m.	During the morning a considerable amount of sniping was carried out by all M.G.	
		10.30 a.m.	It was reported that the Enemy were collecting for a counter attack. Fire was opened for all sweeping to most effective on their counter attack. Ammunition	

Army Form C. 2118.

WAR DIARY
or
INTELLIGENCE SUMMARY.

37 M.G. Coy.

(Erase heading not required.)

Instructions regarding War Diaries and Intelligence Summaries are contained in F. S. Regs., Part II. and the Staff Manual respectively. Title pages will be prepared in manuscript.

Place	Date JUNE	Hour	Summary of Events and Information	Remarks and references to Appendices
La Clytte	8	2 p.m.	2 Guns from 58 M.G. Coy were sent up to strengthen the right flank	so
			of " 58 " " " left "	"
		6.30 p.m.	Rifle fire & other enemy activity by 50 M.G. Coy. No Guns retained in the OLD RESERVE LINE	
	9	9.15 a.m.	Heavy enemy barrage was put on on Front & Support Lines, but no counter attack developed. S.O.S. was sent up for artillery assistance.	
		10.30 p.m.		so
		10.45 p.m.	4 Guns from 58 M.G. Coy retired & 2 of our left Guns	
29		1.10 a.m.	2 Guns from 58 M.G. Coy relieved 2 of our left Guns.	
		1.30 a.m.	" " " " " " " " " " Guns completed relief.	
		10.30 a.m.	By this hour the whole of the Teams were collected in the OLD RESERVE LINE about H.12.a.6.5½	
#			Casualties: 1 O.R. killed, 4 O.R. wounded. 1 O.R. wounded. Handed to A.D.	
La Clytte.	10		In the afternoon the Teams moved down to rest billets at La Clytte joining up with the reserve & transport of the Company.	20
"	11.		The Divisional Band inspected the 37th Bde.	20
"	12.		All gun material cleaned &etc.	20

WAR DIARY
INTELLIGENCE SUMMARY

57 M.G. Coy

Army Form C. 2118.

Place	Date June	Hour	Summary of Events and Information	Remarks and references to Appendices
KLONDYKE FARM.	13th		The Company & Transport moved to billets at KLONDYKE FARM. (about M.24.d.7.6.) Belgium. France 2D.	
	14		Limbers washed & repaired. O.C. Coy went up the line to reconnoitre gun positions, into a rest &c.	
In Line	15th		Relieving 56 M.G. Coy. The Coy relieved 56 M.G. Coy into the line. Two sections in front line "support" in GREEN LINE " " in OLD BRITISH FRONT RESERVE LINE. Positions occupied as follows:— A. O.22.b.2.8. E. O.22.a.55.65. B. O.22.c.2.8. F. O.22.a.6.9. C. O.16.c.3.4. G. O.22.a.1.7. D. O.22.a.55.75. H. O.22.a.15.60. Advanced Coy. H.Q. O.7.d.35.05. Pack Mules supplied for the purpose of carrying up of Stores &c. the last two teams relieved by day. Relief completed by 10.15 p.m. Weather Fine. Visibility Good. Activity. Our Artillery active. Considerable enemy activity. Enemy action. Intermittent shelling during night Enemy put a good deal of Heavy Shells fire on OOSTAVERNE Road.	

WAR DIARY or INTELLIGENCE SUMMARY

Army Form C. 2118.

59 M.G. Coy

Place	Date	Hour	Summary of Events and Information	Remarks and references to Appendices
In LINE	16/9		Weather fine. Visibility good. Enemy Artillery started a barrage on our front line about 9.30 p.m. when opened a fire back on ONRAET WOOD to 9.45 p.m. Then ceased. Till 10.15 p.m. Enemy carried out slight counter battery work in respect of GRAND BOIS with OUTTAVERNE WOOD. Hostile aircraft very active from 8.30 p.m. – 9.30. Flying low on our lines. Our Artillery responded vigorously to enemy bombardment between 9.30 & 10.15 p.m.	(a)
	17/9		Weather. Generally fine. Heavy showers during early part of night, also some rain in afternoon at 3.30 p.m. Our Activity. Held guns Kept up fire considerably during night. Intermittently during day. Hostile Activity. Fire on our front line fairly frequent during day except... Shelling of about intermittent fire at 11.0 p.m. Anti-aircraft positions shelled at O.13.6.10.05.	(a) (a)
	18/9		Weather. Misty fine morning. Overcast with heavy rain, clearing later. Our Activity. Own Artillery engaged hostile area during the day. Fire was slackened throughout evening hours, which started till dawn.	(a)

A 5834 Wt W4973/M687 750,000 8/16 D.D.&L. Ltd. Forms/C.2118/13.

Army Form C. 2118.

WAR DIARY
or
INTELLIGENCE SUMMARY.

59 M.G. Coy

(Erase heading not required.)

Place	Date	Hour	Summary of Events and Information	Remarks and references to Appendices
In LINE	10/10/17		Hostile Artillery 10.0 pm Enemy shelled ROOZEBEEK with H.E. shrapnel. 0.15.d. 90.95. DENYS WOOD shelled intermittently during night	20
			A.A. patrol fired at 0.15.c. 30. 85. 0.20.b. 50. 20.	
"	19/20		Weather In clouds during night, rain early morning. Day overcast with some sun. Own Activity. Normal. Hostile Activity. ROOZEBEEK shelled during night. BUTTERFLY Track N.E. of OOSTAVERNE WOOD shelled with shrapnel during the morning.	20
	20/21		109 M.G. Coy relieved this Coy in the trenches from G OLD BRITISH RESERVE LINE arriving there about 2.30 pm M.4.30 from. This Coy proceeded to WESTOUTRE at M15.c.6.5. arriving 7.30 am	20
MISC.6.5	22.		Guns & gun material cleaned.	20
	23"		The Divisional General inspected the Bn.	20
	24.		Church Parade.	20
	25.		Coy Training.	20
	26.		Divisional Horse Show	
	27.d		Coy Training.	20
	30.			20

Watson H.M
Lieut.
O.C. 59th M.E. Coy

SECRET. Appendix A   "G1060   Copy No. 5

Ref Map G.X.3
WYTSCHAETE 1/10000

57th BRIGADE
PRELIMINARY INSTRUCTIONS FOR THE OFFENSIVE
PART I.   No.1.

31st May 1917.

1. **GENERAL PLAN OF ATTACK.**

    (1)   The IX Corps will take part in an offensive, which has for its object the capture of the MESSINES-WYTSCHAETE Ridge.

    (2)   Zero day will be notified later; the attack will be preceded by several days bombardment and will be carried out in four bounds marked in colours on G.X.3 (already issued).

    First Bound .... RED.
    Second   ,, ... BLUE.
    Third   ,, ... GREEN.
    Fourth   ,, ... BLACK.

    (3)   The 19th Division will be the left of the three attacking Divisions of the IX Corps. The 49th Brigade, 16th Division, will be on our right and 124 Brigade, 41st Division (X Corps) on our left.

II. **PLAN OF ATTACK BY 19th DIVISION.**

    (1)   The 19th Division will attack as follows :-

        58th Brigade on Right)   To capture RED, BLUE
        56th Brigade on Left)   and GREEN lines.
        57th Brigade   to capture the BLACK LINE and
                                 establish an outpost line beyond
                                 OOSTAVERNE WOOD.

    (ii) Divisional Boundaries are :-

        Right Boundary.   German Line at N 18 b.23.53 - VIERSTRAAT-
                           WYTSCHAETE Road exclusive, to NORTHERN
                           BRICKSTACK O 13 c 32.88 - SOUTH CORNER
                           GRAND BOIS O 13 c 92.70 - OBVIOUS AVENUE
                           inclusive - ESTAMINET CROSS ROADS
                           O 20 a 30.87.

        Left Boundary.   German lines at O 8 a 00.80 - House
                           O 8 a 80.05 - MARTENS FARM O 8 d 60.05
                           exclusive - BONDULLE FARM O 15 a 10.50
                           exclusive - House O 15 c 55.95 (exclusive)

    (iii) (a) The RED LINE is to be reached at Zero plus 35'.
          (b) The BLUE LINE is to be reached at Zero plus 1 hr. 40 min.
          (c) After a halt of 2 hours on the BLUE LINE the GREEN LINE
               is to be reached at Zero plus 4 hrs 10 min.
          (d) The BLACK LINE is to be captured by the 57th Brigade
               at Zero plus 5 hrs.

III **PLAN OF ATTACK BY 57th INF. BDE.**

    (1) Assembly.

        (a) On Y/Z night the 57th Brigade will assemble as follows :-

        Brigade Hd.Qrs.   N 12 b 6.8.

III (i) (a) (con).

10th Worc.R. Hd.Qrs. N 11 b 9.0. Old Reserve Line.	7.4	WYTSCHAETE BEEK between N 12 c 4.4. and N 12 c 8.9 NEW RESERVE LINE from its junction with POPPY LANE to N 12 a 3.4.
8th Glouc.R. Hd.Qrs. N 12 a 1.7.		WYTSCHAETE BEEK N 12 a 2.1 to NEW RESERVE LINE N 12 a 3.4. to S. REDOUBT (exclusive)
10th R.War.R. Hd.Qrs. N 6 c 1.9. Existing Left Bn.H.Q.		NEW RESERVE LINE S.REDOUBT (inclusive) and any portions of the WYTSCHAETE BEEK in front of this.
8th N.Staff.R. Hd.Qrs. N 6 d 2.9. DEAD DOG FM.		WYTSCHAETE BEEK about BOIS CON FLUENT NEW RESERVE LINE S.P.7 (exclusive) to P & O Trench.
82nd Fd.Co.R.E.(Attd)		P. REDOUBT and SLEEPY HOLLOW.
"B" Coy, 5/S.W.B. (Pioneers) (Attd)		W REDOUBT.
57th M.G.Co. Details.		W REDOUBT.
57th T.M. Battery		SLEEPY HOLLOW.

(b) During the approach to the Assembly Area and until Zero hour, no bayonets will be fixed and no talking or smoking permitted.

(c) Tracks for the advance from the VIERSTRAAT-BRASSERIE road to the Assembly Areas will be reconnoitred by all down to Platoon Commanders

(d) Wire will be cut by Battalions concerned where necessary in front of VIERSTRAAT SWITCH and OLD and NEW RESERVE Lines and on both sides of BOIS CARRE C.T.
Bridges over VIERSTRAAT SWITCH, NEW RESERVE LINE and WYTSCHAETE BEEK will be placed where required, by 82nd Field Co. R.E. All platoon commanders will make themselves acquainted with the position of these bridges.

(ii) Approach March to GREEN Line.

(a) The 57th Brigade will advance to the GREEN Line in artillery formation. The leading sections will cross over our present front line at Zero plus 3 hours and will reach the BLUE Line about Zero plus 3 hours 40 min. where the Brigade will halt until Zero plus 4 hours, remaining in Artillery formation under any cover available.
At Zero plus 4 hours the advance will continue to the GREEN Line, which will be reached at Zero plus 4 hrs 30 min.

(b) Boundaries for Battalions are as follows :-

10th Worc.R.

	ON RIGHT.	ON LEFT.
German front line	N 18 b 23.53.	OBLIGE LANE (O 7 c 10.15)
RED LINE	NORTHERN BRICKSTACK (O 13 c 32.88)	OBLIGE AVENUE (O 13 a 80.50.
BLUE LINE	S. Corner of GRAND BOIS. (O 13 c 92.70)	Junc. of OBSTRUCTION SUPPORT and OBSTRUCTION DRIVE. (O 13 b 35.35)
GREEN LINE	ESTAMINET Cross Roads (O 20 a 20.80)	O 14 c 50.45.

- 3 -

III (ii) (b)(con).

	ON RIGHT	ON LEFT
8th Glouc.R.		
German Front Line	)	- CRATER (0 7 c 4.8)
RED LINE	-) Left Boundary	- N Corner of GRAND BOIS (0 8 d 35.10)
BLUE LINE	-) of	- N.E.Corner of GRAND BOIS
	) 10/Worc.R.	(0 13 b 80.65.)
GREEN LINE	-)	- 0 14 a 90.00
10th R.War.R.		
German Front Line	-)	- OBIT ALLEY (0 7 b 15.15)
RED LINE	-) Left	- Junc. OBSTRUCTION SWITCH and
	) Boundary	OBSTRUCTION AVENUE (0 7 d 75.50)
BLUE LINE	-) of	- 0 8 c 60.00.
GREEN LINE	-) 8/Glouc.R.	- 0 14 b 45.20.
8th N.Staff.R.		
German Front Line	-) Left	- 0 8 a 00.80.
RED LINE	-) Boundary	- (to be notified later)
BLUE LINE	-) of	- CATTEAU FARM 0 8 c 9.4.
GREEN LINE	-) 10/R.War.R.	- 0 15 a 00.60.

(c) On arrival at the GREEN LINE battalions will shake out into attack formation.

(iii) (a) The 57th Brigade will advance from the GREEN LINE under the Artillery barrage at Zero plus 4 hours 40 mins. and will assault the BLACK LINE.
NOTE: The 16th Division will advance from the GREEN LINE at 4 hrs 20 mins. while the 41st Division will advance at 4 hrs.40 mins.

(b) Each battalion will advance in 4 waves on a two company front per battalion. The 2 rear waves will wear moppers up badges (white)

(c) The barrage will lift off the BLACK LINE at Zero plus 5 hrs. and will dwell 300 yards beyond. Patrols will be immediately pushed out as far as the barrage permits.

(d) At Zero plus 5 hrs 30 mins. the barrage will creep forward at the rate of 100 yards every three minutes and will pile up on the line 0 27 d 8.9 - 0 21 central - 0 15 d 1.7 until 6 hrs 30 mins when it will cease unless recalled by S.O.S. Signal (Red Very Lights). At this hour, Zero plus 5 hrs 30 mins., Battalions will push forward strong patrols, strength 1 platoon per battalion, which will follow under the barrage, and will establish themselves on the line 0 21 a 2.3 to 0 15 c 55.95. These platoons in each case will be supported by a second platoon per battalion.

(e) The 16th Division on the right and 41st Division on the left are pushing out similar patrols and it is important that touch should be maintained with both Divisions. To ensure this on the Right and to ensure that OOSTAVERNE SUPPORT is cleared of the enemy, the O.C. 10th Worc.R. will direct his patrols to proceed in a S.W. direction from the ESTAMINET.

IV CONSOLIDATION

The BLACK LINE will be consolidated immediately it is captured by digging a new trench 100 yards to 150 yards in front of OOSTAVERNE TRENCH. The 82nd Fd.Co.R.E. and "B" Coy 5/S.W.B. (attached) will follow the 57th Brigade and will assist in this work. These troops will work under the orders of the O.C. 82nd Fd.Co.R.E. and will be employed in :-

- 4 -

    (a) The construction of three (or four) strong points ~~and~~ *in* the BLACK LINE, the positions of these will be fixed by the O.C. 82nd Fd.Co.R.E. in consultation with Battalion Commanders in the BLACK LINE (~~New Line~~).
        NOTE: The 56th and 58th Brigades are constructing strong points in the GREEN LINE near O 14 c 3.3, O 14 c 6.6, O 14 b 3.5 and O 14 b 9.5.

    (b) Preparation of tracks and C.T's from the GREEN LINE forward.

    (c) Fixing sign boards to facilitate communication in the enemy's trenches.

    (d) Searching for possible sources of water, and dugouts and rendering dugouts which have been partially destroyed serviceable. *(e) The BLACK LINE is to be wired as early as possible*

    (e) Wire and material required for work on strong points is to be dumped at the junction of STUART TRENCH and the WYTSCHAETE BEEK from which it can be carried forward without delay by the 82nd Fd.Co.R.E., by "B" Coy 5/S.W.B. and by small Brigade Carrying Parties to a point near the BLACK LINE that will be subsequently notified.

V. MACHINE GUNS.

    Two sections (8 guns) of the 57th M.G.Coy. will follow the 57th Brigade in the advance and will be employed in supplying covering fire during the advance from the GREEN to the BLACK LINE, during the subsequent consolidation and in assisting to cover the advance of the patrols sent out at Zero plus 5 hours 30 mins. These guns will be under the orders of the /57th M.G.Co. and will be subsequently disposed for the defence of the Strong Points and the BLACK LINE. This should be done in consultation with the O.C. 82nd Field Coy., R.E.

VI. STOKES MORTARS.

    Four Stokes Mortars will accompany the Brigade in the advance following immediately in rear of the Battalion Commanders. These Mortars will be placed at the disposal of Battalion Commanders, one mortar to each Battalion.

VII. ARTILLERY (to be forwarded later).

VIII. POSITIONS OF BATTLE HD.QRS. before AND after ZERO.
    (a) Advanced Divisional Headquarters.   SCHERPENBERG.
        58th Bde.Hd.Qrs. (Right)   N 10 b 3.9.
        56th Bde.Hd.Qrs. (Left)   N 12 b 6.8.
        57th Bde.Hd.Qrs.   N 12 b 6.8.
        NOTE. For the position of Battalions' H.Q. see para 3 (ii).

    (b) Battalion Commanders will move in rear of their battalions as far as the GREEN LINE and will remain there until the BLACK LINE is taken when they can establish their headquarters further forward if necessary.

    (c) The 57th Inf.Bde. will establish an Advanced Report Centre in the RED LINE one hour after the capture of the BLUE LINE, i.e. Zero plus 2 hours 40 mins. As soon as possible after the BLACK LINE has been captured, 57th Bde.H.Q. will move forward to the Report Centre referred to above, the Advanced Report Centre being simultaneously moved forward to the BLACK LINE. Advanced Report Centres of the 58th Bde and 56th Bde will be established in the RED LINE.

IX. In making references to times before or after which operations will commence, the following nomenclature will be adopted in future :-
(a) <u>Referring to days</u>.

'Z' day is the day on which operations take place.
One day before 'Z' = 'Y' day,
Two days before 'Z' = 'X' day,
Three days before 'Z' = 'W' day,
Four days before 'Z' = 'V' day,
Five days before 'Z' = 'U' day,

Days before 'U' day will be referred to as 'Z' - 6, 'Z' - 7, 'Z' - 8, etc.

One day after 'Z' = 'A' day.
Two days after 'Z' = 'B' day.
Three days after 'Z' = 'C' day.

Days after 'C' day will be referred to as 'Z' plus 4, 'Z' plus 5, 'Z' plus 6, etc.

(b) <u>Referring to hours on 'Z' day</u>.

Zero is the exact time at which operations will commence, and times will be designated in hours and minutes plus or - from Zero, even if they encroach on 'Y' day.

X. In making references to times before and after which operations take place the symbols + and - will not be used, but the words 'plus' or 'minus' will be written in full.
In referring to times before or after Zero hour the words 'Zero plus' or 'Zero minus' will be inserted to prevent possible confusion with clock times.

XI. All Commanders down to Platoon Commanders, will keep in touch throughout with the Commander of the similar formation on his flanks. They must know the disposition and action being taken by their neighbours and more particularly so when the units on the flanks belong to another Division.

XII. Commanders are reminded of the necessity of impressing on all ranks under their Command that it is of the utmost importance to keep Divisional Headquarters constantly informed of the state of affairs in order that higher authority may be informed and arrangements made in time to take advantage of success as well as to give efficient support.

XIII. The necessity of pushing forward to their objective regardless of the progress of units on either flank must be impressed on all ranks. It should also be made known to them that the care of the wounded is not in their province as special people are detailed for this purpose.

XIV. All men should be warned against the probable misuse of white flags and signs of surrender by the enemy. They have also been known to sham death and then to shoot into the back of our assault. The possibility of the enemy using ruses, such as giving the order 'Retire', must be impressed on all ranks.

XV. In order to avoid casualties, the whole of the Infantry for the attack up to the BLUE LINE should get rapidly across 'NO MAN'S LAND' and as few troops as possible will be left in our own front and support lines.

XVI 56th and 58th Brigades will be responsible that all preparations are made to facilitate the advance of the infantry through our front system of trenches in the areas allotted to each for assembly.

C.R.E. will provide any ladders and bridges required. They should be placed in trenches at points where they are required and only put in position after dark on Y/Z night.

Care will be taken to conceal any previous preparation for the removal of wire.

XVII Each platoon commander and platoon serjeant will carry a yellow and black flag in order to assist the artillery in locating their own infantry.

The N.C.O. of each bombing squad will carry a yellow and red flag.

Strict orders will be issued that these flags are not to be stuck in the ground in order to avoid mistakes which might be caused by flags being left behind in evacuated positions.

XVIII The S.O.S. signal will remain RED signal cartridges as at present. GREEN 1" and 1½" cartridges will be kept in reserve for use should it become necessary to make a change

XIX In the event of any Brigade being held up, the units on the flanks will on no account check their advance, but will form defensive flanks in that direction and press forward themselves so as to envelop the strong point or centre of resistance which is preventing the advance. With this object in view reserves will be rushed in behind those portions of the line that are successful rather than those which are held up.

XX The numbers to be left behind by units going into the attack will be as laid down in S.S.135, Sec. XXX.

They will be accommodated in the camp at M 4 c 5.0. and will rejoin their units when they come out of the line. In the event of G.O's.C. Brigades considering that it is necessary in order to maintain the efficiency of any particular unit, to send forward any officers or men, they will refer the matter for the Divisional Commander's approval.

XXI POPPY LANE, BOIS CARRE Trench and CHICORY LANE will be reserved as IN Trenches.

STUART trench, P and O trench will be reserved as OUT trenches.

The 57th Brigade will provide the police posts necessary to control traffic throughout the whole length of these trenches from Zero hour.

After Zero hour no one except officers of the Divisional or Brigade Staffs will be permitted to use these trenches in an opposite direction to the traffic.

****

SECRET.

EXTRACT FROM 19th DIVISION OPERATION ORDER No.136.

Reference Map 1/20,000 Sheet 28 S.W.   4th June 1917.
and Special Maps G.X.5, G.X.7,
G.X.8 and G.X.9

OBJECTIVES OF BRIGADES.   1.

5th Objective —
(Right — Junction Railway and OIL TRENCH
      O 21 a 2.8.
(Left — House O 15 c 55.95.
      (exclusive).
to be gained as soon as possible.

METHOD OF ATTACK.   2. The 4th and 5th Objectives will be taken by the 57th Brigade, which will assault on the whole Divisional Front with its 4 battalions in line, each battalion formed in 4 waves.

The 57th Brigade will move off in sufficient time to reach the BLUE LINE by Zero plus 3 hours 40 mins., i.e., cross the old British Front Line not later than Zero plus 2 hours 40 mins.

The Bde. will halt on the BLUE LINE and advance from it in sufficient time to reach the GREEN Line by Zero plus 4 hrs. 40 min. and pass straight through the 58th and 56th Brigades and take the 4th Objective (BLACK LINE).

The advance from the BLACK LINE to the MAUVE LINE by the 57th Brigade will be made as follows :—

Cancelled

On gaining the BLACK LINE, Battle patrols will be immediately pushed out, under cover of the Artillery Barrage and will occupy the North Western edge of the OOSTAVERNE WOOD and OOSTAVERNE SUPPORT TRENCH.

At Zero plus 5 hrs. 20 min. the Artillery Barrage will move forward at the rate of 3 minutes per 100 yards and will pile up on the line Road Junction O 27 d 6.9 - O 21 central - O 15 d 1.7.

Under this barrage the Battle patrols closely followed by strong re-inforcements, will move forward and occupy the MAUVE LINE.

LINES TO BE CONSOLIDATED.   3. All objectives will be consolidated but particularly the

    RED LINE as a reserve line.
    BLACK LINE as main line of resistance.
    GREEN LINE as a supporting line to the BLACK LINE.
    MAUVE LINE as an Outpost line.

These lines will be strongly entrenched and wired.

STRONG POINTS.   4. Strong points will be constructed approximately as follows :—

    GREEN LINE.— O 14 c 3.3; O 14 c 6.8; O 14 b 3.3; O 14 b 9.8.

    BLACK LINE.— N 14 c 8.2; N 15 a 3.1; and at two intermediate points to be selected by Field Company Commander in conjunction with Battalion Commanders holding this portion of the BLACK LINE.

- 2 -

ATTACHED TROOPS. 5. To assist in the construction of strong points the following technical troops are allotted to the Brigade :-

To 57th Inf. Bde. - 82nd Fd. Co. R.E.
One Company Pioneers (5th S.W.B.)

ACTION OF DIVISIONS ON FLANKS. 6. On the right flank of the Division the advances by 16th Division to the successive objectives RED, BLUE and GREEN LINES will be made simultaneously with the advances by 19th Division. The advance by 16th Division to the BLACK LINE will be made at Zero plus 4-20, viz:- before that by 19th Division.

On the Left Flank, the objectives of the 41st Division and times to reach them do not always correspond with those of the 19th Division.

Special instructions as to the advance of the 41st Division have been issued to G.O.C. 56th and 57th Inf. Bdes. and C.R.A. (Appendix 'A')

ARTILLERY. (a) At Zero plus 5.30 three Artillery Brigades of 19th Divisional Artillery Group will move forward to positions about REDOUBT FARM and N 11 b 9.9., and at Zero plus 6.30 one artillery brigade will move forward to a position in N 11 b. These brigades will support the advance of the troops of 16th Division from the MAUVE to the COSTAVERNE Line

MACHINE GUNS. 7.(a) 2 Sections of each Brigade Company, together with the 34th Machine Gun Company (11th Div.) will form part of the Corps Machine Gun barrage which covers the advance of the infantry as far as the BLACK LINE.

(b) The 56th, 57th and 58th M.G. Companies less 2 sections each will remain under the command of Brigade Commanders.

After Zero plus 5 hours the sections mentioned in (a) will rejoin their companies as quickly as possible under order to be issued by Brigade Commanders.

TANKS. 8. One section of "A" Battalion, Heavy Branch, Machine Gun Corps (TANKS) will co-operate in the attack by the 19th Division.
The section will start from a rendezvous on Z day about MOATED GRANGE and will move North of the DIEPENBAAL BEEK so as to arrive about CATTEAU FARM to advance from the BLUE LINE when the Infantry assault is made from the BLUE LINE at Zero plus 3-40.
One pair will advance by ZERO HOUSE - ONRAET FARM, S.E. edge of ONRAET WOOD to ESTAMINET.
One pair will advance by OBTUSE CRESCENT - EVANS FARM to BONDULLE FARM.

G.O.C. 57th Inf. Bde. may call upon the O.C. Section to assist in clearing upon any points which may impede the advance of the Brigade to the BLACK LINE or to the MAUVE LINE.

R.E. AND PIONEERS. 9. Parties of one officer and 10 other ranks of 1st Canadian Tunnelling Coy. R.E. will be attached to each Infantry Brigade on Zero day to search for and mark habitable dugouts and repair partially destroyed dugouts in the captured ground.

CONTACT AEROPLANES. 10. Contact aeroplanes (Type R.E.8) of 53rd Sqn. R.F.C. will fly over the line and call for flares at the following hours :-
Zero plus 0-45.
Zero plus 2 hours.
v Zero plus 4-20.
Zero plus 5-20.
Zero plus 6-50.
Zero plus 11 hours.
These aeroplanes are marked by a black flap attached to

- 3 -

the rear of each lower plane.

SYNCHRONIS- 11. - From June 5th watches will be synchronised as soon as
ATION OF possible after 9.am., 12 noon and 6.pm. from Div.H.Q.
WATCHES. by telephone with Inf. Bdes. and C.R.A.

The telephone will not be used for synchronisation within 3,000 yards of the front line.

An officer will be sent to RIGHT Bde.H.Q. and to C.R.A. with the correct time from Div. H.Q. at 10.pm. on night Y/Z. An officer 56th and 57th Bdes.. will attend at RIGHT Bde.H.Q. at this hour.

SPECIAL 12. Notes by the Divisional Commander for the guidance
INSTRUCTIONS. of infantry in the attack are issued with these orders.

DIVISIONAL 13. Adv. Div. H.Q. will be established at SCHERPENBERG
REPORT from 6.pm. on Y day.
CENTRE.

SECRET.

Copy No 7

19th Division.
G.123/24/3.

57th Brigade
G.831/0/4.

Corrections to
19th Division Instructions for the Offensive
which have already been issued.

18th May, 1917.

1. The hour of leaving GREEN LINE is altered to plus 4-40, and arrival on BLACK LINE to plus 5 hrs.

   Amend first two paras. of para. 2 (2) (d) to read as follows :-

   (d) The advance from the GREEN LINE to the BLACK LINE will take place at <u>zero plus 4-40 min</u>. (16th Division advance from the GREEN LINE to BLACK at plus 4-20.). There will therefore be a halt of <u>30 minutes</u> on the GREEN LINE.

   The BLACK LINE is to be reached at zero plus 5 hrs.

   Amend time on Map G.X. 3 to read plus 5 against BLACK LINE instead of plus 4-45.

   Amend para 2 (8) (i) to read

   (i) 19th and 41st Divisions advance at 4-40 from BONDULLE FARM and form junction at House O 15 c 55.95. (inclusive to 41st Division) at 5.

2. Para 2 (5)

   Amend the co-ordinates of "Point where trench tramway cuts OBSTRUCTION SUPPORT" to read O.17.b.65.50.

19th Division.
18/5/17.

sd/ E.HEWLETT, Lt.Col.,
General Staff.

6.   In making references to times before or after which operations will commence, the following nomenclature will be adopted in future :-

   (a) Referring to days.

   'Z' day is the day on which operations take place.
   One day before 'Z'   =   'Y' day,
   Two days before 'Z'   =   'X' day,
   Three days before 'Z' =   'W' day,
   Four days before 'Z' =   'V' day,
   Five days before 'Z' =   'U' day.

   Days before 'U' day will be referred to as 'Z' - 6, 'Z' - 7, 'Z' - 8, etc.

   One day after 'Z'   =   'A' day,
   Two days after 'Z'   =   'B' day,
   Three days after 'Z' =   'C' day.

   Days after 'C' day will be referred to as 'Z' plus 4, 'Z' plus 5, 'Z' plus 6, etc.

   (b) Referring to hours on 'Z' day.

   Zero is the exact time at which operations will commence, and times will be designated in hours and minutes plus or - from Zero, even if they encroach on 'Y' day.

7.   In order to prevent leakage of information and to ensure that other methods of communication are practised, all communication by telephone and messages sent on buzzer will cease in advance of present battalion headquarters until the hour of Zero. The telephones which may be used by Corps and Divisional Signal Companies and Army Area Parties will be exempt.

   The following methods of communication will be permitted in front of battalion headquarters :-

   Pigeons.
   Visual.
   Runners.
   Fullerphone for 'S.O.S.' calls.
   Rockets for S.O.S. calls.

   N.B. All Fullerphones in front of battalion headquarters will either be issued without handsets, or have the microphones removed from the speaking circuits.

   Existing 'S.O.S.' lines, battery to company, with the exception of buried lines, will be recovered, and the batteries connected to battalion headquarters only. These lines must be recovered to save cable and lessen the probability of messages being carried forward by induction. In cases where the retention of these lines is desired by the artillery for observation purposes, special sanction for their retention will be given by Divisional Commander.

   The necessary orders to ensure that no message is sent by pigeon which contains anything in the address "to" or "from" or body of message, which would be of value if it fell into the hands of the enemy, until after Zero hour.

   (Detailed orders to put these instructions into effect were issued under 19th Division G.123/39 dated 16/5/17.)

S E C R E T.

10th R.War.R.
8th Glouc.R.
10th Worc.R.
8th N.Staff.R.
57th M.G. Co.
57th T.M. Battery.

Battalions, 57th M.G.Co. and 57th T.M.Battery will reach Assembly Areas tomorrow in sufficient time to enable the leading wave to cross the GREEN Line at 9.40.am. (zero plus 4.40). Barrage 150 yds. beyond GREEN LINE.

9.44.am.	Barrage lifts to BLACK Line until			10.am.	
10.00.am.	"	"	100 yds.	"	10.4.am.
10.4.am.	"	"	150 "	"	10.20.am.
10.20.am.	"	"	100 "	"	10.25.am.
10.25.am.	"	"	100 "	"	10.30.am.
10.30.am.	"	"	100 "	"	10.33.am.
10.33.am.	"	"	100 "	"	10.36.am.
10.36.am.	"	"	100 "	"	10.39.am. (zero plus 5-39)

By this time the MAUVE Line is no longer barraged anywhere on 57th Brigade front.

Barrage moves 100 yds. every 3 minutes until zero plus 6 hrs 30 minutes when it stops and is only recalled by 'S.O.S'.

Therefore, battle patrols should be pushed out as soon as possible after zero plus 5 hours 39 minutes.

Care is to be taken that black, yellow and bombers' flags are carried - also flares for all leading waves.

DRESS: Fighting order with caps.

G. Drake-Brockman
Captain,
Bde. Major, 57th Infantry Bde.

4th June 1917.

MACHINE GUN BARRAGE CHART.

Machine Guns doing Barrage Fire will be supplied with a map showing their tasks during the attack. If guns are in pairs with only a few yards interval between them one map will be sufficient for each pair. In this case the right hand gun will take the right half of the task and the left the other half.

The form in which the tasks will be shown should be in accordance with the specimen chart attached. The area covered by the guns of a group will be divided up into Zones and the Zero line allocated to each zone. The Chart should include 10 degrees right and left of Zero. The whole area will have selected targets for harassing fire before Zero day. These will be numbered, and the maps for each pair of guns will include some of these targets. Numbers will not be altered. This will enable concentration of fire on any target by at least half the guns of a group. If necessary the arc of fire could be widened to 15° instead of 10° so as to bring more targets under concentrated fire.

These targets will have noted against them on each map the number of degrees from the Zero line and the Quadrant Elevation.

The area for barrage fire can be shaded as shewn. The line marking the protective barrage in front of each objective will be in RED.

At each 100 yds the Q.E will be entered against the shaded portion.

Arrangements for lifts are thus made easy.

The gunners should carefully study these maps beforehand and practice the lifts and barrages. This is important.

Great care must be exercised in laying out lines of fire and in fixing the aiming mark.

The graphs for shewing the Q.E. for difference in heights in <u>metres</u> are useful as ready reckoners.

19-5-17.   IXth Corps.

WAR DIARY
or
INTELLIGENCE SUMMARY.

Army Form C. 2118.

CONFIDENTIAL.

57th M.G.C. Coy.

WAR DIARY

from 1st July to 31st July.

1917.

Nov 18

Army Form C. 2118.

WAR DIARY
or
INTELLIGENCE SUMMARY.   57. M.G. Coy.
(Erase heading not required.)

Instructions regarding War Diaries and Intelligence Summaries are contained in F. S. Regs., Part II. and the Staff Manual respectively. Title pages will be prepared in manuscript.

Place	Date July	Hour	Summary of Events and Information	Remarks and references to Appendices
Mt WESTOUTRE. (M15.c.6.6.)	1st		Limbers packed & Company got ready for a move up to the forward area, Mt KEMMEL, preparatory to taking over the line. Men cancelled about noon.	S/D.
	2nd		Coy. Training carried out. With 9 men prepared for the Trenches.	S/D.
	3rd		4436 Sgt BURKE R. was granted the Military Medal for gallant conduct in the field during operations against the WYTSCHAETE-MESSINES RIDGE on 7/8th June.	Ref: WYTSCHAETE 7/10,000.
In LINE No. Centre Section 91st Inf. Front			The Coy. headed up via LA CLYTTE to L.mi's relieving Nº 19 M.G.Coy. Coy. H.Q. in GRAND BOIS. 0.13.b.2.8.	
	12		Gun positions taken over as follows:—	
			Nº 1 Section. 2 guns at { O.21.a.3.4½ Known as U1 and U2.	
			{ O.15.b.8.7½ do. Z1 " Z2.	
			Nº 2 do. 2 guns at { O.15.d. O.5½ do. V1	
			{ O.15.d.3.6½ do. V2	
			2 guns O.15.a.4½.7½ do. V3 and V4.	
			Nº 4 do. 2 guns at O.15.c.2.9½ do. W1 and W2.	
			2 " . O.15.a.9.7 do. Y1. Y2.	
			A.A. Position at O.16.b.3¾.	
			Coy H.Qrs) GRAND BOIS. 0.13.b.2.8.	
			Reserve Sec.)	
			Relief completed 11.0 p.m. Transport moved to N.21.a.6.6. Mt KEMMEL.	
			(Belgium : France. 28.)	

Army Form C. 2118.

WAR DIARY
or
INTELLIGENCE SUMMARY.
(Erase heading not required.)

57 M.G. Coy

Instructions regarding War Diaries and Intelligence Summaries are contained in F.S. Regs., Part II. and the Staff Manual respectively. Title pages will be prepared in manuscript.

Place	Date	Hour	Summary of Events and Information	Remarks and references to Appendices
In Line	3/4 Tues		Weather: Night & early morning fine. Later slight rain. Clearing in afternoon.	Ed
			Our Activity: Normal.	
			Hostile Activity: Nora Denys Farm was shelled, also our Front Line.	
			2.30 – 3.15 a.m. Gotha'urne Road shelled	
			4.0 – 5.0 a.m. Eastern edge of J. Denys Wood & Obercom Switch line shelled	
			Remainder of day fairly quiet.	
			M.G. Fire: Our A.A. gun at O.15.a.9.7 fired about 300 rounds at hostile planes.	
	4/4		Weather: Fine, mostly fair.	
			Our Activity: Artillery fairly quiet.	
			Hostile Activity: 7.30 – 8.15 p.m. Batteries just south of Spoil Bank Canal shelled with 4.2"+ 5.9".	
			7.0 – 8.0 p.m. Ground between Zero House & Grand Bois shelled. Shells 5.9".	
			6.0 a.m. 1.30 a.m. Ravine Wood shelled.	Ed
			M.G. Fire: Our A.A. guns fired during the evening of the 4" at hostile planes as follows.	
			O.12.b.5.4. 1000 rds	
			O.15.d. 5.6.3. } 750 rds.	
			D.10.d. 4.7.3.	
			Intelligence: During this respite a 3rd thaw advanced posts were pushed forward by the Brigade about 600 yds in advance of Front Line.	
			16 R. War. R. captured 6 prisoners of 10 Bav. R.	

Army Form C. 2118.

WAR DIARY
or
INTELLIGENCE SUMMARY.
(Erase heading not required.)

57 M.G. Coy

Place	Date July	Hour	Summary of Events and Information	Remarks and references to Appendices
In Line	5/6		Weather. Fine.	C.D.
			<u>Our Activity</u> Normal. Between 11.30 a.m. + 12.30 p.m. our Howitzers fired on our posts in the vicinity of Bug Wood, apparently owing to the fact that a light was dropped by an aeroplane on it.	
			<u>Hostile Activity</u> - Chiefly confined to counter battery work. OOSTAVERNE WOOD + SONSO FARM were shelled intermittently, also an M.G. position around 0.21.a.3.4.	
			<u>M.Gs</u> Hostile aeroplane M.G. action again on our front line 1000 rds fired by one M.M. H.S.S.	
	6/7		<u>Hostile Activity</u> Before RANINE WOOD were shelled. An intense machine gun fire to Am 2 on Enemy outposts fired. Van Hulleg put up a what barrage during attack. Fire on M.G.'s fired (2 am cold). A.A. Fire 12.50 rds. 1 Gun out of general activity	S
	7/8		<u>Hostile Activity</u> 2.15pm hostile trench mortars of OOSTAVERNE shelled 10.0 - 10.30pm FRONT LINE shelled & rally to front of RAVINE WOOD, also DEVH FARM 2pm - SUMMER FARM and IN DER STERKTE CROSSEST shelled.	S
			<u>M.G. Fire</u> Night firing carried out on Transbara, about 0.17.a. 5.9 (750 rds) A.A. fire 3.600 rds.	

Army Form C. 2118.

WAR DIARY
or
INTELLIGENCE SUMMARY.
(Erase heading not required.)

37 M. G. Coy

Place	Date	Hour	Summary of Events and Information	Remarks and references to Appendices
IN LINE.	July 9/9		Hostile Activity? 7.0 - 7.30 p.m. OUTSKIRTS Neuve shelled.	20
		9.0 p.m.	GRAND BOIS shelled with 4.2 & 5.9's.	
			Coy. H.Q. came up for a bit of strafing.	
		3.0 a.m.	DENYS FARM & Wood shelled	
		M.G.	Barrage fire was carried out to support this night 23 rounds	
	9/10	Activity	The 9-Glana. R. attacked our 9 hostile outposts previously intended in upper ½" 21	
			Barrage fire covered out by H.G.'s ZERO (9.0 pm) to ZERO plus 15 mins on	
			line running roughly O.17.d. 1.3 to O.23 C.9.3 als Same firing sniped	
			Then to ZERO + 30 mins guns shifted to a line O.17.d. 7.0 to O.23.a. 5.7	
			2 guns at O.15.d.6,7½ ⎫	
			1 " O.15.a.0,3½ ⎬ guns sniped intermittently	
			1 " O.15.a.3,6½ ⎭	
			37,500 rds fired	
			During the evening 6 or 7 enemy M.G.'s were heard up opposing our front	
			2 guns about O.16.d.8.2½	
			2 " O.22.b.9.3.	
			Heavy firing carried out on around 2000 rds fired	
	9/10/17		Enemy shelled our old 9' outpost continually	
		11.0 p.m	T.M.'s fired at the TOWER	
		7.0 - 9.30 a.m	O.15.a.0.5. shelled.	
			At the commencement of the Barrage for Zero at O.15.c.9.7½ was hit	22
	9/10		out by an enemy shell. 2/Lt M.B. THORNTON + 1.O.R. killed 1.O.R. wounded	

WAR DIARY or INTELLIGENCE SUMMARY

Army Form C. 2118.

57. M.G. Coy

Place	Date July	Hour	Summary of Events and Information	Remarks and references to Appendices
IN LINE	11/12.		58 M.G. Coy relieved the Team in the Line. Relief complete 10.15 P.M.	AA/8
			2 Teams were left behind for A.A. work, one in OATEY WOOD the other near EVANS FARM.	BELGIUM and FRANCE Sheet 28
KEMMEL	12.		The Coy moved to Billets at KEMMEL. (N.21.C.7.5).	AA/8
	13.		Guns cleaned.	
			A working party of 1 Officer + 50 O.R. reported to YORK HOUSE siding for work on an Ammunition Dump. Remainder	AA/8
"			of Coy were employed in strong points in line and allotted (area bounded by KEMMEL-VIERSTRAAT RD, S. DIV. BOUNDARY	AA/8
			& gull through N.17.d.&.a. D WYTSCHAETE. 2 R.S.M.)	
"	14.		Parades as previous day.	AA/8
"	15.		" " " 2/Lt A. OLIVER joined the Coy	AA/8
"	16.		" " " "	AA/8
"	17.		Working Party cancelled. Company training	AA/8
"	18.		Coy training	AA/8
"	19.		The G.O.C. 57th Bde. inspected the Coy less Transport. The 2 Teams left behind on A.A. work, rejoined on	AA/8
			the return (on 11/12) and were relieved by 56th M.G. Coy.	
"	20.	5. P.M.	The Coy moved up via VIERSTRAAT to the line and relieved No: 58 Coy who had 8 guns in the line and 4 guns in reserve.	BELGIUM and FRANCE 28.
			of No:58 Coy, Coy H.Q. on the DAMMSTRASSE - O.9.a.8.2. No:1. SECTION and 4 guns left as Transport Lair in reserve.	
				(N.21.d.6.6)
			The 12 gun positions as follows:- No: I Section :- O.15.b. 86.73 - Known as Z.3.	WYTSCHAETE 1/10,000.
			O.15.a. 96.73 " " Z.4.	
			O.16.a. 72.53 " " Z.5.	
			O.16.a. 90.90 " " Z.5.	
			No. II Section :- O.10.a.10.48 " " 1	AA/8
			O.10.a.88.70 " " 2	
			O.11.a.16.03 " " 3	
			No. III Section :- O.11.a.41.13 " " 4	

Army Form C. 2118.

WAR DIARY
or
INTELLIGENCE SUMMARY.
(Erase heading not required.)

57. M.G. Coy

Place	Date July	Hour	Summary of Events and Information	Remarks and references to Appendices

IN THE LINE.	20.		No. 4 SECTION :- O.9.d. 87.25 - KNOWNS 5
			                                     O.9.d. 93.70 " 6
			                                       O.10.a. 19.19. " 7
			                                       O.10.a. 58.47. " 8
			
			 Relief completed 11. P.M.
			
			 No. 4478 A/Cpl. T. LANGDON and No. 9582 Pte. J. LANE were granted the Military Medal for gallant conduct on the first enemy operation on the 9/10 June.
				ON 34
				
				 ON 35

"	20/21.		WEATHER. Misty. Fine but cloudy. Day fine but windy, only brightening late. HOSTILE ACTIVITY. About 8 P.M. area bounded by DAMMSTRASSE, DENYS WOOD, RAVINE WOOD & DENYS FARM - ROSE WOOD RD shelled. The tripod at No. 5 position was blown up at 9.45 P.M. & Shears S.A.A. Dump was first on RAVINE WOOD. Then shelling continued intermittently till 4 A.M. Day quiet only occasionally shelling. Several enemy planes flew low over our line during day but returned to enemy lines on being fired at by our coy guns on A.A. mountings at No 6. 7 + 8 position. OUR ACTIVITY. Our artillery continuously active, mostly firing on back area. M.G.s. No. The guns at No. 5. 6. 7. + 8 positions fired 250 rounds at enemy aircraft - enemy any sight. The guns of 5 + 6 positions fired from O.9.d. 72.83 on heavily handed over for night firing over, by 56 Coy from 11 P.M. to 3.0 A.M. a Lett gun fired 7 positions from O.10.a. 30.25 and guns fired of positions from a wet sport on bus taken over by 56 Coy. It owner of Toronto fired 30Rds.	ON 36 Ref WYTSCHAETE 1/10000 ON 37
"	21/22.		WEATHER. Night fine clear. Rainy showers at Day break. Clearing later. Day hot + clear. HOSTILE ACTIVITY. Enemy Artillery active 9.45 P.M. & 3.15 A.M. At first a number of gas shells about DENYS F.M. & ROSE WOOD. Bt About 12.30 A.M. RAVINE WOOD, PHEASANT WOOD and DAMMSTRASSE shelled. During day activity below normal. AERIAL ACTIVITY occurred among enemies machines no enemy planes being over our lines.	ON 38

Army Form C. 2118.

WAR DIARY
or
INTELLIGENCE SUMMARY.
(Erase heading not required.)

57. M.G. Coy

Instructions regarding War Diaries and Intelligence Summaries are contained in F.S. Regs., Part II. and the Staff Manual respectively. Title pages will be prepared in manuscript.

Place	Date	Hour	Summary of Events and Information	Remarks and references to Appendices
IN THE LINE	21/22 July		OUR ACTIVITY. Our Coating were firing actively & periodically throughout the 24 hours. Most hostile bay on battn. Our Aerial Activity was considerable and during the night our planes drew enemy fire from position behind HOUTHEM + 10 search lights were observed at work from Mes direction. Our M.Gs fired 300 rounds at Enemy air-craft from guns A+ position in action on Mer 20/21. From 0.9.d.7.2.83 – 2000 rounds were fired at 0.18.b.65.95 – 5.12.L.2.8. From 0.10.a.30.35 – 2800 rounds were fired at 0.18.d.73.55 – 0.18.d.65.95.	M14 WYTSCHAETE 1/10,000
			WEATHER. Warm & Fine – Visibility bad.	
			HOSTILE ACTIVITY. Enemy's reply to our offensive (as detailed below) was described about 10 minutes after barrage. He then shelled rapidly with heavy calibre shells until 8.4 p.m. & after that slow until about 10.30 p.m. At 7.20 a.m. in the morning he attacked very heavily & our barrage (mentioned below) having previously between 3 and 5 a.m. shelled fairly heavily the vicinity between ROSE WOOD and DENYS FARM. During the remainder of the day the Artillery was fairly quiet. The Enemy Aerial Activity was about Normal. Four Kite balloons were up till 7.30 in the Evening. 22 And Plan & were Action seen. – M.Gs very quiet during the 24 hours.	A14/2
	22/23		OUR ACTIVITY. Our Artillery were very active during the night and fairly busy during the day. Our Aerial Activity was considerable. One enemy aeroplane was brought down at 10.20 p.m. in our lines. M.Gs. At 7.5 p.m. 2 guns of Mis Coy (23 and 24) took part in supporting an attack of 174 S. Lancs. on Junction Bldg. according to orders issued by the D.M.G.O. Mountain Farm = 3000. – At 7 a.m. 25 and 26 guns togethr with gun 5, 6, 7 + 8 were moved to 0.16 a 17.95. in order to support attack by the 112 Brigade on Building at 0.23 a.19. Target supported in accordance with orders issued by the D.M.G.O. Member of rounds fired = 8,500. Rapid fire over ordered until 7.30 a.m. + from thier to S.Bowler. At 5h later the 11th & 10th War Gunsbook & 5th permanent junction. During the night 5,6,7+8 guns fired in eight team. Total rounds fired 4,500. During day 2.00 rounds were fired at Hostile aircraft. During the morning between The Coy had 1 o.R. killed & 2 o.R. wounded by shell fire	M14/2

WAR DIARY or INTELLIGENCE SUMMARY

Army Form C. 2118.

57. M.G.C Coy

Place	Date	Hour	Summary of Events and Information	Remarks and references to Appendices
IN THE LINE	July 23/24		**WEATHER.** Fair, warm and rather HAZY.	
			HOSTILE ACTIVITY. Enemy very active during the 24 hours. Gun shells the prominent features of OAK RESERVE and Antwerpstellung throughout. ROOZEBEEK VALLEY and ROSE WOOD were continually shelled between 1 and 2 P.M. In reply to our Barrage at 10. P.M. Enemy put up an extensive barrage (mainly Shrapnel) including ROSE WOOD. H.E. and gas shells & T.Ms on our front line and M.E. on Batty 0.18.c.central. He traffics on 10.15.P.M close to Mac Cup Z.3 v Z.4 position. Between 12.30 A.M and 2 A.M the DAMMSTRASSE was heavily shelled with Light Trench M/Gs shells. During day Enemy Artillery was active then usual. Several Enemy Planes flew low over our line during early morning. Enemy M.Gs. inactive.	ANY WYTSCHAETE 1/40,000
	"		**OUR ACTIVITY.** At 6. P.M a short practice barrage was put up by our guns. At 10. A.M. a heavy Artillery fire was put up. At 12. Noon WHIZ FARM DUGOUTS at 0.13.A.30.95 engaged by our Lewis. At 2. P.M. 0.7.a.95.80 momentary upper. The guns of the Coy at 5.6.7.8 positions fired on Enemy tracks 0.18.a.7.1 & 0.18.c.00.35. and 0.18.a.80.55 & 0.18.d.35.45 during the night. Total rounds fired 3330. 800 rounds were also fired by Vickers guns during the day on Enemy Aircraft. 1. O.R. wounded by Shell fire. 1 O.R. admitted to F.A. suffering from effects of gas shells.	ANY
	24/25		**WEATHER.** Fair night. Rain fromt 5.A.M. to Noon.	
	"		**HOSTILE ACTIVITY.** – At 8.30. P.M. Enemy shelled our front support lines for 1/2 an hour and at 9. P.M. put up WOOD at 9.30. Gas shells formed part of the barrage used in both occasions. During the night intermittent Shelling on. At 3. A.M up to 4.45. A.M. RAVINE WOOD was again heavily shelled about the DAMMSTRASSE Two bombardment was continued through with less intensity up to 12.15.P.M. Enemy M.Gs fired a few bursts onto RAVINE WOOD in reply to our guns as mentioned below. Enemy Planes crossed our lines flying very low between 5 and 8. a.m. One Kite (Balloon) was seen for a short time only about 3.30.P.M.	ANY
	"		**OWN ACTIVITY.** Our guns retaliated heavily to enemy bombardment and continued active during the day.	

Army Form C. 2118.

WAR DIARY
or
INTELLIGENCE SUMMARY.
(Erase heading not required.)

57. M.G. Coy

Place	Date	Hour	Summary of Events and Information	Remarks and references to Appendices
IN THE FIELD.	July 24/25.		**M.Gs.** — The Coys guns at 57.6.7 & 8 probable fired on night targets as last night. Rof rounds expended = 6,000 — Also 600 rounds were fired during the day at Enemy aircraft.	AMS/t.
"	25/26		**WEATHER.** Night calm — Cloudy from 10.30 P.M. onwards. Windy, snowy bright later. Visibility poor. **HOSTILE ACTIVITY.** Less than usual. At 10.30 P.M. ROSE WOOD shelled with 5.9s. At 3.45 A.M. DENYS WOOD shelled with H.E. Only about 60 shells during day. **AERIAL ACTIVITY.** — Nil. **OWN ACTIVITY.** During the night our artillery very active. During daylight less than usual. **AERIAL ACTIVITY.** Very marked. Our planes being continually over enemy lines. **M.Gs.** The same 4 guns as yesterday fired 6,000 rounds at same angle. Ammo.	WYTSCHAETE 1/10,000. AMS/t.
"	26/27.		**WEATHER.** Fine. Visibility good. **HOSTILE ACTIVITY.** — Enemy fairly quiet. Enemy at 9.45 P.M. heavily shelled RAVINE WOOD and OLIVER TRENCH during considerable damage to the latter, with 5.9s. From 10.45 P.M. was shelling of the totally darkness. and between 10 and 11 P.M. attention was turned to our front line mainly. Very sharp and heavy used. During the bombard against the guns at 0.10d.10.4.8 was discharged. Another gun Kepler [?] was set up northwest of tree [?] from 0.9a.95.70. The remainder of the night the Enemy kept fairly quiet. During the greater part RoseWood and RavineWood were again shelled with 5.9s. — **AERIAL ACTIVITY.** Less than usual. **OWN ACTIVITY.** Our Artillery was very active during the night and west of the day. Heavy firing on our right was continued during the morning. **AERIAL ACTIVITY.** — Our Planes were very active. At about 3 P.M. one was seen to fall near OOSTAVERNE. **M.Gs** 5,000 rounds on front line supports Enemy track during the night from 57.6.7 & 8 probable. Casualties — C.S.M. died of wounds — 3 O.R. wounded. Enemy Planes during the day.	CASt.

Army Form C. 2118.

WAR DIARY
or
INTELLIGENCE SUMMARY.

(Erase heading not required.)

57 M.G. Coy

Place	Date	Hour	Summary of Events and Information	Remarks and references to Appendices
IN THE LINE.	July 27/28		WEATHER. Night fine very dark. Day bright and clear. Wind light S.S.W. HOSTILE ACTIVITY. — Enemy reasonably quiet. Batteries in rear of Coys 5, 6, 7 & 8 position shelled with small calibre shells 9–9.45 P.M. Enemy opened Enemy bombardment at 1.35 A.M. over our subject sept. 400 yds. West being opposite mostly TOOL FARM. During this time he also the vicinity of the Coys 2, 3 and 4 position with 5·9s and go about the latter very numerous. At 1.30 A.M. a S.O.S. rocket was seen from a point near the right crest of the barrage line of 2·4·6 gun which was mostly opened fire following on the line roots side of the right crest. Too open the again was fired and so we further opened more heavy fire from and returned to shoot irregular bursts. The Enemy continued to shell this area very heavy. Fire S.O.S. became so thick as to shew our gun number from another. Fire the S.O.S. was over again but much further to the right. The guns at 2·6 also fired 250 rounds when the first S.O.S. was observed. At 3.30 A.M. ROSE WOOD was heavily shelled for a short time. During the day Enemy batteries reasonably quiet. AERIAL ACTIVITY. Three enemy Kite Balloons known between 2 and 2.30 P.M. Planes were not heard during the night. Activity unknown. Enemy plane noticed over our lines 10.30 A.M. Few Enemy search lights activity about 10 P.M. OWN ACTIVITY. Our guns were not so active as usual during the night. At 5.7 A.M. we put up a barrage in front of the divisions on our left. This ceased 5.45 A.M. Slow firing carried on during the day. M.Gs. In addition to firing on S.O.S. lines mentioned above the Coy guns at 5, 6, 7 & 8 positions fired 1030 rounds at suspected enemy tracks during the night. This Coy position at the following points. Kruystra for 500 rounds from R.A. Batteries during the day. Cwt Kemmel by 2·4·6 Coy during the night. 0.10d.10.48/0.10d 08.70/0.nd 16.03/0.11d.41.13.	Q34 OS 34 OS 34 2 WYTSCHAETE 1/10,000

WAR DIARY
or
INTELLIGENCE SUMMARY

Army Form C. 2118

57. M.G. Coy

Place	Date	Hour	Summary of Events and Information	Remarks and references to Appendices
IN THE LINE	July 28/29		WEATHER. Night fine and clear. Day overcast & very threatening. Wind light N.E.	
			HOSTILE ACTIVITY.- At 9.45 P.M. Enemy opened heavy bombardment on our right. At 9.30 S.O.S. sent up but veered away from right & our arc opened fire both supports and support trench. Enemy generally quieter during day as yet. Considerable artillery activity though the sniper shelling the CANNISTRASSE at intervals and also another over a good number of our shells. Also a great deal of heavy shrapnel over our own. During day two other enemy aircraft over very active during night.	A134
			AERIAL ACTIVITY. - very small. M.Gs. Slightly more active than usual during night.	WYTSCHAETE 1/10,000
"	"		OWN ACTIVITY. Very active during. Ground specially on our left and continued steadily up to M.M. During the day usual activity displayed.	
			AERIAL ACTIVITY. very little. Small arms. M.Gs. Nos. 5, 6, 7 & 8 guns fired at night on Enemy tracks 6,000 rounds. At Enemy Planes during day 700 rounds.	
"	29/30		WEATHER. High Fair - Day- damp with overcast.	
			HOSTILE ACTIVITY. Conditions Normal. Very little shelling now by Enemy except on back areas.	
			AERIAL ACTIVITY. Nil.	
"	"		OWN ACTIVITY. Our Artillery fired steadily and purposefully during all the period covered but mostly took order shell order.	A13A
			AERIAL ACTIVITY. Nil. M.G.S. 3,000 rounds fired during the night on Enemy tracks from four stations 5·6·7 & 8.	

Army Form C. 2118

WAR DIARY
or
INTELLIGENCE SUMMARY
(Erase heading not required.)

57. M.G. Coy

Place	Date	Hour	Summary of Events and Information	Remarks and references to Appendices
IN THE LINE.	July 30/31		**WEATHER.** Damp & overcast. Clear, heavy clouds, some rain. The 2 Sections of the Coy which had been out of the line were moved up during the early evening & took up positions for barrage fire by order of the D.M.G.O. The guns at 5, 6, 7, 18 positions remained at their previous night firing test prior to ZERO hour. Also took up positions for barrage fire. All these 12 guns and those in supplementary & emergency constructed by the Coy for this purpose. The guns at 23, 24, 25 & 2.6 positions had active 4.7m in the barrages from their positions. 8 guns were about 0.10.C.22.02 & 0.10.C.25-32. 2 and 4 guns about 0.10.C.15.40 & 0.10.C.1.55. **HOSTILE ACTIVITY.** Prior to ZERO hour the enemy was quite the same aimed. RAYNE and ROSE WOODS received their usual amount of shells. After ZERO the enemy retaliation on the Mouth of the barrage positions and at 23 & 24 the enemy shelling with heavy calibre guns heavily became Z3 & Z4 positions. No natural damage was done. During the day there was no shelling of ROSE WOOD.— Up to 10 AM the enemy continued to shell the neighbourhood of the barrage positions pretty heavily when it somewhat died down. From 2 PM onwards the hostility was very heavy & persistent increasing in intensity as the day drew on. RAYNE & PHEASANT WOODS and DENYS FARM were also heavily shelled. **AERIAL ACTIVITY.** Enemy planes flew over RAYNE WOOD at about 2 P.M. supper these Spotted the Coys barrage guns and the result was the heavy shelling experienced referred to above. **M.G.s.** The enemy machine guns cannot be accurate.	WYTSCHAETE 7/10.000 OOH OPERATION ORDERS No.14 ATTACHED ADH

Army Form C. 2118

WAR DIARY
or
INTELLIGENCE SUMMARY
(Erase heading not required.)

37. M.G.C Coy

Place	Date	Hour	Summary of Events and Information	Remarks and references to Appendices
IN THE LINE.	31/7/17		OWN OPERATIONS. ZERO hour was fixed for 3.50 A.M. at which time an attack was launched by the 38th Brigade which was preceded by an Artillery barrage. The attack appeared to be unexpected. The whole of the guns of this Coy opened fire at ZERO at the rate of fire and on the lines ordered by the O.C. M.G.C.O. and continued doing this stage in accordance with such orders. At about 2 P.M. the S.O.S. line was towards movement in occurrence with further orders issued by the O.C. M.G.C.O. and the Bgd. Guns ceased fire. 6 Our Artillery after the first noticed fire and barrage, continued heavy concentrations for the next over the 24 hours. For the purpose of carrying out hill fallen, 32 crews from the Infantry Bttns of the 37th Inf. Brigade were attached to this Coy for this operation. Up to completion of this date in the morning this Coy casualties during the operation were ZERO hour. Our casualties 4 S.O.R. wounded. One of the attached men machine guns were killed and wounded.	WYTSCHAETE 1/10000 See OPERATION ORDERS No. 14 ATTACHED

Arthur B. Hayward
for O.C. 37. Sh. G. Coy.

SECRET.

Operation Order No. 14.   HOUSE.

Reference 1/10,000 Map,
Sheet S.W. 2.

I. General.

1. The IX Corps, in conjunction with Corps on right and left, will undertake offensive operations on Zero day, the date of which will be notified later.

2. The intention is to create the impression of a serious attempt to capture the WARNETON – ZANDVOORDE line.

3. The immediate object of the IX & X Corps is the capture & consolidation of the BLUE LINE (roughly O.35.a.7.1 – O.s. b.88.20 – O.12.a.35.60 – O.6.b.2.0.)

4. Attack against that portion of the BLUE LINE from HOUSE at O.32.d.05.65 to ROAD at O.11.b.55.00 will be made at Zero hour by 19th Division, and by 2 battalions of 37th Division.

   Attack by 41st Division (X Corps) on the left will be made simultaneously with this attack.

   Attack on line South of the HOUSE at O.32.d.05.65 will be made by the 37th Division at a later hour.

5. Attack on this immediate front will be made by 56th Brigade, and troops will assemble for attack on the night Y/Z, in existing trenches on the line O.28.c.40.35 to O.11.a.5.1.

6. The 57th Inf. Bde. will be in support.

II. Machine Guns.

1. The following Machine Guns will be used for barrage:-

   (a). 57th M. G. Coy.   –   16 Guns.
   (b). 58th   -do-   –   16 guns.
   (c). 246th   -do-   –   4 guns.
   (d). 19th M. M. G. Bty.   –   6 guns.
   (e). 37th Division   –   4 guns.
                     Total.   46 guns.

2. The 56th M. G. Coy. will remain at the disposal of the G.O.C. 56th Inf. Bde.

III. Particular Work of 57th M. G. Coy.

1. Ten Guns will open fire at Zero on the line O.17.b.9.0. to O.11.d.9.7. and will search the ground for 300° E of this line until Zero plus 14 minutes. At Zero plus 14 minutes these guns will lift on to the line O.18.a.4.0 to O.12.c.4.6, and will search the ground for 300° E of this line until

1. 'Zero plus 40 minutes, when they will lift onto the line O.18.b.4.0. to O.12.d.4.6., & will continue firing on and E of this line throughout "Z" day.

2. Six guns will open fire at Zero on the area immediately round SPUD (O.18.b.2.9) MURPHY (O.18.b.2.7) & PAT (O.18.b.45.45.) Farms. This fire will be maintained throughout "Z" day.

3. For full particulars regarding above – O.E., times of lifts, rate of fire, S.O.S. lines etc. – see Appendix.

IV. Positions of Guns, & General Instructions.

1. 8 Guns will be placed in prepared emplacements from O.12.C.22.02. to O.11.C.28.82.
   4 Guns in prepared emplacements from O.10.C.15.40. to O.10.C.1.58.
   2 Guns in present 23 and 24 positions – DENYS FARM.
   2 Guns in or about present ROSE WOOD positions.

2. For distribution of Sections see Appendix.

3. On Y/Z night all guns will move from their present positions to their appointed barrage positions.

4. Section Officers must reconnoitre barrage positions & get their sight lines laid before Y/Z night.

5. All Belt boxes (at present not in use in the line), loose belts (filled) in S.A.A. boxes, & 96 boxes of S.A.A. are dumped in Dug-out at rear ENGLEBRIGH Fm. This dump must be known to each gun team.

6. On Y/Z. night Section Officers will draw from above dump and ensure that each gun team has at its gun position 20 belts (filled) & 6000 rds S.A.A.

7. Section Officers must also arrange for 2 Petrol tins full of water to be at each gun position.

8. Each gun must have a spare barrel.

9. As Sections have become somewhat intermingled owing to late reliefs, an hour will be given later at which all teams are to arrive at new positions, when Section Officers will immediately sort out their own teams, so that each Section will be under its own Officer & N.C.O.

10. Advanced H.Q. will be in Dug-out at O.10.C.00.82, which will be in telephonic communication with present H.Q., & so with Brigade.

11. Each Section will supply One Runner who will report to Advanced H.Q.

12. All Spare Parts Boxes now in line must be returned to Coy. H.Q., and First Aid Cases packed in usual manner for attack.

13. On Y/Z. night rations will be called for as usual by the teams in the line.

14. As many maps as possible will be supplied to Section Officers, showing barrage lines

V. Miscellaneous.

1. It is possible that the 87th Bde. may be called upon to take a more active part than that of Support Brigade.

2. In such an event Section Officers must be prepared to advance with their guns at a moment's notice, so that all available guns can be brought up immediately the Objective is gained, & to assist defence of the newly captured line entrusted to them while the infantry are at work digging in.

   In the absence of orders being given on the spot, the guns should be placed preferably in advance of or in rear of the line, to avoid shelling.

3. It is therefore most essential that belts emptied by barrage fire are immediately filled, & in case of an advance as many belt boxes as possible should be taken forward, & the remainder dumped in a central position near barrage emplacements.

4. Do not place the guns near well defined points. Get 100" or 200" in front or behind.

5. Send back reports on situation - to Advanced H.Q. Early information is most essential.

6. When once a position is taken up, on no account is it to be yielded to the enemy, even if troops on flanks have given way.

7. In case of an advance the O.C. will go forward with the guns. Second in Command to remain at advanced H.Qrs.

8. Acknowledge.

W. Churchill Capt.
O.C. 87th M.G. Coy.

28/7/17.

Copies to:
   Lt. Tudor.
   2nd Lt. Duck
   " West
   " Rogerson
   " Lawson
   " ~~Adams~~

N.B. 2nd Lt. LAWSON will be in charge of No II Section during these Operations.

Army Form C. 2118.

WAR DIARY
INTELLIGENCE SUMMARY
(Erase heading not required.) 57. Coy M.G. Corps. Vol 19

Place	Date	Hour	Summary of Events and Information	Remarks and references to Appendices
				WYTSCHAETE 1/10,000.
IN THE LINE. Coy H.Q. 0.9.a.7.1.	August 1st		**WEATHER.** Fair and cold. Much rain. Atmosphere misty. Wind S.W. veered to fresh. **HOSTILE ACTIVITY.** ARTILLERY - On the whole unusually quiet. During the evening Coy's barrage position shelled. AERIAL - Enemy planes flew over Coy's barrage position just prior to morning "Stand down". M.Gs - Enemy machine guns fired occasionally in direction of Coy's barrage position. **OWN ACTIVITY.** ARTILLERY - Our Artillery were very active, especially on our left. At 4 A.M. a heavy bombardment on the left. AERIAL - Own planes were active and over the enemy lines back & there over lines. M.Gs - Up to morning "Stand down" the Coy's guns fired irregular bursts harassing fire on enemy lines. Rounds expended 3000.-	Ack.
"	2nd		**WEATHER.** Cold and raw. Fairly clear & sunny. Mist & rain and mud 7 a.m. **HOSTILE ACTIVITY.** ARTILLERY Very slight. DENYS FARM shelled 6 P.M. and again at 4 P.M. Shooting was good. AERIAL. Nil. M.Gs Same as on the 1st. **OWN ACTIVITY.** ARTILLERY. Our guns for less active than usual. AERIAL. Nil. M.Gs. A proportion of the guns of this Coy fired harassing fire from barrage position during the time units in the sector 16,000 rounds being expended.	Ack.

WAR DIARY or INTELLIGENCE SUMMARY

Army Form C. 2118.

(Erase heading not required.) 57th Coy. M.G. Corps.

Place	Date	Hour	Summary of Events and Information	Remarks and references to Appendices
IN THE LINE	August 3rd		**WEATHER.** Wet and overcast. **HOSTILE ACTIVITY** ARTILLERY. Enemy shelled our front line slightly at 11 P.M. Between 11 P.M. and 12.30 P.M. He DAMMSTRASSE was lightly shelled. AERIAL. Nil. M.G.s. An enemy gun fired a few bursts during the night over our barrage position. **OWN ACTIVITY.** ARTILLERY. Between 11 and 11.15 p.m. great artillery displayed and a considerable fire was kept up during the start of the night. During the day activity was rather normal. AERIAL. Nil. M.G.s. During the night this Coy. gun fired 3,000 rounds harassing fire on barrage lines.	WYTSCHAETE 1/10,000
	4th		**WEATHER.** Mist. Lintricks of sunshine. Wind N.W., mostly poor. **HOSTILE ACTIVITY.** ARTILLERY - All the day salt and position of this Coy. were shelled throughout the night. ROSE WOOD was shelled and also RAVINE WOOD. The majority of the shells were H.E. and H.V. The main areas were shelled during the day as previous returns. AERIAL. 3 enemy planes were over our lines at 5. P.M. but were took & there are lines on our planes failing in an appearance. M.G.s. Action against front line posts of left Batt. of DENYS FARM. **OWN ACTIVITY.** ARTILLERY. - Enemy lines barraged from 3 to 3.7 P.M. - AERIAL. Very slight. M.G.S. - This Coy. guns fired 3,750 rounds on night lines. During the night this Bayte established post at O.N at 27. 57, 32. 68, 38. 80 and 44. 90 and got	OBK 2 OBK 2

Army Form C. 2118.

WAR DIARY
or
INTELLIGENCE SUMMARY

(Erase heading not required.) 57th Coy. M.G. Corps.

Place	Date	Hour	Summary of Events and Information	Remarks and references to Appendices
IN THE LINE	August 5th		WEATHER. Fine night but windy. Day bright & sunny. Evening overcast & cool.	WYTSCHAETE 1/10,000
			HOSTILE ACTIVITY. ARTILLERY.- Shelled DENYS, RAVINE and ROSE WOODS and ROOZEBEEK VALLEY - 8 & 9 P.M. Shelled ENGLEBRISH FARM. Continuous shelling during night of RAVINE WOOD and OLIVE TRENCH. Fairly light. At 3.30 A.M. a number of gas shells fell in vicinity of DAMMSTRASSE. At 4 A.M. intense bombardment of left Battalion area commenced up to attack at 5.30 A.M. on HOLLEBEKE and FORREY FARM. The enemy shelled HOLLEBEKE at 5.30 and 200 metres east again with a loss of 15 prisoners. During the day Enemy particularly active. The vicinity of the DAMMSTRASSE was shelled for a short time just before noon. AERIAL. How early when nipping went about after which Enemy planes were numerous. M.G.S. much more active than usual. A gun covered the attack on FORREY FARM. This Coy barrage position came into use at about 5 A.M.	M3f
"	"		OWN ACTIVITY. ARTILLERY. Opened fire on S.O.S. lines after attack on FORRET FARM. During the day our guns were active firing on enemy in E of GYM FARM. AERIAL. Now very much activity later after sunset had closed. M.G.S. 3 guns of this Coy returned the front line going by No. 3E Coy at midnight. One gun was placed just S. of GYM FARM and 2 just S. of GREEN FARM. 3 guns were also mounted for A.A. work as stated in mounts position previously taken up when Coy came out the line on 26.7.17. Night firing of a harassing nature was carried out from guns in ROSE WOOD, DENYS FARM and barrage position. Number of rounds expended 4,000. During the day harassing fire was kept up from barrage position around O.12 central, Houthem square and point. 2,000	M3f

2449 Wt. W14957/M90 750,000 1/16 J.B.C. & A. Forms/C.2118/12.

WAR DIARY or INTELLIGENCE SUMMARY

Army Form C. 2118.

Place	Date	Hour	Summary of Events and Information	Remarks and references to Appendices
IN THE LINE	6th August		**WEATHER** — Day dull, clearing later, light shower 5-7 log to 9. Corps.	
			HOSTILE ACTIVITY	
			ARTILLERY Intense bombardment with all calibres 9.25 pm to 10.15 pm and 2.10 am to 3.40 am - a few heavy shells were used - during the day enemy gun were very active Areas usual	
			AERIAL at 10.30 pm hostile aeroplane in neighbourhood of DENYS FARM	
			OWN ACTIVITY	
			ARTILLERY Our guns replied to our S.O.S. at 9.15 pm and to enemy bombardment at 2.10 am - quicker than usual heavy the day	
			MACHINE GUNS 7 guns of the regt. replied to an S.O.S. at 9.15 pm by firing on the S.O.S. lines - on which they continued to fire at a slower rate than at first firing 17,000 rounds during the night	
	7th		**WEATHER** Fine and warm - clearing at 4 pm - no wind	
			HOSTILE ACTIVITY	
			ARTILLERY Minimally quiet during night. 10 rounds H.E. (naval) on OOSTAVERNE SPUR at 11 am. Area behind DAMMSTRASSE shells between 11 am and 1 pm – DENYSWOOD shells will keeping growing day	
			M.G. \ very little	
			AERIAL /	

WAR DIARY or INTELLIGENCE SUMMARY

67 Coy M.G. Corps

Place	Date	Hour	Summary of Events and Information	Remarks and references to Appendices
IN THE LINE	7th (cont?)		OWN ACTIVITY — ARTILLERY Battery fire at intervals — heavy from active a while from Lille AERIAL M.G. 5 guns of this coy fired on hostile lines from 8.55 p.m to 5.40 a.m. - 9,050 rds fired	
"	8		ENEMY ACTIVITY — ARTILLERY Less active than usual, a few fired lightly. M.G.'s Shells on Bath support line for 1 hour. SNIPERS more active than usual AIRCRAFT Slight activity	
			OWN ACTIVITY — AIRCRAFT Intermittent shelling of enemy lines both by night and day M.G. Slight activity 9 guns of this coy were relieved by an equal number of guns of the 112 M.G. coy and were billeted in area by 6.0 p.m. Remaining 3 guns (in front line) were relieved by 3 guns of 112 M.G. Coy during night 8-9 and were also withdrawn on by 6.0 a.m. — All our teams	Refer Ref. FRANCE Sh.I 28
	9th		advanced and coy H.Q's moved to camp M26 C 2.7	

WAR DIARY or INTELLIGENCE SUMMARY

57 Coy M.G. Corps

Place	Date	Hour	Summary of Events and Information	Remarks and references to Appendices
M26 C.22	10th August	10.10 am	Lt. A.B. HAYWARD proceeded to join Coy (named) as 21 M.G. Coy. Coy. foot inspection — 2.30 pm. packing limbers.	
"		7 pm	Cleaning of clothing and equipment — clothing parade. Coy moved to BAILLEUL by route march entraining 8.30 pm till 11.15 pm. Moved by train at 11.30 pm to WIZERNES arriving at 3.45 am. Detraining till 6.15 — Breakfasts 6.20 am	
"	11th	7 am	Moved by route march to WATTERDAL arriving in billets by 10 am.	
WATTERDAL	12th	9.30 am	Section parades for cleaning fire arms spare parts — Pay parade — Coy attended Brigade parade of inspection by Army Commander	R. Aug/16 14 Feb/1916 G.A.
"	13		2/Lt V.W. RUSSELL joined for duty with the Coy.	
"	14th		M.G. Training 9.30 am to 12.30 pm. C.O.E. expressed his desire that troops should have an easy day. Football in afternoon	
"	15th		M.G. Training 9.0 am to 12.30 pm and 2.0 pm to 3.30 pm — Football 5.30 pm to 6.30 pm.	
"	16th		M.G. Training 9 am to 12.30 pm — cleaning gun & limbers in afternoon	

Army Form C. 2118.

WAR DIARY
or
INTELLIGENCE SUMMARY

(Erase heading not required.)

5-7 by Lt H. G. Cope

Instructions regarding War Diaries and Intelligence Summaries are contained in F.S. Regs., Part II. and the Staff Manual respectively. Title Pages will be prepared in manuscript.

Place	Date	Hour	Summary of Events and Information	Remarks and references to Appendices
WATERDAL	17th August		M.G. Training 9-5 am & 2-30 pm — clearing trails, timber in afternoon	
"	18th		Bn. Coy training RSM parade for prospective recipients of medal ribbons away by Div. Commander. 10th HARLETTES R.S.C. Sports	
"	19th		Church parade — R.S.C. Sports	
"	20th to 21st		Work in timber — Battn. exercise — Divl. Sports	
			Tactical scheme by 6 Coys. of the Bgd. with 10th R. War. Regt. in attack on JUNCTION BUILDINGS – TINY FM + GROENE INDE CABARET on Training Ground 1 mile E.N.E. of HARLETTES Remainder of Coys. range — (E16/p50/55) Owl area in afternoon	refer back HAZEBROUCK 5A
	22nd		By turns of Bn., Coy. moved to COLOMBERT changing billets on R. 5.6.&7.	Refer back CALAIS 13
COLOMBERT	23rd August		M.G. Training 9.0 am to 3 pm.	
"	24th	9.0 am	Working timber — clearing guns returning carts in afternoon checking training & pans in afternoon	
"	25th	9.30 am	Tactical scheme on high ground ½ mile N. of COLOMBERT STA. Bn. Transport Show & Cricket match vs afternoon	
"	26th	9 am	Physical Training and range with M.G.3 — rifle another practice transport moved to LARTS (HAZEBROUCK 5A) at 11.25 am	
"	27th	9 am	Route March till 12-10 — afternoon football	

2449 Wt. W14957/M90 750,000 1/16 J.B.C. & A. Forms/C.2118/12.

WAR DIARY
or
INTELLIGENCE SUMMARY

(Erase heading not required.) 57 Coy. M.G. Corps.

Army Form C. 2118.

Place	Date	Hour	Summary of Events and Information	Remarks and references to Appendices
CALOM BERT	28th	8.45 a.m	Coy. moved by 'bus to billets near STAPLES arriving at 7.30 p.m. Transport formed at 4 p.m.	(HAZEBROUCK STA)
STAPLES	29th	9.0 am	Coy & Transport moved by route march via HAZEBROUCK - STRAZEELE - billets in MERRIS arriving at 2.15.	
MERRIS	30th		Horse lines fixed - limbers drawn in field 200y S of MERRIS church -	
"	31st		Gun & Spare parts cleaned in afternoon. In Q. training 9 - 12.30 & 2 - 3.	

A Shufflewro
W. for O.C. 57 M.G. Coy.
31/5/17 MERRIS.

WAR DIARY
or
INTELLIGENCE SUMMARY
(Erase heading not required.)

Army Form C. 2118

57 Coy. 1st/1st C. Corps M.G.C.

Place	Date Sep/17	Hour	Summary of Events and Information	Remarks and references to Appendices
MERRIS	1st	8.30am	Coy went to NCOs B com Rifle range & fired classification practice. Coy including transport kept fit etc in afternoon spotclean. Change of billets. Guns cleaned in afternoon.	Ref HAZEBROUCK 5A H.H.
"	2nd	9.0am	Coy carried out a Barrage scheme for which, to all ranks the Coy Nuc. gunners w. with Barrage took the road with 12.2 guns etc cleaned in afternoon.	H.H.
"	3rd	9.0am	Coy paraded & marched to field about MOOLENACKER & took part in 68th attack & refused on a Brigade scheme. Guns etc cleaned in afternoon. Teams & men rest in H.Q. kitchen.	H.H.
"	4th	9.30am	Coy carries out a barrage fire scheme in field 200 x S of MERRIS Church. - afternoon inspection of Respirators by Div. Gas N.C.O.	H.H.
"	5th	9 am	Coy Training in morning - guns cleaned in afternoon.	H.H.
"	6th	9am	Coy moved to Camp M 13.6.79. near WESTOUTRE	Refer Sheet 28 H.H.
WESTOUTRE	7th	9am	Physical Training & barrage scheme including marching over land by Coy.	H.H.
"	8th	9 am	Physical Training & repetition of yesterdays scheme with adjustments.	H.H.
"	8th	9am	Coy attended a flank from the (5th) Officers scheme in BOESCHEPE TRAINING AREA (MT KOKERE 5LE)	"

WAR DIARY or INTELLIGENCE SUMMARY

Army Form C. 2118

57th Bny. M.G. Corps

Place	Date	Hour	Summary of Events and Information	Remarks and references to Appendices
WESTOUTRE	Sept 10th		Physical Training or Revelin. fine & fair material along rail. Camp at WESTOUTRE	
"	11th	10 am	Coy. moved to BUTTERFLY FM (N.19.a.6.9)	
N19.a.6.9	12th		Preparing gun spare material for the line in the morning – 8 guns of the line both on & position of 112 Coy M.G.C. in afternoon relieving.	
IN THE LINE	12th/13		WEATHER. High oak – Day dull – visibility fair up to 2000x – wind E.S.E. road ACTIVITY (ARTY) Dull slight – Hill 60 YELMING ZILLEBEEKE shelled slightly – Done for shells between 1 am + 2 am. (AIRCRAFT) Considerable activity on both sides – Enemy aircraft were busy all night – They picked up one of our 'planes after 10 m heavy shells. 2 enemy 'planes came over our line at 5:30 a.m (M.G.) Very settled	
"	13/14		50 rounds A.A. were fired from our M.G. at CATERPILLAR position Remainder of Coy & Transport moved to Camp at N.15.a.8.9 WEATHER. Slight mist rising at intervals. Wind S.E. strong – Day fine between ACTIVITY (ARTY) Enemy artillery only indulged in indiscriminate shelling Our S.O.S. was sent up twice on left at 3:15 a.m. – an artillery reply promptly (AERIAL) SLIGHT – our planes very active. (M.C.) One enemy M.G. active firing eight against line CORNER JUNO. – I.36.a.5.0. and against Ruilway cutting I.35.a. R.S. firing at extreme range	Sheet 2& Report HALLEBAST Trench Meth

WAR DIARY or INTELLIGENCE SUMMARY

Army Form C. 2118

57 Coy M.G. Corps

Place	Date	Hour	Summary of Events and Information	Remarks and references to Appendices
IN THE LINE	13th (cont'd) 14/9/15		M.G.s (cont'd) M.G. carries out harassing fire against enemy tracks during night (2500 rds.) Working party sent up from camp to work on barrage position.	
"			WEATHER Dark night - some rain - fine day - visibility indt.	
			ACTIVITY (Arty) Enemy enjoyed his usual targets - a little of our position barrage at 8.30 a.m. an enemy retaliation indicated on KLEIN ZILLEBEKE otherwise normal activity. (Aerial) 13 enemy planes found our guns in a S. direction at 12 noon. which we heavily engaged by M.G.s gun fire M.G. Gun activity than normal - we fired 7000 rounds on enemy tracks.	
N.15.D.89	16th		Coy. relieving lay at M.G. by 11.10 a.m. 15/9/17. Moving to camp N.15.D.89. Cleaning guns - equipment etc. Working party sent this afternoon on barrage position.	Rifles Sheet 28 ∥
"	17th		Cleaning guns - examining belts, filling belts - inspection of Iron Rations - fatigue parade - Carrying party sent to barrage position with material.	∥
"	18th		Practice barrage scheme and prepared all equipment for action.	∥
"	19th	9.0 a.m	Various inspection preparation for action. In afternoon 4 Secs of this Coy. moves up to intermediate position about THE CATERPILLAR Rifles These teams moves to assault positions about KLEINE ZILLEBEKE Hollebeke map	

WAR DIARY
or
INTELLIGENCE SUMMARY
(Erase heading not required.)

57 Coy. A.C. Corps

Army Form C. 2118

Place	Date	Hour	Summary of Events and Information	Remarks and references to Appendices
	19/Apr 1?		Getting into position by 1 a.m. (20h)	Ht
IN THE LINE	20th	5.40 a.m.	This Coy took part in a M.G. barrage and attack of a line WOOD - FM - NORTH FM (approx). 6 guns took part in the barrage under 2/Lt ROGERSON and 2/Lt RUSSELL - 4 guns went forward behind the last wave of the first line of attack & 4 guns behind the last wave of the attack. The former under 2/Lt WEST to establish GREEN LINE and latter under Lt DUNT to take up position between BLUE and GREEN lines. 2 guns under 2/Lt OLIVER advanced under escort of 1 platoon of N. STAFFS REGT under Lt CARVER M.C. to serve on junction with the Div. on our left. Nine last named guns did exc'dent'y good work & the men of the unit are spoken of in very high terms by 2/Lt CARVER M.C. especially Sgt. WRIGHT - L/Cpl RIDDOCH & Pte GOMERSALL D.C.M. This battle lasted until 8 o/c am and towards of the day we consolidated such on our front. All enemy weapons became non active owing this night but at long range. Relief of tell SAK covered cradle - nothing extraordinary happened on our front. HH	Refer hypo HOLLDRIKE

Army Form C. 2118.

WAR DIARY
or
INTELLIGENCE SUMMARY.
(Erase heading not required.)

67 Coy M.G. Corps

Place	Date	Hour	Summary of Events and Information	Remarks and references to Appendices
IN THE LINE	22nd Sept		There was several severe H.E barrages by the enemy during the day, apparently to interfere with our communication. This Coy was relieved during the night & early morning (23) by 112 Coy M.G. Coy. All reach forward to camp near SEIGE FARM) on N 15 D 29.	Refer Map SHEET 28
N 15 D 29	23rd	9.am	Cleaning of guns, gun material & personnel	Htt
	24th	9.am	Guns boiled out - ammunition cleaned - clothing issues & exchanges	Htt
		P.m.	Physical Training	
	25th	9.am	Cleaning - afternoon - a football field was prepared	Htt
	26th	9.am	Physical Training - preparing guns etc. to section	Htt
	27 to		LT GRIFFITHS R. & 2/Lt WARD A.E. joined Coy. Football in afternoon. 8 guns of the Coy were to the line of take over from 112 M G C	Htt
IN THE LINE	28th		One of time Section of guns was pulled out of action en route at 3.45 am and the arrived at JACKSON'S DUMP in place thereof at 6.0 am. This relief was completed by 10.6. a.m. Coy was found snug in battle dress except for one W. of hut GATE R.PILLAR - ETANG DE ZILLEBEKE	Refer heat map HOLLEBEKE

Army Form C. 2118.

WAR DIARY
or
INTELLIGENCE SUMMARY.

(Erase heading not required.)

57 Bde. Hy. A. Cps/o

Instructions regarding War Diaries and Intelligence Summaries are contained in F.S. Regs., Part II. and the Staff Manual respectively. Title pages will be prepared in manuscript.

Place	Date	Hour	Summary of Events and Information	Remarks and references to Appendices
IN THE LINE	Sept 28		Shore enemy artillery was very active with all sorts of shells - including gas shells. Civilian houses wrecked at SEIGE FM and cook house & latrine were moved to 100x distance from during shelling on far side. Football in afternoon.	#
	29th		Pour considerable artillery activity on both sides and several S.O.S signals were replied to very promptly by troops on the right – Guns & men's equipment were cleaned at SEIGE F^m Football in afternoon	#
	to 30		Shells been fairly quiet day & night – except for a heavy barrage on our left 4 a.m. – 5 a.m. Back area bombed severely at night.	#

Lewis Newman
Lt Col.
In Ct. 57 Bde/ Coy

A 5834 Wt.W4973/M687 750,000 8/16 D. D. & L. Ltd. Forms/C.2118/13.

WAR DIARY or INTELLIGENCE SUMMARY

Army Form C. 2118.

57th Coy Aus G.C.of/o 19/10/21

Place	Date Oct	Hour	Summary of Events and Information	Remarks and references to Appendices
In the line	1		4 guns of the Coy in the left sector 4 guns in BULGAR WOOD. Barrage fire in front of Sircet. All officers in sector under command of O.C. 58 In Fd Coy. We had 12 in the line. ACTIVITY (Enemy) Artillery very active against MT. SORREL, ZWARTELEEN, SHREWSBURY and track leading to I 29 d 30 e. Aircraft flew very high & very seldom in our lines. Machine gun & trench fire.	Refer HOLLEBEKE B.10000
"	2		Enemy activity normal - fire against RAILWAY CUTTING by HILL 60, HILL 60 & RIFLE DUMP. There was considerable enemy aircraft activity.	HOLLEBEKE 1:10000
"	3		4 guns of this unit moved into Barrage position about I 25 a 7.7. Our new line positions were dug every day by 5th Coy. Both men & track heavily shelled by enemy during day with all Barrage position very heavily shelled during whole day. 4 light bombs were dropped on the British working & formations.	Rft
"	4		July on this sector & prpts. advance of 27 Div. A lyddite indirect & screen the gas. In the afternoon a plane taken British lyddite stores overhead every fermen - the plane as obviously German - & then returns	Aft

WAR DIARY
or
INTELLIGENCE SUMMARY.

(Erase heading not required.) 57 Bgy RFA G. Corps

Army Form C. 2118.

Place	Date Oct	Hour	Summary of Events and Information	Remarks and references to Appendices
In the line	5		Barrage guns moved to [crossed out] T.30.C.9.5 - attempted gun flashes considered aerial activity on both sides - enemy artillery fairly active. Target - parapets round tail of SBIGE Fm Bretivin	Rifle HOLLEBEKE I.10.c.0.0 SHEET 28 NE
"	6		Owing to heavy casualties sustained in attack and 2 position were taken over by 5 Bgy through relieving men to our relieving. Personnel relieved - Quiet night	MA
"	7		4 Gun team relieved. 1/Lt. POPE went to S.H.E. to 2/Lt. In y. Scott RM. Both consisted of barrage from 6 in mortar (11.6/1.st & 2 of 37th bgs) Gave a fairly good finish. Jackson's Dump shelled heavily on interval during night - gone none Weather cloudy - Quiet, even.	MA
"	8		Aerial warfare active from a great altitude artillery very active from about midday in rally. T.30.e. after hills I mile track quiet night	Rifle ZILLEBEKE I.10.c.0.0 MA
"	9		Weather fine - visibility poor. Great aircraft activity on both sides about 5 pm an enemy plane was brought to earth with one of ours about 2 mile due E of T.30.e.9.5 - at 6.5 p.m our S.O.S signal was	

WAR DIARY
INTELLIGENCE SUMMARY

Army Form C. 2118.

57th Coy 4th Army Corps

Place	Date	Hour	Summary of Events and Information	Remarks and references to Appendices
In Billets	9th (contd)		Sent by Division in an effort to reply to vigorous fire immediately by our artillery the G.S.	
			They send every given till at trench in I.30.c. Hostile artillery was very active both by day & by night - night firing was carried against our communication by h.q.'s of this unit - 5000 yds. The commonest of trenches hq's were taken over from 6th D.L by 6.E. 57 Coy as HILL 63. Every artillery again very active against communication by day & night especially between 8 pm & 8.30 pm. Still they far became made was inferior to Wistle areas. Every aeroplane were on several occasions flying low very high speed N.W. It still bv & fairs in within radius of R.E.'s. One of our flew was brought down by enemy A.A. some distance S.E. of I.30.c. Except for artillery activity reports above night was v. quiet.	HOLLEBEKE
	10			
	11		During event were again very active against the communication & during morning fire a considerable amount of heavy shell against our heavy batteries in vicinity of LA CHAPELLE The night was extraordinarily quiet except for some few shells	HOLLEBEKE

Army Form C. 2118.

WAR DIARY
or
INTELLIGENCE SUMMARY.
(Erase heading not required.)

57 Bry M.G. Corps.

Instructions regarding War Diaries and Intelligence Summaries are contained in F. S. Regs., Part II. and the Staff Manual respectively. Title pages will be prepared in manuscript.

Place	Date	Hour	Summary of Events and Information	Remarks and references to Appendices
In the line	Oct 11 (cont⁴)		fires between 7 & 7.30 p.m. against dark tracks between ZWARTELEN & MT. SORREL. Enemy artillery action at intervals during day. Fairly particular attention to cutting J 25.c 90.25, & all dumps in this area of work tracks to SHREWSBURY FOREST.	Afts
"	12th		Our own artillery on left were very active. Down early increasing to a barrage of some fire about 5 a.m. then later until 8.15 a.m. On our own front our activity was slight. Enemy aeroplane numerous when returned in the evening.	Refer HOLLEBEKE 1/10,000. Afts
"	13th		Enemy rifles fired to our barrage in early morning. He was active with 5.9 & 4.2 shells against MULKTRACK, RIFLE DUMP & CUTTING at J 25.a. 6.7. At 1.20 p.m. & 8.30 & on 10 p.m. to replies on barrage by shelling were when indiscriminately. He paid some particular attention to COKES COTTAGES on artillery very slight. In g. activity nil.	Afts

A 5634. Wt. W4973/M687. 750,000. 8/16. D.D. & L. Ltd. Forms/C.2118/13.

WAR DIARY
or
INTELLIGENCE SUMMARY.

Army Form C. 2118.

57 Coy M.G. Corps

Place	Date	Hour	Summary of Events and Information	Remarks and references to Appendices
In the line	Oct 14		Weather showery during day, raining very much during night. Heavy battle going on every night and guns on both sides were up(loud). The enemy's use of incendiary shells was of at least a marked increase. Enemy planes were in large formations between 6 a.m. & 7 a.m. The above of enemy K.B's were marked. At 2.30 p.m. an assault of an air battle over Pheone (undec7ps) was brought about on him. At 11.30 p.m. in reply to our S.O.S. there was an intense by fire lasting about 1/2 hr. The collision OD sent up the S.O.S. for at least 5 min. The enemy sent over a good many fm. shells from 9 p.m. to 2 a.m. on HILL 60 & Valley I 30 c, far and hinterland & phosgene. Horserign clouds were much practically up north. There was no bombardment of stand position during day. ... some enemy M.G. fire. The Middle Coy was x. Transhuil fired on both sides. 2 enemy K.B's were up towards of day. Enemy shells HILL 60 HILL 60 + Valley I 29 c +30 c very much in led with _____ ..... shell – Rail damage was also done	Rifle HOLLEBEKE I.10,110
"	15			

WAR DIARY
or
INTELLIGENCE SUMMARY.
(Erase heading not required.)

Army Form C. 2118.

57 Fd [?] M.G Corps

Place	Date	Hour	Summary of Events and Information	Remarks and references to Appendices
In the line	15 (cont)		Coy H.S. to multitrack Quecktren Trenches to SHREWSBURY FOREST.	[?] MOLES BRIDGE I. 10.000
	16		Movement a Green censor know from S.E. of 2 AND VOORDE in a northerly direction at 2.20 pm — returning at 2.30 pm. Enemy continued his fair shell bombardment up till 7 a.m. The hostility been slow + chill. Day V.Q [?] quiet on both sides. At 4.30 pm 8 Teums of the coy relieved 6 Teums in the line - 2 of 3 Coy Teums. C.P. 58 M.G Coy took over HQ at HILL 60. History Hidel granted to No 24/70 Pt HOLMES W 815-029 " Honeyball J	
	17		Barrage portions were dealt fairly heavily, a good many gas shells being employed. Bulgar Wood Trench slow shelled. Casualties 1 OR wounded.	[?]
	18			[?]
	19		Fairly quiet day. Nothing of importance taking place except P.O.S. going up in [?].	[?]

WAR DIARY
or
INTELLIGENCE SUMMARY.

(Erase heading not required.) 57 Coy M.G.C.

Army Form C. 2118.

Place	Date	Hour	Summary of Events and Information	Remarks and references to Appendices
In the line	21st		Back area shelled with gas shells. Hostile fumes carried out normal harassing.	AO
			Following awards made: Military Cross Capt W.L.W. KNOX LITTLE. D.C.M. 257 WRIGHT. F. M. Medals Pte. RIDDOCK. F.L. Pte. SOMERSALL W. D.C.M	AO
	22.		Misty quiet early morning. The front line positions were fairly heavily shelled. Our artillery opened heavy enemy munitions allowed light fire shot off R.W Day & 4.30 from enemy artillery active later. Station relief carried out	
	23rd		1am. 4pm stand to. 1am 7 germans walked into one of the BULGAR WOOD Teams (I.N.C.O. & 6 men). All were taken prisoners (I.N.C.P. & N.C.O. & 12 O.R.) were shot up for the purpose of carrying them up for positions for forthcoming operations	AO
	24.		Quiet day (Ready) sent up to complete teams for four times. Working	AO
	25.		O.C. Coy took over command from O.C. 60 M.G. Coy 2 Extra gun teams were sent up for barrage work	AO

Army Form C. 2118.

WAR DIARY
or
INTELLIGENCE SUMMARY.   37 M.G. Coy
(Erase heading not required.)

Place	Date	Hour	Summary of Events and Information	Remarks and references to Appendices
In the field	26th		Barrage carried out by 6 [Frames?] of this Coy's in conjunction with operations on the left.	[illeg]
"	28.		Inter Lutgan Relief carried out	B

B.S.D. [illeg]
37 M.G. Coy

Army Form C. 2118.

WAR DIARY
or
INTELLIGENCE SUMMARY.   57 M. G. Coy

(Erase heading not required.)

Place	Date Nov	Hour	Summary of Events and Information	Remarks and references to Appendices
In the Field	1st		The Divisional Commander presented medal ribbons to the undermentioned of this Coy. Military Medal: Capt W. K. W. KNOX-LITTLE D.C.M. 4533 Sgt WRIGHT F. M.M. 6313 Cpl RIDDOCH J L 80305 Pte HUMPHRYS H T.	
	2nd		Intra Sentin. Relief carried out.	[20]
	3/4		Western Mntg. Hill 60 + Mt SORREL were shelled from H.F. in smaller units down. A few guns shelled with heat into BULGAR WOOD. Some E.A. flew low over our lines.	[20]
	4/5		Western Mntg. Barrage gun positions Hill 60 and heavily engaged. A lot of gun shelling going west. Cemetery. 2.O.R.i wounded (gas).	[20]
	5/6		Western. Night. Wet day. Only first visibility good aft. 10.30am. Night my guns Barrage position was shelled fairly heavily. We saw shells during the day into Trench, Mt SORREL, Hill 60 received a rather intensive. E.A. active flying low.	[20]
	6/7		Western. Dull + showery. Night Shoot on the Dolote Some gas shells fell in vicinity of the Barrage positions. A number of heavy fell round Mt SORREL Bank area. Track shelled yesterday marked. Our Artillery fired a heavy barrage on the Hoff at 5.10 am. One A.P.M. g. fired at Sastburg potato dump on very low on our lines.	[20]

Army Form C. 2118.

WAR DIARY
or
INTELLIGENCE SUMMARY.   59 M.G. Coy

(Erase heading not required.)

Instructions regarding War Diaries and Intelligence Summaries are contained in F.S. Regs., Part II. and the Staff Manual respectively. Title pages will be prepared in manuscript.

Place	Date	Hour	Summary of Events and Information	Remarks and references to Appendices
In the Field	7/8		The 112 M.G. Coy relieved us in Barrage Trench & the two left half Guns in BULGAR Wood. The remaining 2 were withdrawn. Relief completed 6.50 p.m. All Transport returned to Transport lines at SIEGE FARM.	fd
"	9:		Weather showery day spent in general cleaning up & packing of kits on 59th Inf. Bde. relieved by 112 Inf. Bde. 9/10.	fd
"	10:		The Camp at SIEGE FARM was handed over to 112 M.S. Coy. The Transport was despatched overland by road to MERRIS. The Company entrained for to billets at MERRIS.	fd
"	11:		Guns cleaned	fd
"	12:		The Transport under Brigade arrangements went to BECOURINCHEM & entrained at CAESTRE. Infantry at EBLINGHEM marched to billets at BECOURINCHEM.	fd
"	13		Coy paraded 9.15 for rifle inspection – remainder of day spent in cleaning billets, techanaships & unpacking guns & gun material & cleaning limbers	Refer. SHEET Sh. G.6.
"	14	9.30 a.	10 min arm drill, stalking exercise carries out & 2/Lt 9 Coy & 2/Lt Taylor officers were photo'd. Return as follows. Lu. 2/Lt R.B LAWSON - No. 2 y/e CAME W.3 2/Lt W.W. WARD with Lt LA DUNT a medium mortar with broken Sam - fired a short turn burst from 4.20 pm. to 4.30pm.	fd fd fd

A 8831 Wt. W 4973/M687 750,000 8/16 D. D. & L. Ltd. Forms/C.2118/13.

Army Form C. 2118.

WAR DIARY
or
INTELLIGENCE SUMMARY.
(Erase heading not required.)

57 Coy. M.G. Corps.

Place	Date Nov.	Hour	Summary of Events and Information	Remarks and references to Appendices
RAEQINGHEM	15th		M.G. Training & Inspection Drill Order after 14/11/17 - Football in afternoon	Refer. SHEET 36 c & 36d
"	16		Further limber team making chains. Training as for 15/11/17. Training in anti-fly bomb.	
"	17th		Route March in full M.O.C. 63K Test hillness - Football match afternoon B.H.Q. v TM Batty combined	
"	18th		Inspection of small kit – Church for C of E 6.30 – 12.30 & 2.3 Limber clean	
"	19		M.G. traps training – Recreational train	
"	20		Repairing – Recreational train. M.G. Traps Training. Limber cleaning. Football	
"	21		M.G. traps Training. Football – arrears 6.30pm	
"	22		M.G. and Infantry training. Football match opp 246 M.G.C 2.30pm	
"	23		M.G. + Infy Training for school demonstration class attended by 40 officers	
"	24		Route march – march discipline. Sen school (demonstration class attended) by reconnaissance officers	
"	25		Kit inspection. Church parade. 2/Lt. Copeland 2/Lt Wood, e.s. 2nd Lt & 1 Cpl	

WAR DIARY
or
INTELLIGENCE SUMMARY

Army Form C. 2118.

57 Coy. M.G. Corps.

Place	Date	Hour	Summary of Events and Information	Remarks and references to Appendices
MACQUINGHEM	25		The (Temp) officer IX Corps School (Refresher) Offs Drill course M.G. Staff's Training as usual. Bathe at BLARINGHEM in afternoon — 2/Lt LAWSON & IV DARE 2nd Lts to IX Corps School	Mr. FRANCE Sheet 5/6 36 A 36 A
"	26		M.G. Staff's training except for 40 O.R. R.E. working party centinuing +20 O.R. + 10 M.G. in afternoon — Baths at BLARINGHEM.	※
"	27		M.G. Staff's Training as usual.	※
"	28		" " " "	
"	29		" " 2 Secs 70 rounds elementary.	※
"	30		Route march — Anard Cenceptus — Creation Inglis wear tracera.	

[signatures]

Herewith VERDICT

5th December 1917

A A Bromitt
Mayor

WAR DIARY
INTELLIGENCE SUMMARY

Vol 23 57 Coy. M.G. Corps

Army Form C. 2118.

Place	Date	Hour	Summary of Events and Information	Remarks and references to Appendices
RECINGHEM	Dec 1	8.30	Coy turned on Exercise - 1/2 Coy to range - 1/2 Coy M.G. & Infy training - 2.30 pm football match Officers 2.4b Coy - 1.00	Ref Sheet 36a France
"	2		Church parade. Services in the evening & Christmas in evening	
"	3		B.H.Q. Tuf O'War (Coy) Coy Canteen. 5 M.Gunners pulled against R.Van a Tussen	
"	3		Coy walking parades. - 1/2 Coy to range with rifles - remainder Limber Drill - Skew foot inspection at 2.30 pm	
"	4		Limber Drill - M.G. & Infy training - football match between Coy & Transport Sec. & Section 3 lag race in afternoon	
"	5	9.15-12.15	an attack scheme was carried out - Baths in afternoon cancelled. Time occupied in preparing for come home	
"	6		Part Cleaning Limber Packing limber for war	
"	7		Coy moved by motor lorries to ST OMER - entraining thereby for three POMMIER area	Ref A2/5 Draw ft. 52 Ref Sheet 57C
POMMIER AREA	8		Coy arrived by motor lorries Ettrick marched to ETRICOURT with	

Army Form C. 2118.

WAR DIARY
or
INTELLIGENCE SUMMARY.

(Erase heading not required.) 57 Bde. R.G.A. Corps

Place	Date	Hour	Summary of Events and Information	Remarks and references to Appendices
ETRICOURT	8		Levels arriving at 11 p.m. — 1 Newport never defective	off
"	9th		Bty. moved up by detachments to IK 36 & 1.3 to relieve 18th Bty	Map 57c N.E.
			In C.A. – 16 Guns in the line – 8 in pool and 8 Barrage.	off
			Weather – fine	
IN THE LINE	10		Activity. A few rounds of enemy artillery activity – wire & dump	
			position shelling. RIBECOURT shelled with 5"G3	
			gun/howitzers	
			Aerial activity slight on both sides – our enemy 'planes	
			fell on Fleurus at 3:45 pm. apparently brought down by high I.A.	
	11		Weather – moist, slight rain	
			Activity very little of importance – usual intermittent shelling on	
			little Oise – enemy M.G.s slightly active against patrols	
			of our front line by night	
	12		Weather – dull, red wind from N.E.	
			Activity. Our artillery fired intermittently, shot on crash all day.	SECRET 17c
			Enemy – their frequency increasing during early evening 12/7/19	

WAR DIARY
or
INTELLIGENCE SUMMARY.

(Erase heading not required.) 57 Bde M.G. Corps.

Army Form C. 2118.

Place	Date	Hour	Summary of Events and Information	Remarks and references to Appendices
IN THE LINE	Dec 12 (cont.)			Ref. Sh 57cNE
"	13		Activity. Both activity chiefly ground RIBECOURT & BM 827 line etc - night in early morning 2gram truck Wind N.E. Enemy artillery very active during morning - noon & on indiscriminate shelling with stuff of small calibre - Heavy shrapnel put over RIBECOURT at intervals all day - Enemy aircraft on our line + tattoo old Jerry direction 15' at a time were observed - Our M.G. fire on RIBECOURT during night direction uncertain. Our artillery did very little except to a barrage between 3.45' + 6.45' a.m. - Our barrage from flanks on S.O.S. line between 5.30 + 6.30 a.m. - Considerable A.A. work brought one during dawn by L.Guns.	
"	14		Weather. Low cloud - Visibility poor. Activity. On a request of our alarm our artillery put a 1am barrage all along the front - There was no reply by enemy on this particular front - but a good on left (verbally) & on right	

Army Form C. 2118.

WAR DIARY
or
INTELLIGENCE SUMMARY.
(Erase heading not required.)

5-7 Coy. M.G. Corps.

Place	Date	Hour	Summary of Events and Information	Remarks and references to Appendices
IN THE LINE	14 (cont.) Dec		The Germans put up a barrage on the left, from about 8.0 am to 9.0 am. Our artillery replies will presumably to the barrage otherwise there was no activity. Our M.G's (barrage guns) fired on areas — L.R.D.0.2 — L.9.C.1.2. — L.14.D.9.7 — L.15.C.0.6. & on sunken road from L.13.R.9.0 to L.14.B.0.2. & c.0.8. on each side of same from 5.30 pm to 7.30 pm. & from 6.15 am — 8.45 a.m.	Ref. sheet 57C NE
			Weather cold finish.	
"	15		Slight activity on both sides during day & night. This company relieved 56 M.G.C. in Res. Boe area — 56 taking over left Bde. Sector — relief complete 2.27am 16th.	
			Weather Dull spots — low visibility — fresh N. wind	
"	16		EAST FORK Avenue shelled during night with light H.E.S & on front line slightly to our right heavily shelled. Several enemy planes of low flying over our lines — one at least Armoured car driven off by fire from left	

D.D.S.I., London, E.C.
(A-83) Wt W362/M1072 559/000 4/17 Sch 9?a Forms/C/2118/14

WAR DIARY
or
INTELLIGENCE SUMMARY.
(Erase heading not required.) 57 Coy. M.G. Corps.

Army Form C. 2118.

Place	Date	Hour	Summary of Events and Information	Remarks and references to Appendices
IN THE LINE	16 (cont'd)		Our heavies shelled NINEWOOD from 6 p.m. to 6.30 pm. A squadron of 6 of our machines reconnoitred MARCOING area from early afternoon	Ref. Sheet 57 C N.E.
"	17	Weather	Dull & very windy. Wind N.N.E.	
		Activity	Enemy shelled support trenches & communication trenches till light about morning. Several enemy aeroplanes were times back from our lines — one especially returned in great haste diving underneath. Our batteries did their usual harassing fire day & night.	
"	18	Weather	Day apparently particularly in LAVACQUERIE DIRECTION. top of NEUF BOIS — slight fairly fried. Both supply — touch bright — wind E.N.E.	
		Activity	Enemy shelled our position in L.32.B+D lightly during day — aeroplanes & M.G's very quiet. Our artillery carried out usual harassing fire & shoot burst during day & night.	

Army Form C. 2118.

WAR DIARY
or
INTELLIGENCE SUMMARY.
(Erase heading not required.)

157 Coy. A & Corps

Place	Date	Hour	Summary of Events and Information	Remarks and references to Appendices
IN THE LINE	Oct 19th		WEATHER: Fine, mild S.E wind - wind 6-9 am night.	Refer NINE WOEL 1:10:000
			Every child P.M line with 4.2 from "HOD" & Mutual	
			ACTIVITY: Ourou Day & RIBECOURT in early evening.	
			Enemy Aircraft very active all day flying high	
			Own artillery carried out harassing fire with 18/an.	
			In short bursts every day & night.	
	20		WEATHER: Cold - Rain quiet. Lgt N.E wind.	
			ACTIVITY: Every shelled SUNKEN ROAD at L.26.a. 70.20 into	
			until with every Gay. Trenchlaw very quiet during	
			shelled roads & tracks immediately east of RIBECOURT	
			every in S. of front, active of east support & rear	
			own own night	
			Own artillery very quiet - Period situation quiet. Ack	
	21st		WEATHER: Day Bright, CB observation. Moonlight night	
			mild N.E wind.	
			ACTIVITY: Enemy artillery shelled reserve lines during day with	

Army Form C. 2118.

WAR DIARY
or
INTELLIGENCE SUMMARY.
(Erase heading not required.)

57 Bty An F.C.

Place	Date	Hour	Summary of Events and Information	Remarks and references to Appendices
IN THE LINE	21		Sills of Manroux Calibre	REF NINE WOOD Pin Eve
			Our artillery very slack - quiet. Day + night quiet on the whole	
	22		WEATHER: Wind N.E. mild. Day slightly misty.	ATT
			ACTIVITY: Enemy artillery shell R.13.50 S.W. at intervals during day + night. Ideas (railway) were sticking to our Rn line getting rifle with N.F.A. & FK20 & H.2 Host. Enemy MG & scattered tracers all over in front. Our artillery quiet. Otherwise quiet.	
	23		WEATHER: Day very bright. Night clear. Wind NE cold. Sunny (Whig) Gang(s).	ATT
			ACTIVITY: The front line - KAISER SUPPORT + NINEWEPEN LANE Ray against front line during day + MARCOING - RIBECOURT trenches been shelled all day for no apparent reason. 50 or 60 'Planes' were over our group + second on the Early evening - all very high	

WAR DIARY
or
INTELLIGENCE SUMMARY

Army Form C. 2118.

57 City M.G. Coys

Place	Date	Hour	Summary of Events and Information	Remarks and references to Appendices
IN THE LINE	23		T.M. & activities of our F. line	Ref/M+ NE WOD 1:10000
			M.G.s trained	
			Our artillery active. Our aircraft active. Our heavies active	
			fair weather all day	X
			WEATHER — wind N.E. night cheerful	
			From O.P.	
		2H	Enemy heavies shell Ridge shaft & Rifle shaft - Marching	
			Valley all day — 3am enemy M.G. barrage on	
			our left with a lot of shells turning in	
			Aircraft normal	
			T.M. & M.G. slight	
			Own artillery shell NINEWOOD & ARCONVE Dpt	
			with.	
			R.F.C. brought down E.A. (1) behind our line at 3 p.m.	X
			Winter patrols scattered by M.G. is fire	
IN THE LINE	25		WEATHER Unseven weather — with some hail & snow hail	
			ACTIVITY Enemy artillery more active than usual during X-mas	

WAR DIARY
or
INTELLIGENCE SUMMARY.

Army Form C. 2118.

Place	Date	Hour	Summary of Events and Information	Remarks and references to Appendices
IN THE LINE			Morning	
			Quiet. Not - M.G + T.M.S quiet.	
			Enemy infantry attempted to fraternise (not use la)	
			been warned + circular just a step to this by rifle	
			fire. (One German appears on parapet with both +ba etc.)	
	26		Night very quiet	
			WEATHER: Fine - visibility for lewis + m.m.	
			ACTIVITY: Enemy very quiet all day + night.	
			Our artillery quiet. A aacof actr very late + returning	
			Our enemy back with	
			WIND - South - 10mm NE	
	27		WEATHER: Cloudy + overcast times shelling mainly with light shells	
			ACTIVITY: Enemy thrice quiet	
			Our artillery strafed NINEWOOD area snipers	
			Afternoon	
			T.M.S + batteries on front of L21D'49	
			Our Lewis guns very active against enemy forward work	

WAR DIARY
or
INTELLIGENCE SUMMARY.
(Erase heading not required.)

Army Form C. 2118.

57 Bde Hr. A. Corps

Place	Date	Hour	Summary of Events and Information	Remarks and references to Appendices
INTELLIGENCE	27th		6-7 pm enemy put up claims of red & white flares over fire - no return of [?]	(Minutes)
	28th		WEATHER Bad - fine [?] about 10 AM - visibility poor returning - no action of [?]	
			ACTIVITY Enemy commenced shelling SW of Russécourt from 10.30 - 11.30 am. 300 SW of Russécourt	
			H.E. Shells. Some unseen infantry firing late afternoon East of YN, some 2 of shrapnel over TRESCAULT	
			Aircraft activity slight - 5 over our lines enemy morning, three were engaged by Lt A+AA Stations SW	
			Our side very quiet day except for our own [?] (4 in number) from	Sgd
	29th		WEATHER Sunny and [?] very [?] during day	
			ACTIVITY Enemy aircraft few on our lines 9 am till 11 am.	

WAR DIARY
or
INTELLIGENCE SUMMARY.

(Erase heading not required.)

57 Bde M.G. Coy.

Army Form C. 2118.

Place	Date	Hour	Summary of Events and Information	Remarks and references to Appendices
FRONT LINE	29th	(cont)	Enemy L.G.s fired short bursts at day - but no particular target found (to answer). Our own O.C. MGs quiet except for usual harassing fire by our L.M.G. outposts.	MMGC [illeg] note-sos
			Wind W and N.E.	##
"	30th		**WEATHER** Wind W and N.E. **ACTIVITY** Very slight artillery activity by enemy of [?] PIRECONAT. 3 Enemy 'planes flew very low over our lines & fired on 2 occasions during morning - they were engaged by A.A. and M.G. fire. Slight enemy [?] except for evening T.M. activity. 40th new Ct. On artillery aircraft very quiet - 40th on M.G. fired on a [?] field (battery at L.7.a.15.35) during the night (300 [?] 5000)	
"	31st		OTS arrived bet 2 hrs. Enemy harrass on right [?] Div's front from 6.30-8.30 a.m. Enemy T.M. shafts on front line during morning	##
			WEATHER **ACTIVITY**	

Army Form C. 2118.

WAR DIARY
or
INTELLIGENCE SUMMARY.
(Erase heading not required.)

5-7 Coy M.G. Corps

Place	Date	Hour	Summary of Events and Information	Remarks and references to Appendices
(IN THE LINE B1 (cont.))			10th Jany 1918. Enemy aeroplanes were totally inactive during whole of enemy trench small bursts of fire every day. Our artillery inflicted considerably of enemy barrage in reply to the enemy retaliation. All other arms were quiet during day & night.	MINORIES 1.10.1918

J. M. H——
A/Capt M.G.C.

Army Form C. 2118.

WAR DIARY
or
INTELLIGENCE SUMMARY.
(Erase heading not required.)

57 Coy M.G. Corps

Place	Date	Hour	Summary of Events and Information	Remarks and references to Appendices
IN THE LINE	1918 July 1		WEATHER Cold frosty - visibility bad due NE	Appx NINE ATTACHED HEREWITH
			ACTIVITY Enemy Artillery very active, especially in early morning + late evening.	
			Target especially enemies - valley S.E. of RUYECOURT & high ground about 13.13.2.	
			Aircraft nil	
			Inf Patrols continuously brought say enemy cliffs on ANGLE ROAD to the right.	
			" Drafts to enemy heavy fire western, our artillery firm	Appx
			Our M.G.'s co-operated	
			L.O for 1 W—	
2			WEATHER 45°27 wind N.E.	
			ACTIVITY Enemy Artillery very quiet Artillery peaceful in all respects	
			M.G. normal	
			Our Artillery inflicted enemy front line at STAND TO evening & morning - all other arms quiet	Appx

Army Form C. 2118.

WAR DIARY
INTELLIGENCE SUMMARY.
(Erase heading not required.)

57 Coy. 2nd L.G. Corps

Place	Date	Hour	Summary of Events and Information	Remarks and references to Appendices
IN THE LINE	3rd July		WEATHER Clear & hot — Fresh N.E. wind	Ref. Machine Gunner Corps Special Instr.
			ACTIVITY Enemy shelled RIBECOURT very heavily up to mid-day.	
			Aircraft — Enemy had seven planes reconnoitring our lines at	
			one time during day — other activity nil.	
			Own — Artillery carried harassing fire at intervals — Own aircraft	
			very quiet — In front of this company from 200-300 at enemy	
			aircraft seen.	
			Enemy used 5" 12 B's M.G. throughout the day.	
	4		WEATHER Clear — visibility v. good.	
			ACTIVITY Enemy artillery were v. objectionable — especially on KAISER SUPPORT —	
			FRONT LINE during whole day	
			Aircraft were v. active — apparently "spotting" with v. little	
			hostilities. Enemy fired a prolific no. of rounds from M.G.'s	
			against our 4 planes. One was heard to hum at R.E. in	
			our shells of all calibre were directed against enemy lines	
			day & night. Our own planes returned in safety	✓

WAR DIARY
INTELLIGENCE SUMMARY
(Erase heading not required.)

Army Form C. 2118.

57 Bde. Aus G. Corps

Place	Date	Hour	Summary of Events and Information	Remarks and references to Appendices
IN THE LINE	4th		at 10.41 am with the exception there is was bright down by day	
			fire continues N. of NINE WOOD from otherwise fairly peaceful	
	5		WEATHER Very red – Visibility fair	
			ACTIVITY Enemy very active – slight indiscriminate fire on the front. M/G fired – a few rounds directed against the CHATEAU in COULLIST WOOD.	XX
			M.G. fire in large volume seen railway R.E. B. This comes from ORNE to S.W. + on HIGHLAND RIDGE	
			Rain practically nil	
6			WEATHER Smoky will rain at intervals from freshens Wind S.W.	XX
			ACTIVITY Enemy fairly quiet during day except for considerable L.T.M. Activity against SUNKEN ALLEY in evening. Artillery quiet at night – slight shelling of battery positions. considerable M/G activity	

Army Form C. 2118.

WAR DIARY
or
INTELLIGENCE SUMMARY.
(Erase heading not required.)

57 Coy M.G. Corps

Place	Date	Hour	Summary of Events and Information	Remarks and references to Appendices
IN THE LINE	6		ACTIVITY Our: Very quiet in all respects. Our aircraft	
			WEATHER Fine - visibility fair - wind changed to S.S.E.	Sept MINE records files also
	7		ACTIVITY Enemy Artillery fired fairly heavy — our aircraft except for a few shells	
			to BULLET WOOD.	
			M.G. Very active during night — most troublesome from N.N.E.	
			range uncertain but long	
			Our: Desultory shelling, otherwise nil.	✓
	8		WEATHER Rain	
			ACTIVITY Enemy artillery fairly — some indiscriminate shelling — our	
			gunner quiet — night quiet	
			M.G. Unusual active — larger	
			T.M. Shells support line during morning	
			Our: Slight — Aircraft active between 8-4 p.m in	
			small numbers.	
	9		WEATHER Fog — Wind N.W. visibility low.	
			ACTIVITY Enemy artillery nil — Aircraft active from N.West	

Army Form C. 2118.

WAR DIARY
or
INTELLIGENCE SUMMARY.
(Erase heading not required.) 57 Bay M.G. Corps.

Instructions regarding War Diaries and Intelligence Summaries are contained in F. S. Regs., Part II. and the Staff Manual respectively. Title pages will be prepared in manuscript.

Place	Date	Hour	Summary of Events and Information	Remarks and references to Appendices
INCHY-LES-	9		NOTHING to be observed at our front	
			M.G. normal	
			ACTIVITY our Nil.	
—	10		WEATHER Very dull — rain at 3.30 p.m. Wind towards North. Loose	※
			ACTIVITY Enemy Artillery were active giving gun & quick bursts	
			Two of Batty positions likely for scrapped — fired	
			during night	
			M.G. normal	
			Our fixed day & night	
			Lines — against showing — Thaw — Wind S.O.	
—	11		WEATHER Sunny Artillery very active going day far shells fell in	※
			TUNNEL WOOD — Enemy fired heavy guns with flat shells	
			T.M. & action as usual targets	
			Aircraft normal M.G. slightly below normal.	
			Enemy sent up in this usual coloured lights & signals	
			Green lights — several single double red & some golden rain	

WAR DIARY
or
INTELLIGENCE SUMMARY.
(Erase heading not required.)

Army Form C. 2118.

57 Coy. M.G. Corps

Place	Date	Hour	Summary of Events and Information	Remarks and references to Appendices
IN THE LINE	1918 May 12		WEATHER Fine, visibility good – but cloudy from S.E. bright strong wind. ACTIVITY Enemy Artillery very active in White over during day – he dropped some gas shells (lach?) in COUILLET WOOD – he also used a few whizz bangs over our White area again first half of night. Enemy T.M's unusual active & target during the day appeared to be 9 Gordons billets area over White area & morning – especially on our right. Aircraft – Nil. ACTIVITY OWN Artillery opened at 6.18 am along whole front with 18 Pdr, H.E. & shrapnel – firing unsimultaneous extra heavy rate of fire (& shown) to White Sap. Quiet night except from 8.30 pm to 10.30 pm – otherwise our front side quiet. Stiff concentration by night – otherwise Coy. night as usual.	(of WIND)(WIND)("ROPE & Shell")
"	13		WEATHER Fine. ACTIVITY Enemy arm'm was quiet during day & active (practically all strong) at night. Our Artillery firing by arty. by day & night. Our M.G's fired active on concentration by night – otherwise Coy night as usual. Wind NNW.	#
"	14		WEATHER Fine +ish. ACTIVITY Enemy during day. Enemy M.G's put most of Hutson or E.B. WORK – During night COUILLET WOOD around the line there (shell shelled)	#

WAR DIARY or INTELLIGENCE SUMMARY

Army Form C. 2118.

57 Coy 2nd G.C. of P.

Place	Date	Hour	Summary of Events and Information	Remarks and references to Appendices
(14/1/18 cont'd)			**ARTILLERY** continued - shell violently T.9 Cues	Ref. Nile M.C. 1:10,000 Sh 36
			S.A. very active at a great height. 01.40 a.m. the flare dropped 8 bombs on L.32 D.B.C. - Enemy K.B. up from Douchy till Dusk at 8 M.B. of 77° from L.32 D.70.85 M.G.s. T.M.'s Quiet	
			ACTIVITY (own) will below normal (very quiet). Shafts to Screw Observing Pbns. up to morning in usual numbers	Off
IN THE LINE 15			**WEATHER** Dull - visibility low - Wind N.W., later becoming S.W. Rain strength Enemy artillery active on O.P. shots with guns + heavy Trench Guns - Quiet night. E. aircraft nil - T.M.'s slight in Support area. Th 9s very active as usual locally during night	
			" Our artillery very quiet - M.G.s T.M.s + aircraft - Nil	S.A.
IN THE LINE 16			**WEATHER** Rainy - visibility v. low	
			ACTIVITY Enemy artillery very quiet both by day + night - Heavy Trench Guns will seen left in sight - T.M. very active during day on SUNKEN ALLEY + CENTRE AVE. + BATT. LANE (normal). Aerial activity nil M.G.s fairly quiet. Except in usual searching traverses. E. aeroplanes	

WAR DIARY
or
INTELLIGENCE SUMMARY.
(Erase heading not required.)

Army Form C. 2118.

57 Coy M.G. Corps

Place	Date	Hour	Summary of Events and Information	Remarks and references to Appendices
IN THE LINE	16th (Cont'd)		ACTIVITY Our Artillery (chiefly shelling of Enemy Front line by 18 pdr)	Ref NWR WSD 11:00am Sh. 82.
"	17th		WEATHER Dull stormy - misty, poor visibility. W.	
			ACTIVITY Practically nil on both sides. A slight exchange of Rifle & M.G. Fire between 6.30 pm & 11 pm.	
"	18th		WEATHER No change	
			ACTIVITY Enemy again quiet during day - slight shelling of our Support lines at night - T.M.s (Enemy) still some performance. Reply by our Trench Mortars - Enemy unful. Our Artillery & Field Heavy Day - very active in Evening harassing Enemy night. Aircraft T.M.s nil. In G. front on enemy Column eating during night	
"	19th		WEATHER Clear - no wind	
			ACTIVITY Enemy Artillery very quiet in day, some shelling of Wickeboard Wilfred Track in R.H.A. area. T.M.s opened on front line W & BH.D. Enemy in G.s Front an extensive movement of troops at our flares which were up in large numbers	

WAR DIARY or INTELLIGENCE SUMMARY

Army Form C. 2118.

(Erase heading not required.) 57 Bgd. A.M.G. Coy.

Place	Date	Hour	Summary of Events and Information	Remarks and references to Appendices
INCHY	19th (cont'd)		Enemy MGs observed (very?) about in 2's & 3's in great number evidently to cover medium gun attempts which were made to barrage - None checked. Quiet night.	Ref WINE WOOD (illegible)
			ACTIVITY ours Very quiet by day & night. One M.G.s fired on enemy communications.	##
"	20		WEATHER Dull - rain - light S.W. wind	
			ACTIVITY Enemy very quiet. Our guns - very skilful on our wood support from wood. Shelling on our part. Sharp artillery duel in early morning.	##
"	21		WEATHER Bright then early rain later	
			ACTIVITY Enemy (shells) overland traffic again in enemy. Quiet in afternoon a night. In other activity quite	
	"		our slight shell on of enemy lines by day & night. One M.G.s fires on enemy communication by night.	##
"	22		WEATHER Very mild	
			ACTIVITY Enemy activity nil - except for M.G. fire by day, none at night.	

Army Form C. 2118.

WAR DIARY
or
INTELLIGENCE SUMMARY.
(Erase heading not required.) 57 Coy A. G Corps

Place	Date	Hour	Summary of Events and Information	Remarks and references to Appendices
INTRE LOOS	22 (cont)		ACTIVITY Our Aif by day & night	
"	23		WEATHER Bright — rain by night	
			ACTIVITY Enemy Artillery quiet, lively on Suffolk lines by day — Shells VILLERS- PLOUICH from 8-12 p.m. for 2-3 hrs. Other towns worried.	
			" Our usual shelling of enemy lines & last number & our aircraft too on enemy lines & last number on reserve — Night Quiet	
"	24		WEATHER Cloudy, some rain — how wind S.S.O.	
			ACTIVITY Enemy artillery dropped 4/M. N.G. Fan shells in COUILLET WOOD 2.30 p.m — 3 p.m Our "E" Battery at L.32.D.6.3 (5.9in shells) heavily with 5.9's Our troops stand up. Our K.B. up just further side MARCOING. A.G. worried by night	
		"	Our. Artillery put a few salvos of shrapnel over MARCOING On our two sam 25.000 into on enemy communication on account of suspected relief by enemy.	
"	25		WEATHER Very fine — Bright moonlight night	
			ACTIVITY Enemy Shelled R.3.C. (RIBECOURT & back area) firework	

WAR DIARY
or
INTELLIGENCE SUMMARY.

Army Form C. 2118.

57 Coy M.G. Corps

Place	Date	Hour	Summary of Events and Information	Remarks and references to Appendices
IN THE LINE	25 (cont'd)		M.G.s paid particular attention to tracks at night. Enemy "Spotting" planes at work by day & night.	N/NE/NW(?) 1:10,000
			ACTIVITY (cont'd) Very quiet. One hour went on swept him by our m.g.s before received with showers of M.G. bullets -	
			between 10-12 p.m. from either side.	A/H
"	26		WEATHER Fine with slight mist and bright night.	
			ACTIVITY Enemy snipers very active at short range. Otherwise both sides very quiet by day. A good deal of artillery & m.g. fire exchanged by night.	A/H
	27		WEATHER Very dusk all day. Dull after-noon.	
			ACTIVITY E. artillery only fired a very few rounds into our back area & very late afternoon. m.g. active on usual targets by night. Our activity practically nil except barrage between both m.g. mounts while enemy trying to heavy mist.	A/H
	28		WEATHER Very fine. Slight S.W. wind. Sunny & still.	
			ACTIVITY On 2 Batteries each of 1 R.O.B.O.S. in each.	

WAR DIARY
or
INTELLIGENCE SUMMARY.

Army Form C. 2118.

57 by M.G. Corps

Place	Date	Hour	Summary of Events and Information	Remarks and references to Appendices
IN THE LINE	28		Morning front will probably covering most of extreme area. Fair day. Clouds later R.B. up Approx direction MAUNIERES from shell & isolated bombs E.9 H.9 fire on the R.P. (R 3 A 19). Heavy bombs Planes passed over towards our back area from 7.30 pm onwards. Fairly quiet.	
			ACTIVITY OUR. Practically nil. by day & night.	
			WEATHER. Visited fair — night bright, full.	
			ACTIVITY. Very little artillery activity except tracks over shells to the heavy shelling of the T.M. posture in R.9 & T.M.'s quiet — M.G.'s active during day on a usual target L.A. exited our own lines in the mozen patrol, and R 2'5 & 3' o in the position apparently nothing — a for very troubling flares covered toward our back area in the evening.	
	29.		OUR Our artillery very quiet. T.M.B. Quiet, active in	

WAR DIARY
or
INTELLIGENCE SUMMARY

Army Form C. 2118.

57 Coy. A.C.C

Place	Date	Hour	Summary of Events and Information	Remarks and references to Appendices
INFANTRY BARRACKS	29th		ACTIVITY QUIET. On arrival Confirmed of 57th - Sentries on Night	Appx
"	30		WEATHER Fine bright night	
			ACTIVITY Enemy Artillery active at intervals - intermittent shelling in forward areas. Enemy aircraft active particularly on the Railway & Ravine in R3 - Aircraft seen + flights of 6 m on the all day	
			" OUR Artillery particularly active, trench mortars & enemy's communication - otherwise quiet on our side	Appx
	31		WEATHER fine sunny & bright	
			ACTIVITY Enemy Artillery more active than usual on forward areas especially CENTRAL AVE, TRATTY LANE (R.4.9.) aircraft flying low over L36 + R4 - 5 K.B's up all day	
			" ENEMY Very active from 5:30 to 7:30 am against back areas. Otherwise our activity was very little	Appx

Stanley Harris
O.C. 57 Coy C

Do 95/2086/4

19TH DIVISION
57TH INFY BDE

57TH LT TRENCH MORTAR BTY
FEB 1918- MAR 1919

TRENCH MAP.
WYTSCHAETE.
28 S.W. 2.
EDITION 5.A
Scale 1:10,000.

INDEX TO ADJOINING SHEETS.

57TH L.T.M.B

January ~Feby~ – December 1918

Mar '19.

WAR DIARY
or
INTELLIGENCE SUMMARY.

Army Form C. 2118.

Place	Date	Hour	Summary of Events and Information	Remarks and references to Appendices
HAUSSY	22	6.00	Left Battalion about ½ an hour out of action soon after Zero hour. No other section did not come into action. Enemy Observation being chiefly one section 57" T.M.B. fired a barrage on the F.M.E. DE RIEUX (MAP REF N.2.b.7.8. FRANCE 51A S.E.) ¾ on the Bridge over the RIVER D'HARPIES under cover of which a fighting patrol crossed the Bridge & occupied the farm gaining valuable information.	
	23		1 Section 57 T.M.B. followed attack of 8th Gloucester Regt. & during the attack successfully dealt with hostile 6" Battery about Q.27.c.9.0. (FRANCE 51A S.E.) Hostile machine guns which were troublesome to advancing infantry were also successfully dealt with.	
	23/24		Relieved by 182nd T.M. Battery (VALENCIENNES A.E.5.4)	
	26		to AVESNES LES AUBERT (VALENCIENNES A.E.5.4)	
	27/31		Proceeded by march route to RUBELS et CAUROIR (VAL. A.D.6.2) thence Western Route MC 57 E.M. 0	

Army Form C. 2118.

WAR DIARY
or
INTELLIGENCE SUMMARY.
(Erase heading not required.)

UNIT. 57 L.T.M.B.

Place	Date	Hour	Summary of Events and Information	Remarks and references to Appendices
CAUROIR	2.xi.18	09.35	Proceeded by march route to ST AUBERT. (VALENCIENNES 4F).	
ST AUBERT	3.xi.18	16.10	MARCHED to SEPMERIES. (VALENCIENNES 3G).	
SEPMERIES	4.xi.18	10.10	Proceeded by march route to MARESCHES. (VALENCIENNES 3G).	
MARESCHES	5.xi.18	10.95	MARCHED to JENLAIN. (VALENCIENNES 3H).	
JENLAIN	6.xi.18	10.95	Proceeded by march route to BRY. (VAL. 3I) and relieved 56 L.T.M. 13 in line & on night of 6/7 Nov. Battery H.Q. established in LA FLAMENGRIE. (VAL. 3I).	
	7.xi.18	06.00	One Section followed attack of Left Bn. of 57 Bde again St high ground East of River HOGNEAU. (57 Bde Order 25?). Opposition slight & guns did not come in to action. Operations continued (vide 57 Bde. B.M. 137 & 57 Bde Order 258). T.M. Battery followed in rear of 10 R. War. R. naming Pack Animals & Wheeled transport to carry forward ammunition.	
MALPLAQUET	8.xi.18	15.25	Enemy M.G. in vicinity of J.2.a.1.3. was silenced by 15 rounds from our T.M. at J.1.b.05.10. (BELGIUM & PT. OF FRANCE 51).	
	9.xi.18	—	Battery in billets at MALPLAQUET (VAL. 3.K).	

Army Form C. 2118.

WAR DIARY
or
INTELLIGENCE SUMMARY.
(Erase heading not required.)

Instructions regarding War Diaries and Intelligence Summaries are contained in F. S. Regs., Part II. and the Staff Manual respectively. Title pages will be prepared in manuscript.

UNIT. 57 L.T.M. B.

Place	Date	Hour	Summary of Events and Information	Remarks and references to Appendices
MALPLAQUET	10.XI.18	09.20	Proceeded by march route to LA FLAMENGRIE. (VAL. 3I).	
LA FLAMENGRIE	11.XI.18 13.XI.18		Rest + Salvage work in LA FLAMENGRIE area.	
	14.XI.18	10.10	Marched to SEPMERIES. (VAL. 3G).	
SEPMERIES	15.XI.18 16.XI.18		Proceeded by march route to ST. AUBERT. (VAL. 4E).	
ST. AUBERT	17.XI.18 18.XI.18		Proceeded by march route to CAUROIR. (VAL. 4D).	
CAUROIR	19.XI.18 23.XI.18		Training and Salvage work in vicinity of CAUROIR.	
CAUROIR	24.XI.18	11.00	Entrained for LONGUEVILLETTE. (LENS 11 S.D.) in accordance with 57 Inf. Bde. Order 265. Marched from	
LONGUEVILLETTE			LONGUEVILLETTE to billets at GÉZAINCOURT. (LENS 11 S.D).	
GÉZAINCOURT	25.XI.18 30.XI.18		Rest + Training in billets at GÉZAINCOURT.	

W. Murphy Capt.
O/c 57 T.M.B.

Army Form C. 2118.

WAR DIARY
or
INTELLIGENCE SUMMARY.
(Erase heading not required.)

5 y L.T.M. Battery

Place	Date	Hour	Summary of Events and Information	Remarks and references to Appendices
GEZAINCOURT	DEC. 1		Rest and Training in billets at GEZAINCOURT.	
	9	10.00	Marched to billets in huts on FIENVILLERS — Map Ref. (LENS 11. S.D)	
			H.E on Rd. M.A.P. REF. LENS 11. 5.C. 90. 53.	
	10-31		Rest and Training.	

Wathly Capt.
O/c 55 T.M.B.

Army Form A 2007.

6

CENTRAL REGISTRY.

Central Registry No. and Date.

Attached Files.

SUBJECT, AND OFFICE OF ORIGIN.

Referred to	Date	Referred to	Date	Referred to	Date
				P.A.	Date

Schedule of Correspondence.

[M3457] W7673/1079 250m 11/14v McA. & W. 21   Forms A. 2007 6

Army Form C. 2118.

WAR DIARY
or
INTELLIGENCE SUMMARY.
(Erase heading not required.)

UNIT 54 L.T.M.B.

Place	Date	Hour	Summary of Events and Information	Remarks and references to Appendices
FIENVILLERS	JAN. 1919		Battery billeted in huts/tents on the FIENVILLERS - HEM Rd. MAP. REF. (LENS 11. SD). The month was spent in Training and Post Educational Classes were held in Shorthand, Arithmetic and at Bonplatin. Six men were demobilised during the month.	
			W.Whaley Capt. O/C 54 L.T.M.B.	

Army Form C. 2118.

WAR DIARY
or
INTELLIGENCE SUMMARY.
(Erase heading not required.)

UNIT. 57th L.T.M.B.

Place	Date	Hour	Summary of Events and Information	Remarks and references to Appendices
FIENVILLERS	1919 FEB. 1-6		Battery billeted in huts on the FIENVILLERS - HEM ROAD (MAP REF. LENS 11. S.D.)	
	7		Moved to CANDAS by march route (MAP REF. LENS 11)	
CANDAS	7-28		Battery in billets at CANDAS (MAP REF. LENS 11) The Battery was employed on fatigues during the month. Seven men were demobilised.	

J M Ruo H
for O.C., 57 T.M.B.

WAR DIARY
or
INTELLIGENCE SUMMARY.

(Erase heading not required.)

Army Form C. 2118.

UNIT. 57 & 61 T.M.B.

Place	Date	Hour	Summary of Events and Information	Remarks and references to Appendices
CANDAS	1919 Mar. 19		Battery in billets at CANDAS (map ref. LENS 11). Employed on fatigues.	
	20		Personnel of Battery returned to the Units from which posted. 1 O.R.	
	21		O.C. & 2 O.R. took the CADRE of the Battery with the tents, equipment &c from the Units and to the 104 Bde Royal Fusiliers from them	

March 21. 1919.

Kinnock Capt.
57th T.M.B.
Capt: i/c O.C.
57th T.M.B.

WAR DIARY
or
INTELLIGENCE SUMMARY.
(Erase heading not required.)

Army Form C. 2118.

Place	Date	Hour	Summary of Events and Information	Remarks and references to Appendices
BELLE CROIX	1917 DEC. 1-6	—	Training in BLARINGHEM AREA. Reference map 1/40,000 FRANCE SHEET 36A.	
BELLE CROIX	7	9 a.m	Battery marched to ST OMER and entrained there for MONDICOURT. Arrived MONDICOURT 5:30 p.m. Detrained there and marched to billets at POMMIER. Ref. Map. 1/40,000 Sheets HAZEBROUCK 5A and LENS 11.	
POMMIER	8	6:30 p.m	Advance party proceeded to ACHIET-LE-PETIT for billeting purposes. Rest of battery marched to LA CAUCHIE and embussed there for ETRICOURT picking up advance party at ACHIET-LE-PETIT en route. Arrived ETRICOURT 6:30 p.m. — billets there for night.	
ETRICOURT	9	5:30 p.m	Battery marched to billets at FINS. Ref. Map. FRANCE Sheet 59C 1/40,000	
RIBECOURT	11		Relieved 18". T.M.B. in the line. H.Q. at L.25.d.15.80. (MARCOING SY6 NE4)	
	14	3 p.m	2 Guns at L.21.d.95.95 and 1 gun at L.20.b.65.90 fired 7 rounds registering on S.O.S. lines.	
	15		Relieved by 516 L.T.M.B. Billeted in RIBECOURT CATACOMBS L.25.a.2.45.10.	
	17		Battery marched to HAVRINCOURT WOOD and occupied tents at T.18.d.45.10.	
	19-21		Rest in 9 in Div. reserve at Reserve — HAVRINCOURT WOOD.	

Army Form C. 2118.

WAR DIARY
or
INTELLIGENCE SUMMARY

(Erase heading not required.)

Place	Date	Hour	Summary of Events and Information	Remarks and references to Appendices
	DEC. 22		Relieved 58 L.T.M.B. in the Right Sector of 19th Division al Front. Six guns laid on S.O.S. lines taken over	
	26	12.5 a.m	A second gun installed at L21d 35.35. Fired 20 rounds on Enemy Trench Mortar Located at L22a 25.15.	
	28	12.20 a.m	15 Rounds fired from No 4 gun silenced enemy machine gun firing from L22 c 15.50.	
	30	1.15 a.m	No 4 gun in action at L21 c 80.25 registered with 3 rounds on DAGO HOUSE.	
	31		Still in line.	

W A Huxley? Lt
O/C 57 T.M.B

Army Form C. 2118.

WAR DIARY
or
INTELLIGENCE SUMMARY

(Erase heading not required.)

57 L.T.M.B.

Instructions regarding War Diaries and Intelligence Summaries are contained in F. S. Regs., Part II. and the Staff Manual respectively. Title Pages will be prepared in manuscript.

Place	Date	Hour	Summary of Events and Information	Remarks and references to Appendices
	1.2.18		The Battery had 6 guns in the Left Sector of the 19th Divl. Front.	
	2.2.18	12 Noon	Seventeen Rounds from our T.M. at L.34.a.10.60 silenced enemy trench mortar at L.34.b.0.9. MAP REF: MARCOING 57c. N.E.4.	
	7.2.18	10.30 am	Our 3" Stokes Trench Mortar at L.34.a.10.60 fired 20 rounds on hostile machine gun at L.28.a.16.10. Two direct hits were observed.	
	13.2.18	10.45 pm	Relieved by 190th L.T.M. B. 13 (63 Division) + proceeded to TRESCAULT where Railway intrainment on Light Railway for ROCQUIGNY. Detrained at there and marched to Camp at N.18.b.0.4. MAP REF: FRANCE Sheet 57c.	
	14.2.18		57 T.M. Battery in Corps Reserve with 19th Division for Rest and Training.	
BEAULENCOURT	18/2/18 to 28/2/18		Training & Employment. (4 hours per day) N.18.b. { Steady Drill Musketry Bayonet fighting S.B.R. Drill Bombing Gun Drill Manual of Employment Firing Practice Instruction in use of Stokes 3" T.M. + Shell } MAP REF. FRANCE Sheet 57 C.	

F. Stuart Capt
OC 57 TMB

Army Form C. 2118.

WAR DIARY
or
INTELLIGENCE SUMMARY.
(Erase heading not required.)

Instructions regarding War Diaries and Intelligence Summaries are contained in F. S. Regs., Part II. and the Staff Manual respectively. Title pages will be prepared in manuscript.

Place	Date	Hour	Summary of Events and Information	Remarks and references to Appendices
BEAULENCOURT	1/3/18		5g L.T.M. Battery in Corps Reserve with 19 Division for rest	5g L.T.M. B
	4/3/18		& training. Training & employing (Strong Discl Musketry	
			(4 hours per day) Bayonet fighting	
			N.18.6. S.B R Drill	
			Bombing	
			MAP FRANCE	
			Sheet 57c	
			(Gun Drill Motor & Explosive	
			Fuzing & Aiming	
			Instruction in use of	
			Stokes 3"T m & shell)	
BARRASTRE	7/3/18		Battery transferred by rode march to SALAMANCA	
		0100.	CAMP. BARRASTRE - HAPLINCOURT road. MAP REF. FRANCE 57c.	
	8/3/18		Training as above continued	
	20/3/18			
	21/3/18		Enemy attack launched on 3rd Army front.	
		6pm	5g I.J. Bde attacked to regain lost portion of 2nd	
			System between Eastern portion of DOIGNIES Sq.J16B to the	
			CAMBRAI - BAPAUME ROAD at J10A.00.30.	
	23/3/18		Two Stokes Mortars installed in defence post in hand	

WAR DIARY or INTELLIGENCE SUMMARY

Army Form C. 2118.

Place	Date	Hour	Summary of Events and Information	Remarks and references to Appendices
BEAUMETZ LEZ CAMBRAI	21/3/18	8.30/9	at T.20.d.5.6.	
	22/3/18	4 a.m	Enemy attacked under protection of knee-high barrage, and advanced in masses through our defensive trenches. The emplacement at T.20.d.5.6. were blown in and whilst situation was beyond our hopes guns were disabled and abandoned. Enemy who engaged with rifle fire. Subsequently the enemy were again engaged with rifle fire from a position along the track J26.c.2.9 - J26.b.2.0. Owing to the rapid advance of the enemy on the left it was found necessary to withdraw. 6 Reserve guns were picked up at O5.c.8.8. and the Battery reorganised at O5.c.2.9.	
		6/pm	Personnel remaining of with Battery bivouced to BANCOURT in accordance with orders received to concentrate in I.36.c. (FRANCE SHEET 57 C).	
BANCOURT	23/3/18	10 a.m	Battery shelled out of camp & occupied old huts at J.39.b.6.2	

Army Form C. 2118.

WAR DIARY
or
INTELLIGENCE SUMMARY.
(Erase heading not required.)

Place	Date	Hour	Summary of Events and Information	Remarks and references to Appendices
BANCOURT	24/3/18	11 a.m.	Orders were received to proceed to transport lines of guns on 3 lorries was dispatched as Battery strength was now reduced to 60%. Few horses were received at Transport lines to assist in pulling limbers.	
		4 p.m.	Marched to MIRAUMONT with Bde Transport via WARLENCOURT BAUCOURT and IRLES. (Map Ref: FRANCE Sheet 57 D)	
MIRAUMONT	25/3/18	9 a.m.	Proceeded to COIGNEUX with Bde. Transport via PUISIEUX - SERRE - COLINCAMPS - COURCELLES - BERTRANCOURT - BUS LESARTOIS.	
COIGNEUX	26/3/18	9 a.m.	Proceeded to WARLINCOURT with Bde Transport via COUIN, PAS, and GRINCOURT. Night was passed in fields at 26a.2.9.	
WARLINCOURT	27/3/18	10 a.m.	Proceeded to LA CAUCHIE with Bde. Transport.	
		4 p.m.	Continued march to BIENVILLERS au BOIS. Bivouacs in E.1.b central.	
BIENVILLERS	28/3/18	12 a.m.	Marched with Bde Transport to FAMECHON where billets were obtained for night. Route via POMMIER, ST. AMAND and PAS	
FAMECHON	29/3/18	9.30 a.m.	Battery marched to DOULLENS via THIEVRES, ORVILLE, AMPLIER and AUTHIEULE.	

Army Form C. 2118.

WAR DIARY
or
INTELLIGENCE SUMMARY.
(Erase heading not required.)

Instructions regarding War Diaries and Intelligence
Summaries are contained in F. S. Regs., Part II.
and the Staff Manual respectively. Title pages
will be prepared in manuscript.

Place	Date	Hour	Summary of Events and Information	Remarks and references to Appendices
DOULLENS	29/3/18	2.30 a.m	Entrained for STRAZEELE. (Mob. Ref. HAZEBROUCK 5A)	
		12 am	Arrived STAZEELE & marched to billets in KEMMEL by Lorry.	
KEMMEL	30/3/18		In Billets at KEMMEL.	
	31/3/18			Wattrelly lent to O/C 57 T.M.B.

WAR DIARY 57th T.M Batty

Army Form C. 2118.

INTELLIGENCE SUMMARY.
(Erase heading not required.)

Place	Date	Hour	Summary of Events and Information	Remarks and references to Appendices
	1-1-18		In the line to the 5-2-18. (Left Sector)	
	5-1-18		Relieved by the 58" T.M. Batty and proceeded to. (HAVRINCOURT WOOD.)	
	11-1-18		Relieved the 56" T.M. Batty in line. (Right Sector)	
	24-1-18		Relieved by the 58" T.M. Batty and proceeded to (HAVRINCOURT WOOD)	
	30-1-18		Relieved the 56" T.M. Batty in line. (Left Sector)	

J.W. Flannigan Lieut
Commanding 57" Light Trench Mortar Batty

57th Brigade.

19th Division.

57th LIGHT TRENCH MORTAR BATTERY

APRIL 1918.

Army Form C. 2118.

WAR DIARY
INTELLIGENCE SUMMARY.
(Erase heading not required.)

5ᵗʰ L.T.M. Battery

Instructions regarding War Diaries and Intelligence Summaries are contained in F.S. Regs., Part II. and the Staff Manual respectively. Title pages will be prepared in manuscript.

Place	Date	Hour	Summary of Events and Information	Remarks and references to Appendices
KEMMEL	APRIL 1		Relieved 5ᵗʰ Aust. T.M.B. in the Line @ Messines Sector (centre and right sub sector), four guns in the line in posns at O35.a.9.4, O35.a.5.1, U5b3.3, U5d3.15. respectively. (Sheet 28 S.W. FRANCE)	
MESSINES	10.		Enemy attacked in force, gain[ed] possession of MESSINES and hence Sub-Sector in front of it. The guns in the line were lost and 55% of the Battery personnel were casualties.	
	11		Two guns were placed in reserve line at T6b9.3. Battery withdrew from hot line at T6b9.3 and moved to transport lines at M10c.2.3.	
	15		Two guns were placed in position at N29a.5.1 + N29d.1.6 respectively. (FRANCE. Sheet 28 S.W.)	
LINDENHOEK	17	10a.m.	Parties of the enemy attempting to advance from direction of Kagnames Cᵗ & Fmᵉ were engaged by our Stokes gun at N29d.1.6. About 40 rounds were fired and good results observed, the enemy being	

WAR DIARY
or
INTELLIGENCE SUMMARY.
(Erase heading not required.)

Army Form C. 2118.

Place	Date	Hour	Summary of Events and Information	Remarks and references to Appendices
LINDENHOEK	April 17	10am	compelled to scatter frequently, as enemy himself to fire from out Lewis Guns in so doing. Many casualties were caused by our fire. The Stokes Gun at N.27.a.5.1 was disabled by hostile shell fire.	
	18	2.0pm	The remaining personnel of the Battery returned to transport lines at L.29.b.3.7. (Sheet 27 BELGIUM & PART of FRANCE)	
	21		Battery proceeded to camp at F.11.9.3. (BELGIUM + Part of FRANCE 27)	
	24		Battery proceeded to Transport lines at F.19.a.5.3	
	29		Battery moved with Brigade Transport to L.10.3.9.	

Army Form C. 2118.

WAR DIARY
or
INTELLIGENCE SUMMARY.

(Erase heading not required.) 57 L.T.M. Battery.

Instructions regarding War Diaries and Intelligence Summaries are contained in F. S. Regs., Part II. and the Staff Manual respectively. Title pages will be prepared in manuscript.

Place	Date	Hour	Summary of Events and Information	Remarks and references to Appendices
	MAY			
S. JAN TER BIEZEN	1-15		57 L.T.M Battery at 57 Bde Transport lines 27	
			Training was carried out. MAP REF. BELGIUM + PART OF FRANCE L 1 D + 3	
	16	9.45 p.m	Entrained at HEIDEBEKE STATION for CHALONS-SUR-MARNE.	
			MAP. REFS. HAZEBROUCK 5A + CHALONS. 50.	
	18	1 p.m	Arrived CHALONS-SUR-MARNE and proceeded to	
			billets at MONCETZ	
MONCETZ	19-28		Training	
	28	10/m	Embussed at MONCETZ and proceeded to	
			to SARS CHAMBRECY. MAP. REF. SOISSONS 22.	
	29		In billets at CHAMBRECY	
	30		57 T.M. Battery proceeded to POURCY.	
POURCY	31	9 am	Aeroplane and 57 Bde Transport lines to	
			on NANTEUIL-HAUTVILLERS Road 2 kilometres SWest of NANTEUIL	
			MAP REF. CHALONS 50.	

W.H.Halden Capt
OC 57 T.M.B

Army Form C. 2118.

WAR DIARY
or
INTELLIGENCE SUMMARY.
(Erase heading not required.)

UNIT — 57 T.M.B.

Instructions regarding War Diaries and Intelligence Summaries are contained in F. S. Regs., Part II. and the Staff Manual respectively. Title pages will be prepared in manuscript.

Place	Date	Hour	Summary of Events and Information	Remarks and references to Appendices
POURCY	1/6/18		Battery in Billets at POURCY. MAP REF. SOISSONS 22.	
	3/6/18		Two Stokes guns were emplaced in BOIS D'ECLISSES to fire on S.O.S. lines.	
HAUTVILLERS	10/6/18		The 9 guns were withdrawn and harnessed up Battery accommodated in tents in woods 400 x N.W. of HAUTVILLERS.	
	10/6/18		Training.	
	19/6/18			
OGER	20/6/18		On relief of 19th Division by 8th Italian Division proceeded by route march to OGER. Met Reg.	
BROUSSY-LE-PETIT	22/6/18		Proceeded to BROUSSY-LE-PETIT by train. CHALONS 50.	
	24/6/18		Moved with 57 Brigade to P.O.W. camp on the LE MESNIL BROUSSY – CONNANTRE Road.	
	24/6/18			
	29/6/18		Training.	
SEMOINE	30/6/18		Proceeded by Route March to SEMOINE. MAP REF. ARCIS 67	

W. Hopley Capt.
O/C 57 T.M.B.

Army Form C. 2118.

WAR DIARY
or
INTELLIGENCE SUMMARY. 57th L.T.M. Battery
(Erase heading not required.)

Instructions regarding War Diaries and Intelligence Summaries are contained in F. S. Regs., Part II. and the Staff Manual respectively. Title pages will be prepared in manuscript.

Place	Date	Hour	Summary of Events and Information	Remarks and references to Appendices
	July			
MAIZY	1	7.30am	57th L.T.M.B. entrained at MAILY for HESDIN in accordance with 57 Brigade Order No 220	
	2		Arrived at HESDIN & proceeded by motor lorries to billets at MAC.REF. ARCIS 67	
WAVRANS			WAVRANS MAP REF HAZEBROUCK 5A	
	3–10		Training & Rest	
	11	6.AM	Proceeded by Motor Buses to billets at RAIMBERT, in accordance with 57th Brigade Order No 221. MAP REF HAZEBROUCK 5A	
RAIMBERT	12–19		Training & Rest	
	20	9.15am	Proceeded by Motor Route to billets at ST HILAIRE in accordance with Brigade Order No 222	
ST HILAIRE	21–30		Training & Rest	
	30	9.15 PM	Proceeded by March Route to billets at RAIMBERT in accordance with 57th Brigade Order No 223	
RAIMBERT	31		Training & Rest	

W. Hockley Major
O/C 57 L.T.M. Battery

Army Form C. 2118.

WAR DIARY
or
INTELLIGENCE SUMMARY

(Erase heading not required.)

160 L.T.M.B.

Place	Date AUG	Hour	Summary of Events and Information	Remarks and references to Appendices
RAIMBERT	1-4		Training & Rest.	
"	4	4pm	Proceeded by Route March to CHOCQUES to take up position in Reserve in accordance with "57" 2/ Bde order. No 224.	
CHOCQUES	5	5pm	Proceeded to BETHUNE to take over & relieve 9th T.M. Battery in the line.	
BETHUNE	21	12pm	Montana withdrawn (and teams) to billets near N.Q's in accordance with 57 2/ Bde order No 229.	
"	24	4pm	Proceeded by Route March and to Chateau "L'ABBAYE" for Training & Rest.	
L'ABBAYE	29	3pm	Proceeded to Bethune to relieve 56" T.M.B. on Right sector of Divisional front in accordance with 57 2/ Bde order No G. 884.	
BETHUNE	31			

E.H.B. Hannigan 2 Lt
O/c 57. T.M.B.

WAR DIARY or INTELLIGENCE SUMMARY.

Army Form C. 2118.

S-7th L.T.M. Batty

Place	Date	Hour	Summary of Events and Information	Remarks and references to Appendices
LACOUTURE	1918 SEPT 1-2		On right sector of Divisional Front	
	3	5 AM	Our Stokes Mortars cooperated with Infantry in attack on ROUGE CROIX	
RICHBOURG	7-9		Our Stokes Mortars fired 125 rounds on enemy M.G. Posts	
	10	2 PM	Relieved by 58th Bde T.M.B. & proceeded to billets at HINGES (W.8.D.9.5)	
HINGES	11	2 PM	Proceeded to billets at Canal Bank N.23.C.95.25	
BETHUNE	12-15		On Divisional Reserve at Canal Bank N.23.C.95.25	
RUE DU BOIS	16	4 PM	Relieved 56th Bde T.M.B. on right sector of Divisional front	
"	20	5-7 AM	Four Stokes Mortars cooperated in Infantry attack on SHEPHERDS REDOUBT. The DISTILLERY 290 Rounds fired on Co SEVEN SISTERS. Owing to advance of Infantry guns were emplaced to fire on SHEPHERDS REDOUBT. a Capt. Machine gun was captured from SHEPHERDS REDOUBT	
	25	5-30 AM	In cooperation with Artillery our Mortars fired 390 rounds on SHEPHERDS REDOUBT. The DISTILLERY. The DISTILLERY afterwards Two guns were emplaced in REDOUBT for defence	
SHEPHERDS REDOUBT	26	6 AM	56 Rounds fired on enemy M.G. Posts	

Army Form C. 2118.

WAR DIARY
or
INTELLIGENCE SUMMARY.

57 L.T.M. Battery

(Erase heading not required.)

Instructions regarding War Diaries and Intelligence
Summaries are contained in F. S. Regs., Part II.
and the Staff Manual respectively. Title pages
will be prepared in manuscript.

Place	Date	Hour	Summary of Events and Information	Remarks and references to Appendices
	1918 SEPT			
RUE DU BOIS	28	8 P.M.	Relieved by 58th Pdr. T.M.B. Proceeded to Billets at Canal Bank W. 21. c. 95. 85	
BETHUNE	29-30		In Q. H.Q. Reserve Canal Bank W. 21. e. 55. 85.	

A.R. Hannigan Lt.

O/c 57. T.M.B.

Army Form C. 2118.

WAR DIARY
or
INTELLIGENCE SUMMARY.
(Erase heading not required.)

57TH LIGHT TRENCH MORTAR BATTERY.
No. ....
Date: 1/11/18

Place	Date	Hour	Summary of Events and Information	Remarks and references to Appendices
BETHUNE	1918 OCT 1	1330	On relief by 281st T.M Battery proceeded by march route to billets at RAIMBERT (MAP REF HAZEBROUCK 5A)	
RAIMBERT	2	0930	Proceeded by march route to billet at HUCLIER (LENS 11.1 E 3.2)	
HUCLIER	4	2225	Proceeded by rail route to railhead at BRYAS (LENS 11.25 55 R.5)	
	5	0900	Detrained & proceeded by rail route to BAVINCOURT area (MAP REF LENS 11)	
			Detrained & proceeded by road route to billets at SOUASTRE (LENS 11 5 G 88)	
SOUASTRE	7	1950	Embussed for the GRAINCOURT area (MAP REF VALENCIENNES 5.B)	
GRAINCOURT	9	1400	Marched to billets at ANNEUX	
ANNEUX	10	1420	Marched to billets in CAMBRAI	
CAMBRAI	11		Training & Rest in CAMBRAI Area	
	16		Proceeded by march route to St AUBERT VALENCIENNES	
St AUBERT	17/19		57th L.T.M.B. in reserve at St AUBERT	
	20	0250	2nd Section 57th T.M.B were ordered to assault Battalions to cooperate in attack on HAUSSY & ground east of RIVER SELLE & section following the attack on the	

www.ingramcontent.com/pod-product-compliance
Lightning Source LLC
Chambersburg PA
CBHW080852010526
44117CB00014B/2241